Travels with Foxfire

TRAVELS
with
FOXFIRE

*Stories of People, Passions, and Practices
from Southern Appalachia*

PHIL HUDGINS

and Foxfire Student

JESSICA PHILLIPS

ANCHOR BOOKS
A Division of Penguin Random House LLC
New York

AN ANCHOR BOOKS ORIGINAL, AUGUST 2018

Copyright © 2018 by The Foxfire Fund, Inc.

All rights reserved. Published in the United States by Anchor Books, a division of
Penguin Random House LLC, New York, and distributed in Canada by Random House
of Canada, a division of Penguin Random House Canada Limited, Toronto.

Anchor Books and colophon are registered trademarks of Penguin Random House LLC.

"Lillie Mulkey West: Inspiring a new generation of folk singers" first appeared,
in slightly different form, in *The Times* of Gainesville, Georgia.

Due to limitations of space, permissions to reprint previously published
material can be found following page 314.

The Foxfire Fund, Inc.
PO Box 541
Mountain City, GA 30562-0541
706-746-5828
www.foxfire.org

Library of Congress Cataloging-in-Publication Data
Names: Hudgins, Phil, compiler, interviewer. | Phillips, Jessica, 1998– interviewer. |
Foxfire Fund, issuing body.
Title: Travels with Foxfire : stories of people, passions, and practices from Southern Appalachia /
Phil Hudgins and Foxfire student Jessica Phillips.
Description: New York : Anchor Books, a division of Penguin Random House LLC, [2018]
Identifiers: LCCN 2017056227
Subjects: LCSH: Appalachian Region—Civilization. | Southern States—Civilization. |
Country life—Appalachian Region. | Country life—Southern States. | Handicraft—Appalachian Region. |
Handicraft—Southern States. | Appalachian Region—Social life and customs. | Southern States—
Social life and customs. | Interviews—Appalachian Region. | Interviews—Southern States.
Classification: LCC F106 .H83 2018 | DDC 975.8—dc23
LC record available at https://lccn.loc.gov/2017056227

Anchor Books Trade Paperback ISBN: 978-0-525-43629-4
eBook ISBN: 978-0-525-43630-0

Book design by Anna B. Knighton

www.anchorbooks.com

Printed in the United States of America
10 9 8 7 6 5 4 3 2 1

While a great many folks lent their talents to this work, we want to take this opportunity to recognize four individuals for their many years of service to Foxfire. First, Ann Moore, who retired as Foxfire's executive director after nearly twenty years in that role and forty years with the organization. This past year, two long-time board members, Janet Rechtman and Hunter Moorman, retired from their posts. Then, Hilton Smith, a long-time staff member, past interim executive director for Foxfire, and one of the educational innovators behind the Foxfire Approach to Teaching and Learning, retired from teaching.

Janet Rechtman first came to Foxfire in 1998 as a consultant through the organization's strategic planning process. Three years later, she joined the board of directors and was shortly thereafter appointed as board chair—a position in which she served for some seven years. All told, Janet served on the board for seventeen years.

Hunter Moorman was invited to join the board of directors in 1999. Hunter was a former assistant secretary to the US Department of Education and brought an informed perspective on Foxfire's educational programming, specifically teacher development through the Foxfire Approach. In 2009, Hunter was nominated to serve as Foxfire's board chairman, a position he held until 2017. In that time, Hunter guided the organization through its strategic plan for 2009–2015 and helped the organization secure its first NEH (National Endowment for the Humanities) grant in some thirty years.

Hilton Smith was an early adopter of the core practices that would become the Foxfire Approach to Teaching and Learning. He joined the Foxfire staff as an educator in the 1980s and played a pivotal role in developing and defining the approach. Later, Hilton was asked to serve as Foxfire's interim executive director as it navigated a difficult transition in administrative leadership. Years later, Hilton was instrumental in coordinating Foxfire's partnership with Piedmont College, through which many teachers were educated in the Foxfire Approach.

Ann Moore joined Foxfire as its bookkeeper in 1976 and was named president and executive director in 1999. Ann retired from Foxfire in 2016, leaving behind a legacy of selfless, tireless work for this organization. In 2017, the Gate House, which houses Foxfire's museum store and offices, was rededicated as the Ann Moore Gate House, to honor her selfless dedication to Foxfire.

To these individuals and the countless others who have contributed to Foxfire over the years, we dedicate this volume to you.

CONTENTS

Acknowledgments

When I fully retired as senior editor of Community Newspapers, Inc., in April 2015, I wasn't ready to sit down and sort my socks or glue Popsicle sticks together. I wanted a project. I thought of the Foxfire program of Rabun County, Georgia, where I lived for five years while serving as publisher/editor of *The Clayton Tribune*, a weekly newspaper. I had served on Foxfire's community board in the early 1990s and was impressed with the program. For fifty-plus years, hundreds of students in Rabun County have learned valuable skills through Foxfire, which has earned a worldwide reputation, thanks mainly to books and magazines produced by the students themselves.

I visited the Foxfire office on Black Rock Mountain and presented my idea to Ann Moore, then president and executive director of the Foxfire Fund. My proposal was this: I would interview and write stories on people, passions, and practices and compile them for a book, one a bit different from the series Foxfire has published over the years. Ann liked the idea.

In her absence at the next Foxfire board meeting, Barry Stiles, curator of the Foxfire Museum, presented the proposal to board members. The board gave a thumbs-up. Jessica Phillips, then a student at Rabun County High School, was chosen to work with me on the project. This bright young woman did as many interviews as she could work into her busy schedule. I did the rest, gathering stories from five states: Georgia, North and South Carolina, Tennessee, and Kentucky.

You are holding the final product in your hands. It was a lot of work, but, if you'll excuse the cliché, it was a labor of love. Jessica and I interviewed hunters, folk artists, herbs gatherers, musicians, songwriters, historians, farmers, former moonshiners, water dowsers, stock car racers, television executives, authors, storytellers, cooks, a genealogist, a professor, a mule collector, and even an expert on outhouses. And there were others. We met some interesting people, believe me.

We have a lot of people to thank, some for reading and offering suggestions, some for story ideas, some for encouragement. First, of course, we thank Ann Moore, Barry Stiles, and T. J. Smith, now director of Foxfire; editor Kaye Collins, and members of the Foxfire board for giving Jessica and me this opportunity. Without them, this book would still be only a dream. I'd also like to thank editor Tom Pold and Penguin Random House for oversight and publication.

All proceeds from book sales, by the way, go to Foxfire.

Others deserving our thanks include: Johnny Vardeman, Ken Hudgins, Myles Godfrey, Emory Jones, Sharon Hall, cartoonist Jim Powell, Joy Phillips, Teddi Heck, Joseph "Doc" Johnson, Jack Ogle, Tommy Bowers, Jack Frost, Don Elrod, Barbara McRae, George Thompson, and *The Times* of Gainesville, Georgia.

I'd also like to thank my wife, Shirley, for putting up with my obsession with this book.

Introduction

It's a bit daunting, even for a native son, to sit down and try to define Southern Appalachia. Fortunately, that's not the purpose of this book. The purpose is to capture and preserve as much as possible the culture, wit, and wisdom of the people of this region, people who cling tenaciously to traditions and stories and music and events and food and activities (legal and otherwise) and all those other things fading from reality and into reality TV.

If there's any defining in this book, most of it will come from the Southern Appalachian people themselves. And even they wouldn't always agree.

The fact is, says Glen Kyle, Southern Appalachia is not going to survive as what it was. "It's going to survive in memory, perception, song, food, but it's going to be mixed with more modern activities and lifestyle."

Kyle should know. He grew up in a house at the end of a dirt road in mountainous Fannin County, Georgia, the shinbone of Appalachia. He also studied this region as a history major in college and now serves as executive director of the Northeast Georgia History Center in Gainesville, Georgia.

"I would argue," he says, "that it's geography that made the Southern Appalachian culture. Now the geography is no longer an issue." We are no longer farmers who try to grow turnips in rock and corn on a mountainside. Most of us buy our milk in a carton at the store. We don't have to plan our trips to the neighbors' or to church. We now have good roads, so we jump in the car and go.

The land and the people here were interconnected more than in other regions of this country. That's what defined the concept of Southern Appalachia, Kyle says. And now we don't have that. However, many of us still like to think of ourselves as rugged, individualistic mountain folks who cling to tradition like bark to a tree. And you'll meet some in this book who fit that description nicely. You'll also meet people who are serious about preserving family stories and histories, along with others who understand folk art and music, hunting and food, and the nature of this region.

Used to be, if the people of Southern Appalachia wanted to hear music, they learned how to play instruments and entertained themselves. Folk songs and ancient Scotch-Irish ballads that told stories of joy and woe once wafted across the mountains. And then radio came along and changed music everywhere, including, eventually, here. Radio opened up music, says Wayde Powell, Jr., of Dahlonega, Georgia, "but diluted it at the same time, because it was more composite and the various strains [of mountain music] began to disappear."

Southern Appalachian people also entertained themselves by telling stories, but now, with texting, Facebook, and other social media at their fingertips, personal interaction has suffered. Fortunately, though, great storytellers are still around, and you'll read about some of them here.

This is not a travel book, but it is a journey around the Appalachian region. It's called *Travels with Foxfire* because former Foxfire student Jessica Phillips and I traveled a good bit to capture these tales. I found stories in five states—Georgia, the Carolinas, Tennessee, and Kentucky—that showcase the people, passions, and practices of this colorful region.

You'll meet four men who still dig wild ginseng the right way, refusing to harvest it out of season or when the plant is not old enough. (Digging wild ginseng is one of those mountain traditions that found its way to reality television on the History Channel.)

We'll also explore other vanishing practices: doctoring with herbs, watching movies at the local drive-in theater, making moonshine whiskey, finding underground water by dowsing, and even answering nature's call at the privy. Have you ever heard of a priviologist? We interviewed one.

You'll read about moonshine trippers racing cars in a cornfield in the Etowah River bottoms of Dawson County, Georgia. Those races, some say, led to the first organized stock car races and the formation of NASCAR.

We'll introduce you to people of faith. After all, Southern Appalachia has always been the buckle of the Bible Belt. We'll look at Southern gospel singing, funny things that happen at gospel concerts, and at a man who has collected eighteen thousand long-play record albums featuring all kinds of music, including gospel. You'll learn how a lifelong friendship between two country music songwriters developed into concerts of praise for several charities.

If you're interested in the mouthwatering cuisine of Southern Appalachia—and who isn't?—you'll enjoy interviews with some of this region's best cooks. For example, Jessica Phillips interviewed her grandmother, Lazell Vinson, who cooked at the Best Western and the Dillard House in Dillard, Georgia, for twenty-one years. Her and others' recipes are included.

And then there's Dori Sanders, a cook, a novelist, a speaker, a food writer, a peach farmer, a book award winner, a philosopher—all the characteristics of a person who requires two essays to tell her story. You'll enjoy getting to know this outspoken lady from South Carolina farm country.

This introduction, like our stories about food, is just to whet your appetite, urging you to read on. Yes, Southern Appalachia has changed, but change is not all bad. Who wants to return to middle-of-the-night trips to the outhouse? Hardly anyone wants to live the hard, hungry lives of our ancestors, barely eking out a living on an isolated land often too rough to plow.

But much of that old-world honor of the Scotch-Irish lives on. "They will do everything they can to help somebody if they like them," Kyle says. "But if they've been slighted in any way, or they feel like they've been slighted, that's it. It's an all-or-nothing thing."

Seven or eight decades ago, there wasn't much formal education in these parts. For those who could read, there was little to read. Even the Sears, Roebuck catalog found a more useful purpose in the little building at the end of the path. But our ancestors not only survived, they thrived. They thrived by making do, and when change came, they drew on their basic wit and common sense to adapt rather than simply surrender to it.

That's why the Southern Appalachia of old not only offered a culture and lifestyle worth remembering and celebrating but is still the best starting point for exploring what makes the region tick today. We invite you to join us in both the celebration and the exploration.

—Phil Hudgins

Travels with Foxfire

THE WAY IT WAS

The Family Farm

The story of Mama & Papa Hudgins

BELMONT SEEMED like another world to me. It's a little community near the Jackson County line, only about ten miles south of Gainesville, Georgia. Belmont was the home of my grandparents Mama and Papa Hudgins, officially Hattie and Barto.

Their world was so different from mine. I lived on hustling, bustling West Broad Street in Gainesville. Yessir, I lived in a big city. Nearly twelve thousand people lived there in 1950. We got our milk in bottles, delivered to the front door. A cow had nothing to do with it. We bought our cotton in clean rolls. But in Belmont, cotton had to be picked from a little bush, and it had crummy seeds in the middle of it. Why, in Gainesville, you could go to the store and buy bacon and fatback and all those exotic meats. You didn't have to wait till cold weather came, as they did in Belmont, so they could shoot an old hog and cut him up into hams and shoulders and ribs and then cook his fat in a big, black pot till it produced lard for cooking grease and shriveled-up pieces of crisp-fried meat—cracklin's, they called them. They were perfect for giving cornbread a heavenly flavor.

Belmont seemed like a thousand miles away back then. And just about every Sunday, we'd pile into Daddy's 1941 black Ford, which he liked to say didn't have a rattle in it, and drive that thousand miles to see Mama and Papa. And it was great.

Practically every adult who grew up in Southern Appalachia back then

PLATE I   Mama always cooked a big dinner on Sunday.

had a Belmont in his or her childhood. It wasn't that long ago, really. But now small family farms are disappearing every year, leaving only memories for most of us.

I remember Belmont, Georgia, well. I remember when Belmont's roads were paved with two different kinds of material: slick, red mud when it rained and dry, choking dust when it was dry. I liked the rainy-day material better because with it you could still breathe when a car passed as you walked along the road.

I remember that Mama Hudgins cooked on a wood-burning stove, and pancakes seemed to taste better cooked over wood. Her chicken and biscuits would have won any cooking contest. Mama sometimes cooked beans in a black pot over the fire. Occasionally, she would use a Dutch oven, which she'd also use to bake bread on the hearth. The house was heated mainly by two fireplaces: one in the kitchen, where everyone stayed during visits, and the other in Mama and Papa's bedroom. Besides these two fireplaces, there were little kerosene heaters for the other rooms.

These were used when it got so cold, you couldn't sleep. But I don't remember seeing those little heaters lit. It never got that cold, apparently. Oh, it got cold, all right, but when you went to bed, your body literally sank into the feather mattress; you'd pull up eighty-two pounds of cover and you were warm. One thing you had to remember: You needed to get in a position you liked before pulling up the covers, because it took a lot of effort to turn over with all those quilts on top of you. The only thing that got cold was your nose. You had to keep your nose out to breathe. But only the nose.

Mama and Papa always kept a drawer in the pie safe full of heavy, cast-iron toys to play with. There were also empty old cans of Colgate tooth powder and Woodbury talc. These were much more fun than the toys Gainesville had. There was also an Uncle Wiggily game. It must have been fifty years old. And for the little girls, there was a Raggedy Ann, made from some flour sack or something. After Mama and Papa were gone, Raggedy Ann was still there, but even more raggedy.

Papa had mules. Sometimes he had one mule; sometimes he had two. But every mule he had, I remember, was named Bill. Or maybe it's just that I couldn't tell one from another. Anyway, I know that at least one of those mules, Bill, didn't like to be ridden by little boys. He threw me off one day. Bill never did mind me when I hollered out "Gee" and "Haw," but when Papa did it, old Bill would turn to the right or left just as pretty as you please.

Mama's cows wouldn't mind me either. They'd give milk for her, but when I'd pull on those things, just a drop or two would come out. Some-

PLATE 2   Mama Hudgins with some of her great-grandchildren

times Mama would squirt milk into my mouth straight from the cow. It was fun, but it wasn't good. Warm milk was for babies, calves, and sissy kids who caught colds. It wasn't for me.

Mama and Papa grew practically everything they needed. About the only things they bought were the essentials they couldn't grow, stuff like salt, coffee, sugar, cloth, and maybe a few seeds. Papa grew cotton, too, and my brother Kenneth and I helped him pick it, sometimes bolls and all for me, for a quarter a bag. I would have done it for nothing.

Hog-killing time was always fun. Well, the first part of it wasn't. Somebody would shoot that poor thing in the head, and he'd squeal and bleed like crazy for what seemed like a long time. But soon as he quieted down, the rest was enjoyable. The men would cut up that old hog and lay the fat aside to be cooked out as lard and cracklin's in a big, black pot with a fire under it.

During hog-killing time, we kids would play games to keep warm. We'd take a straw or reed and blow up the hog's bladder like a balloon, tie it off, and then kick it around like a soccer ball, although nobody had ever heard of soccer back then. You couldn't do that on West Broad Street in Gainesville.

Papa wanted to kill his hog on Thanksgiving Day, if the weather was cold enough. He and his sons would start early in the morning, about sunup, and by dinnertime, which in the big city is called lunch, Mama and her daughters-in-law would have enough food on the table to feed the whole neighborhood. Mama always killed a hen, cut it up, and cooked it inside the cornbread-and-sage dressing. The chicken and dressing would emerge golden brown and would sit out on the cupboard all day, along with everything else, until suppertime. No one knew until years later that even cooked food should be refrigerated between meals. Or so they say.

Mama and Papa didn't always have a dog, but they always had cats. I don't know where so many cats came from. And there wasn't a tame one in the bunch. They'd sneak out of the cat hole in the smokehouse, tip-paw up to the food Mama had left on a big, flat rock, and eat as fast as they could.

Belmont had all kinds of great games. All it took was imagination. The cellar, where Mama and Papa kept perishables (until the Rural Electrification Administration ran power to their house), was cold and spidery like a dungeon. Then there was a little log cabin way off in the middle of a field behind my grandparents' house. I imagined some famous person grew up in that cabin and someday it'd be a museum. Or maybe a very brave outdoorsman lived there, I dreamed, and he could outfight, outrun, and outhunt any man alive. I was extremely disappointed in later years to learn that two nice little ladies, Sis and Sarah Fowler, sisters, lived in the cabin. There went the museum.

Belmont Baptist Church was famous for its lemonade. I'm sure its members would like to be remembered for greater things, but I remember the lemonade. Belmont had homecomings, and people would bring food like they thought they were going to eat their last meal that Sunday afternoon. And, boy, somebody always brought lemonade, stirred up in a big, tin washtub with lots of ice in it. It was always a bit on the sour side. The first sip grabbed you and shook you all the way down to your shoe tops, which, incidentally, were freshly shined with Griffin liquid polish just for the occasion. The next sip was better, and from then on, it was great. Belmont Baptist Church made me believe in one thing, for sure: When you get thirsty in heaven, they serve ice-cold lemonade from a big, tin washtub.

Not all my visits to Belmont were fun. My brother and I were taken there in 1949, and it wasn't to play kickball with a blown-up pig's bladder. We were sentenced to two weeks at the farm just because we had come down with a bad case of the red measles.

That's right. When our daddy found out that we were breaking out, he gave us two options: You can go stay with Mama Stevens at her house in the city, or you can go stay with Mama and Papa Hudgins down on the farm.

"Why can't we stay home?" I asked pitifully. "You can't stay here," Daddy said firmly.

My brother and I chose the farm. The downside was that the farmhouse didn't have indoor plumbing. Relief normally was a good seventy yards away in a little house behind a fig bush. But each of us had a little pot under our bed for quicker access.

Mama Hudgins put both of us in Aunt Gertie's old bedroom, pulled the shades, turned the calendar toward the wall so we wouldn't strain our eyes trying to figure out what day it was, switched out the lights, and shut the door.

No one called the welfare department to report two little boys being held against their will in a cold, dark room down on a farm. If anyone called to check on us, our grandparents wouldn't have answered. They didn't have a telephone. They didn't have a television. They'd had electricity only a couple of years. As usual, the bedrooms weren't heated—this was in March—but it didn't matter. We had enough quilts to survive a Siberian winter.

Mama and Papa treated us well. Mama fed us homemade soups and other light fare, and as we got better, we graduated to country ham and gravy and biscuits and other delicacies Mama concocted on her wood-burning cookstove. When she decided our eyes were strong enough for the light, she taught us to embroider. And that's all I'm going to say about that.

If it hadn't been for the measles, it might have been a pleasant stay. We weren't forced to scrub floors like Cinderella; we weren't beaten; we weren't scolded. Like whitetail fawns, in our own good time, we simply shed our spots and were good as new. We were ready for civilization again.

Back at home, I found out why Daddy wouldn't let us recuperate at our own house. Snuggled inside a little bassinet in our living room was our baby sister, Elaine, all pink and pretty and without a spot of red measles.

Both the farm and the community had changed a lot when I visited in the summer of 1972 to take a few photographs. Mama was living by herself. Papa had been gone since June 24, 1965. He died about a month ahead of

PLATE 3   Old hand-turned washing machine
sits upside down outside the smokehouse.

his eighty-fifth birthday. An electric stove had replaced the woodstove and Dutch oven Mama used to cook on.

The two fireplaces had been cemented up, and Warm Morning coal heaters stood in their places. The road had been paved. There were no hogs or cows or mules. The smokehouse was empty of meat, but the old salt box was still holding up. The outhouse was still there, though the fig bush in front had grown bigger over the years and completely hid the two-holer, which Daddy or one of his brothers nicknamed Hoschton, after a town not far away.

The old garage was still there at the house—Daddy and his siblings called it a car house—but I don't recall seeing a car anywhere around it. It was built for an A-Model Ford that belonged to Glen, the oldest boy. But the only evidence I saw that an automobile was once parked there was an old headlight. Papa never learned to drive. He didn't need to.

The old hand-cranked washing machine still rested behind the smokehouse, just as it had when I was a kid. The log cabin in the field where the Fowler sisters lived had collapsed a little more in the past twenty-five years. The old Gainesville Midland steam engines that once stopped in Belmont to take on water and passengers were gone.

Mama was eighty-four in 1972. She hadn't changed much in two

PLATE 4   Mama Hudgins always wore her bonnet when she was outside.

decades. She was a little lady, maybe five foot two, and still wore her hair in a bun. I'd seen her let her hair down a couple of times, but only literally, never figuratively. Mama's lace was straighter than a poker. She still worked in her garden, which son Herbert plowed for her, and she always wore a bonnet outside to protect her face from the sun. She still made the best tea cakes and apple pie this side of Appalachia, and she still stood and waved over the ferns and flowers that lined the end of her back porch until her visitors' car pulled out of sight.

Belmont was then, as it still is today, a warm, friendly community that looks after its own. The town still holds some fine homecomings at the Baptist church and keeps farming in its blood with gardens and maybe a milk cow here and there.

Changes had been made in Mama's house, but she probably didn't see much need for them. After she started fading with dementia, a nursing home in Winder, Georgia, became her new home. She left one day and started walking down the highway. Someone who knew her pulled his car up beside her and asked where she was going. "I'm going home," she said. The man convinced her to let him take her back to the nursing home.

Mama really wasn't that unhappy, though. In fact, at the end, she thought all the other people at the home had come to serve her. "You know," she said one day, "I don't have to cook a thing these days. They bring me three meals a day."

Mama had always been an optimistic person. She taught Sunday school for Lord knows how many years and made real wine for communion but wouldn't touch the stuff any other time. I never saw Papa at church, although he was a deacon. Someone said the doctor told him to stay out of crowds because he had a heart murmur, and he took him at his word. Papa didn't say much, and he wasn't warm and affectionate, by any means. I saw Mama kiss him only one time, and that was when he was lying in a casket in the front bedroom of his home. But Papa was an honest man, a good farmer who provided for his family, a trusted justice of the peace, and a grandfather whose surname I am honored to carry.

Hattie Mangum Hudgins, our Mama Hudgins, died on Christmas Eve 1979. She was ninety-one. The family waited until the day after Christmas to hold her funeral. She is buried beside Papa in the cemetery of Belmont Baptist Church.

The four sons and one daughter, Glen, Edwin (my daddy), Herbert,

PLATE 5   Mama and Papa Hudgins with their offspring.
From left, Glen, Gertie, Edwin (author's father), Herbert, and Alton.

Alton, and Gertie, are gone. But I have some things at home to help me remember them, to remember Mama and Papa and their farm. I have Papa's spectacles and his felt hat made by Etchison. I have his New Testament, printed in 1886. Daddy gave me the small glass-front cabinet and table that Papa crafted. I have a couple of churns Mama used for making butter and buttermilk. I have part of a harness the old Bills wore when Papa plowed. I have schoolbooks that Daddy used at Braselton High School and a banjo-lele, which is a banjo ukulele.

After Daddy died, Mother said I could have as a keepsake either his mandolin or Papa's shotgun. But before I could claim either one, someone broke into Mother's home and stole them both. I hope the thief tripped on the way out, the shotgun went off, and blasted that mandolin all to pieces.

The farmhouse that Papa built has been moved to a new location now. Another small family farm is gone. Nothing is left but memories. Memories of gathering eggs for Mama in her chicken house and watching her wring the neck of a nice, fat hen for Sunday dinner; memories of the pear tree in the yard that produced the knottiest but tastiest fruit known to man; memories of the nearby walnut tree from which neighbor Willard Baxter made bowls for us grandkids after it was cut down; memories of going blackberry picking with Mama in the summer, our pant legs and long-sleeve shirts tied off with string at the ankles and wrists and doused with kerosene to discourage chiggers, which usually found other entrances; memories of lying on hay in the loft of Papa's barn, listening to the rain tap-dance on the tin roof; memories of Mama reading the *Katzenjammer Kids* comic strip to us grandkids; memories of sitting with Papa on the back porch and wondering when he would be moved to say something.

It was a different time back then. I'm all for progress and technology, and I don't want to return to the days of cold bedrooms and even colder bathrooms outside, but there was something I learned from my grandparents, something that seems to be missing in a lot of homes today. Mama and Papa were satisfied with what they had. They worked for what they owned, which wasn't much, and they built much of it themselves. They were content. I never heard either of them complain about not having something. Owning stuff was not important. Family was important. There were some things about the good old days, the days of Mama and Papa Hudgins, that were very good. And I miss them.

Moonshining Days

Stories from James Speed's life making illegal liquor

THERE HE IS, early for the interview, sitting on a front-porch bench at Pleasant Hill Baptist Church, a simple white building with wings on each side, forming a perfect cross when seen from the air. "When they Life Flight somebody out of here, they land right here in this parking lot," the man says. The pilot knows he's in the right place when he sees the church shaped like a cross.

Pleasant Hill is about six miles east of Clayton, Georgia, way down winding Warwoman Road in Rabun County, a mountainous place that hugs the borders of the Carolinas. "They say that the further you go down Warwoman, the meaner they are. And I live in the last house." That's James Speed speaking, the man on the porch. He's chairman of the board of deacons. He's here to tell his story about growing up in this neck of the woods and living in the county's Persimmon Community, where he honed one of his greatest skills, making moonshine. "Good moonshine."

"You write it right," Speed tells me before agreeing to be interviewed. "There's been so much written about the people that ain't right. We need to see the truth, whether it hurts or it's good. The true story needs to be told." To get away from ringing phones and other interruptions at home, he'd suggested meeting at the church, an appropriate place to bear one's soul. So we sit down, face-to-face, in the church fellowship hall, and Speed, a bearded,

PLATE 6   Speed packs heat in front of the former sanctuary
of his church. He is a big proponent of the Second Amendment.

PLATE 7   Speed in younger days

barrel-chested bear of a man, begins to tell his story. But not all of it. That would take days.

James Earl Speed was born on July 24, 1952, at Rabun County Hospital. One of the six children—four boys and two girls—of J. P. "Pick" and Mary Grace Cobb Speed, he started working when he was no taller than a baseball bat. He dug worms to fill Prince Albert tobacco tins and got a nickel for each can. His grandmother, Amanda Norton Speed, kept his money in a drawstring tobacco bag. Later, he shucked corn and worked in the cornfields and then at a nearby sawmill. Money wasn't easy to come by. "Life was hard, but happy," he says.

By the time he was in the sixth or seventh grade, Speed was helping his daddy at "the place," where moonshine was manufactured and jugged. He and Donny Ray, one of his brothers, made thirty dollars each one summer, cutting up wood for the boiler with a bow saw and hiding the limbs so that spotter planes looking for stills wouldn't see them. Sometimes, in the fall, they'd work all night and then go to school the next day.

"We worked hard, like I'm doing today," Speed says. "And contrary to belief, Daddy didn't make moonshine all the time." He made it certain times of the year: in the spring and the fall, when the temperature was right for working the beer, or mash. At other times, Speed's father tilled the land, growing corn, potatoes, and other crops. He also worked for Burlington Industries in Clayton, drove a school bus, worked for Pontiac Motors, and did other jobs.

Everybody in the family was expected to do his or her part, and Pick Speed set the standard. If you're going to do anything, he said often, do it right. As for making moonshine, he said this: "Boys, let me tell you something. You wouldn't put off on another man what you wouldn't drink yourself." Daddy Speed wasn't a drinking man, but he sold plenty. And it all went to one man: a taxi driver in Clayton.

"He bought everything Daddy made," James Speed says. "He bootlegged it out from the business in Clayton. Us boys would load stuff on his taxicab, and he'd pay us and he was gone."

When Speed got to high school, he wanted to play football. His daddy said that was okay as long as his chores were done. Many times, Speed followed football practice with milking two cows, feeding twenty-five hogs, and cutting wood for the cookstove. On Fridays, he would walk to the game, play four quarters as a noseguard—"we won, most of the time"—and then walk home to do his chores.

Young people today are pampered, he says. "They got a Camaro, and Mama and Daddy are buying the gas, and they can't make it," he says, his piercing, dark eyes glaring out from under the bill of his camouflage cap. "I understand we're living in a different age. But hard work got me in condition for playing."

After graduating from high school, Speed and his buddies liked to attend local football games, and sometimes they took along a little libation for halftime. For one game, he and his brother Johnny transported a gallon of peach brandy, fresh from the still. "I don't know why we took a gallon, but we did," Speed says. "Well, Johnny took him a drink, and then I said, 'Now you watch out; I'm going to take me a drink.' I got down there and about that time, I heard something go *click, click*." There stood Chester York, the county sheriff, in uniform, with his sidearm, a .38, in his hand.

"I caught you, didn't I, boys?" the sheriff said. "Then he said, 'Go ahead and take you a drink.' So, I did. He said, 'Now you hold the gun on me while I take a drink.'" The sheriff didn't press charges; in fact, the boys poured him up a quart to take with him.

James and Johnny eventually ventured out on their own, figuring they could make more money if they did the manufacturing *and* the selling. Word got around that their product was top quality; after all, they'd learned from the master, their daddy, who followed a family recipe religiously, and they received an offer to make for "other guys," other moonshiners, for six hundred dollars a week. "That was good money back in them days," the 1960s, Speed says. But before saying yes, the brothers sought advice from Daddy. "Boys," he said, "if you're going to take a chance in life, do it for yourself. Don't do it for nobody else." So, they did it for themselves.

James Speed and petite Gail Patterson were married on August 12, 1972—he was nineteen, she was sixteen—and he went to work for her daddy, a moonshiner in the Persimmon Community. He did the making; daddy-in-law Richard Lamar "Pat" Patterson did the selling. "I stayed in the woods all the time," Speed says. "I'd come in, throw a wad of money on the bed to Gail, she knew what to do with it, and I was back in the woods."

Did Gail Speed ever worry about James being off in the woods making moonshine? "No, but then I was raised in it. I didn't see anything wrong with it. I thought they were just going to work."

Speed was arrested only once, while delivering, and charged with transporting nontax-paid liquor. He was sentenced to twelve months. He served only four and was fined five hundred dollars. He never had to pay.

Getting caught making moonshine, or nearly getting caught, keeps a fellow on his toes, he says. "If a covey of quail ain't shot into—and this is documented—if it ain't shot into, they'll all die because they get careless. If they're not afflicted from time to time, the foxes and everything else will get them. Now, here's the moral of the story: If you don't get your tail feathers dusted from time to time, you'll get careless."

James Speed wasn't one to get careless, though he did get nervous a few times. But making moonshine in the woods was exhilarating. "You're out there one frosty morning right after the crack of day, and all of a sudden, somebody jumps out of the bushes and says, 'Hold it right there. ATF.' It's federal officers and their friends. You talk about a butt pucker," he says. "Now you'll get one."

Fortunately for the Speed boys, that didn't happen at "the place." But it could've. James Speed says only he and Donny Ray could do the proofing, getting the alcohol content to a proper level, often by cutting it down with water, preferably good, soft spring water. "You either got it or you don't have it," Speed says of proofing prowess. Brother Mike was never good at working the still, although he is a talented man who can repair anything,

If you pin him down, Speed will admit to making a full-time living from moonshine for about four years. Everything since that time was a "hobby, making something for friends." Besides, making moonshine wouldn't be fun anymore, now that you can get a license in Georgia and other states and make it legally. And pay taxes on it. Speed doesn't think highly of government-sanctioned moonshine. "Anytime the government runs their hand in something, it's not going to come out right." The white lightning isn't as good.

Dwight Bearden of Dahlonega, Georgia, disagrees. An illegal distiller himself for many years, Bearden has been running moonshine legally at a distillery in Tennessee. "This is the highest quality of liquor that you'll find," he says. "When I was in the woods, I had to run more just to survive." But legal moonshine is pulled from the middle of the run, he says, cutting down on the amount of liquor used and improving the overall quality.

Whichever is better, legal moonshine or the backwoods variety, Cheryl Wood, owner of a legal distillery in Dawsonville, Georgia, agrees with James Speed's father about quality. Her grandfather, the late Simmie Free, a moonshiner from Tiger, Georgia, wouldn't sell anything that he wouldn't drink himself, she says, and that's how she wants to run her distillery. Much of the legal liquor, just like her grandfather's, is made the old-timey way, just good corn with no sugar. Trouble is, it's hard to find good corn nowadays, Speed says, because "it's all crossed up."

Some of Speed's customers of the past were a bit crossed up, too, after drinking too much of what looks like water but packs a punch like a heavyweight boxing champion. "It don't take much," he says. "It's like Brylcreem, a little dab'll do you."

He tells about some guys at the Highlands Country Club in Highlands, North Carolina, who wanted a few snorts to take with them on a round of golf. Being inexperienced drinkers of moonshine, they put the stuff on ice, a bad move because cold accelerates the potency, according to Speed. "They didn't make eighteen holes that day," he says.

A man Speed calls Barry the Brit, a frequent visitor to the Blue Ridge Mountains, took a jug of Speed's 'shine back to the mother country for his friends to try. Some of these fellows often took a break from work to enjoy a hunk of cheese and a glass of scrumpy, cider that originated in the West Country of England. But after a couple of drinks of Rabun County moonshine one day, they didn't make it back to work. "Where did you get this stuff?" Speed says, mimicking Barry's friend in his best British accent, punctuated with North Georgia twang. "I got it from this bearded guy over in America who hides in the forest over there, and he makes this stuff," was Barry's answer. "Wow," one of the workers responded, "we've got to move to America."

The stories are funny, and there are many more of them, but Speed knows that heartache and trouble can be alcohol's closest relatives. Speed himself abused the stuff at one time. He became a Christian—"I was saved," in 1971, he says—but then he fell away from the church. He remained a Christian, but he was only ankle-deep in the faith. "I had an uncle I couldn't stand," he says. "I'd have to get drunk to stand him. But finally, the Lord showed me there ain't no future in this, so He got me off the stuff." His life has been changed ever since.

"I was a binge drinker," he says. "The longest drunk I was ever on was three days, and I drank myself sober, if you can believe that. I didn't have no hangover or nothing, but I don't want to think about them days." That was in 1978 or '79, and his son and daughter never knew him as a drinker. He's thankful for that.

Speed grew up in the Warwoman Community, and it was Warwoman people and members at Pleasant Hill Baptist Church who took him and his family in and forgave them. "I wasn't a really bad person, I guess," he says, "but I done my part. But I give these folks a lot of credit. A lot of them are laying up here in the cemetery. I wouldn't be here today, as a deacon at church, if it wasn't for them, more than thirty years as a deacon, and I've taught Sunday school even longer than that.

"I'm not saying that there's much wrong with moonshine. The old moonshiners were some of the finest people that you'll ever meet in your life back in that day. They had their own recipes, but they always done it right." Moonshining was both bad and good, he says. It was bad because the product sometimes was abused. "We wouldn't sell to anyone we knew shouldn't have the stuff." It was good because it put food on the table.

Speed doesn't apologize for his moonshining days, although he's not proud of everything that went on. "It's not what goes in a man that defiles him," he says, quoting scripture, "it's what comes out." He believes in moderation in all things. It's all right to keep a little white lightning around for medicinal purposes, he says. "That was all my grandmother had for medicine. That and Bayer Aspirin. And you could throw the aspirin out the door if you had the other."

The conversation returns to his daddy. "Nobody owes you anything in this life," Pick Speed told his son. "'Get off your hind end and go get it.' Daddy said you use this head for something besides a place to hang your ears on. We always went to him for advice."

Daddy died in 2011, so now it's the son handing out pretty much the same advice, plus a lot more. Memories and stories live on after a man dies, and they're all important to James Earl Speed, a paradoxical fellow who broke the law but who preaches forgiveness and redemption as chairman of the board of deacons. "We can't escape our past," he says. "We're forgiven for it. But we've been there and done that."

―――――

On the night of June 8, 2017, the parking lot was full at Pleasant Hill Baptist Church. Folks had come to pay their respects to the family of James Earl Speed, Sunday school teacher for thirty-five years, deacon chairman, hunter, fisherman, humorist, family man, friend, former moonshiner, and victim of cancer. Among the last words he could mutter to his wife, Gail, were, "I appreciate the good times we had together." "So did I," she replied. James Speed was sixty-four years old.

How Stock Car Racing Started

Dawson County folks talk about the precursor to NASCAR

GORDON PIRKLE knows stock car racing. "I have argued with the Frances [NASCAR leaders Bill France, Sr., and Bill, Jr.] and with Junior Johnson about where racing started," he says while being interviewed in the conference room of the Georgia Racing Hall of Fame in Dawsonville, Georgia, where he reigns as president.

He continues: "It started right down here in the river bottoms in the midthirties. A bunch of liquor guys would meet on Sunday evenings. They had a makeshift track in a cornfield. They were just betting on who had the best driver at the time. But word kind of sneaked out, and people started showing up to watch on Sunday evening."

No one who witnessed those races is still alive, Pirkle says, but he has talked to enough people to know the story is true: What eventually birthed NASCAR started in an old cornfield in the Etowah River bottoms of Dawson County. The makeshift track was located somewhere around what is now Rock Creek Park.

Okay, doubters might ask, how could racing in a cornfield have led to organized stock car racing, which led to NASCAR? Gordon Pirkle has the answer: "Frank Christian of Atlanta could see dollar signs in that, and he went to Atlanta and rented the old horse track at the Lakewood fairgrounds."

The horse track was to become Lakewood Speedway. And right there on that flat dirt track with no banked corners was where the first organized stock car racing, as we know it, took place, Pirkle says. Those Lakewood races evolved into NASCAR races in 1948, after the organization was formed in late 1947.

Robert Glenn "Junior" Johnson disagrees. Johnson, a NASCAR driver in the 1950s and 1960s, has argued with Pirkle that stock car racing started in his home state, North Carolina. "His argument was we didn't have a racetrack here," Pirkle says. "We had a makeshift racetrack. And I don't argue with the Frances. I don't say that this is where NASCAR started. I say this is where stock car racing started. We started ten years before there was a NASCAR. It went over into NASCAR."

On Armistice Day 1938, after the cornfield races went to town, Lloyd Seay of Dawsonville won the first race at Lakewood. Roy Hall of Dawsonville won the second. And then Gober Sosebee of Dawsonville came along, "and they dominated in the early days of racing," Pirkle says.

Racing was going strong on Florida's Daytona Beach in the 1940s, and drivers from Dawsonville also dominated down there. "Five drivers from Dawson County won twelve times," says Pirkle, certain of his facts. "They

PLATE 8   Gober Sosebee with his wife

had three championships from Dawson before NASCAR was formed, and four since it was formed."

Many of the drivers honed their skills hauling moonshine from Dawsonville to Atlanta, often down Highway 9. Seay and Hall, who were cousins, were among them. They transported illegal liquor and then got into racing. Bernard Long of Dawsonville got into racing, won second at Lakewood, first at Daytona, quit racing, and got into illegal liquor. Driver Gober Sosebee was also a moonshine tripper, his son David says, although Gober wouldn't ever admit it.

Pirkle, however, does admit to hauling moonshine in the 1950s, after high school. He drove what trippers call a "slip-by." That's a regular family car, with its springs beefed up to withstand a heavy load. The slip-by driver would drive into Atlanta like any ordinary, law-abiding citizen, perhaps with his wife in the passenger's seat. "You didn't try to race with the law," Pirkle says. "You just tried to slip by."

Raymond Parks of Dawsonville, later of Atlanta, ran away from home at the age of fourteen and soon started hauling liquor. But he eventually decided it was safer and more profitable to hire a crew of drivers to do it for him. Parks, incidentally, was the owner of the car that won the first Lake-

PLATE 9   Raymond Parks's wife, Violet (*right*), and friend, Linda Sharp.
Officials didn't want to recognize moonshine running as part of racing.

wood race, and he went on to form his own team: drivers, a mechanic, and himself, the man with the money. He was the first champion car owner in NASCAR's premier series, now called the Sprint Cup.

When asked how many of the early drivers started out in the moonshine-hauling business, David Sosebee answers, "Why don't you turn that around and say, 'Who didn't haul?'" But later, NASCAR officials, mainly Bill France, Sr., NASCAR's founder, didn't acknowledge the moonshine runners' connection.

"They didn't want to recognize moonshine in any way," says Violet Parks, Raymond Parks's widow, who lives in North Carolina. "But they got Bill France, Jr., who succeeded his father, and they couldn't keep it hidden forever."

Gordon Pirkle has been following NASCAR and other racing events for decades. And if you have any doubt that he's dedicated to the sport, just visit his Dawsonville Pool Room, known for its locally famous Bully Burger and for the memorabilia of Bill Elliott's racing fame hanging on the walls. It's where Pirkle sets off a police siren, perched on the roof of the pool room, to celebrate another racing victory for one of the Elliott boys, Awesome Bill from Dawsonville, back in the day, and his son, Chase, today.

"I pride myself in wanting to keep this history going," Pirkle says, "but it would have died if Bill Elliott hadn't come along."

It was Elliott who brought new life to Dawsonville's racing history, not to mention the Dawsonville Pool Room and, indeed, the whole town. He raced for thirty-seven years and compiled enough victories, forty-four in all, to put him near the top of several of NASCAR's all-time lists. He captured the NASCAR premier series championship in 1988, when he had six wins, fifteen top-fives, and twenty-two top-tens in twenty-nine races. Sixteen times, he was named NASCAR's Most Popular Driver.

The first time Pirkle's victory siren sounded was when Elliott won at the old Riverside International Raceway in Riverside, California. That was 1983, and it has wailed through the tiny town dozens of times since then. The original siren now resides in Charlotte, North Carolina, where it is displayed in the NASCAR Hall of Fame, which inducted Elliott in 2015. So, Pirkle has installed a new siren for Elliott's son, Chase, who has a promising future in racing.

PLATE 10   Charlie Mincey (*left*) and Gordon Pirkle with an old Mincey race car

Sitting across from Pirkle at the Dawsonville racing museum is Charlie Mincey, who, in his eighties, is too young to remember the cornfield races of the 1930s, but he knows the reputations of moonshiners and their driving skills, because he was one of them.

"I always heard tales about how Roy Hall would aggravate the law, and I was the same way," he says, smiling. Mincey started hauling moonshine when he was fourteen, and for the next five years he aggravated a lot of lawmen. "I went to jail just by being identified in a car."

One night, his girlfriend, Carolyn, who was soon to become his wife, wanted to go with him on a liquor run from Dawsonville to Atlanta. "You can't do that," Mincey told her. "It's dangerous." Finally, he told her she could ride with him to Dawsonville to get a load and ride back to Atlanta with friends in another car.

"They left for Atlanta before I did," he recalls. "I passed them on the way back, and the law was shooting at me when I passed them. I told Carolyn later, 'That's why I didn't want you to ride with me.'"

His daddy, who owned a body shop, complained about having to plug all those bullet holes in his son's car.

Mincey says he followed different routes from Dawsonville to Atlanta to keep revenue officers off guard, and he kept different license plates in his car for emergencies. He didn't worry about the Atlanta police. They drove

PLATE 11   Charlie and Carolyn Mincey
visit the racing museum in Dawsonville, Georgia.

six-cylinder cars. "The main ones you had to worry about," he says, "were federal agents. Federal agents would get their motors built at the same place we moonshine trippers got ours built," and their cars were faster. Once they caught a tripper, they'd confiscate his car and sell it in front of a courthouse. "You could go and buy your car back sometimes," Mincey says. "I never did that."

Mincey quit tripping moonshine after being slapped with a federal charge of conspiracy and a sentence of three years on probation. "The judge told me, 'Now, if you come back up here for anything, just running a stop sign or anything, you're going to do that three years out on Boulevard in Atlanta,' where the federal pen was." So, his five years of running liquor ended abruptly. Carolyn, daughter of a Church of God preacher, didn't like his moonshining anyway. Racing she could put up with.

For the next thirty-three years, Mincey was racing somewhere practically every week. He also worked at his father's body shop. How many races did he win? Well, he doesn't know. He didn't keep count. But he won often. And sometimes it was in a moonshine car. He'd given up hauling, but not driving the cars. "That was a lot of fun," he says. "Winning in a moonshine car."

Today, Mincey suffers from back injuries. "I hit so many walls and turned over so many times," he says, "I messed up my back, so I've had it operated on. I still have trouble walking."

In one race, he recalls, his car turned over but flipped back onto its wheels. He finished fifth. The very next week, driving a modified car, he flipped again, but this time the vehicle was demolished. "I was leading the race, but the car flipped over on top of me and rolled all the way to the second turn. I crawled away from that one."

Gober Sosebee saw his first race in 1938 at Lakewood Speedway. He liked what he saw, his son David says, and vowed to see another one. He did, and then he wanted to be a participant.

"Everybody laughed at him when he said he wanted to race," David says. But in November 1939, with money he'd saved working at Atlantic Steel and AAA Laundry in Atlanta, he bought a brand-new 1940 Ford, built in the nearby Atlanta plant.

On Thanksgiving Day 1939, Sosebee took his new Ford to Lakewood and raced to third place. Lloyd Seay was first, and Roy Hall second. All three were from Dawson County. Nobody knows for sure, but David estimates his daddy won more than two hundred times, racing from 1939 until 1964. "Gober was a great driver," Mincey says. "And he could really put on a show for the fans."

That was one of his problems, David says. He didn't do anything halfway. He went all out, not slowing down for anything, and his all-or-nothing attitude hurt him sometimes.

One example was at Daytona in July 1949. Gober sat on the pole and led every lap for the last four. "He was a mile and a half ahead of Red Byron, who won the race," David says. "But he wouldn't slow down. He peeled the right front tire off, and it hit the fuel pump and cracked it. It would still run, but not at speed."

Gober also went all out when he hauled moonshine, although he never touched the stuff. "He was never caught. If you asked him about hauling, he would say, 'Some said I did.'" And that was it.

Anyone who knows anything about automobile racing knows that drivers don't carry passengers. Why would they? They would add unnecessary

PLATE 12   Gober Sosebee ready for a race on July 4, 1947

weight to the car, and what would passengers do, anyway? But it's because of the antics of Gober Sosebee that Bill France, Sr., added that rule to the book: No riders allowed.

Here's the story from Gober's son David: In January 1949, the year after NASCAR was formed, Sosebee, driving a flathead Ford, was running first, but he needed gas. He pulled in for a pit stop, and a crew member attempted to pour gas from a can. Trouble was, somebody had stuffed a shop rag in the neck of the can, and very little gas ended up in the tank.

His next stop, with a few laps to go, Sosebee pulled in again. But this time, afraid he would lose his lead, he banged on the side of the car, yelling, "Got to go, got to go!" So with the car still moving slightly, another driver, Jack Smith, who was out of the race and had joined the Sosebee pit crew, jumped in the right window carrying an Army can full of gas. The pit stop lasted only a few seconds. Sosebee was back in the race. So was Smith.

On the straightaways, Smith poured gas into the tank, which was located behind the driver's seat. Going through the corners, he just held on tight. Sosebee finished the race in first place with Smith still riding in the back. But in scoring the race, officials said there was no way Sosebee could have made two pit stops, as he reported.

Well, he said, I came in and got a rider the second time.

You can't carry a rider, Bill France argued. "Daddy said, 'There's nothing in the rule book that says you can't have a rider,' " David Sosebee recalls. The driver and France argued for about an hour, and France wrote a note in his rule book. That note became a new rule for NASCAR. France still didn't want Sosebee to get the victory. "Daddy said, 'I'm going to tell you that I never knew your mother, and I'm sure she was a fine lady. So that makes you a self-made son of a bitch.'"

Stories like these have circulated for years in Dawson and its neighboring counties. And they may get better each time they're told. Fact is, there could have been more of them if certain drivers from Dawsonville had changed their ways.

"Roy Hall couldn't win any championships because they couldn't keep him out of jail," Pirkle says. "And if Lloyd Seay hadn't have been killed, we'd be up there with the Pettys. Raymond Parks would have stayed in, and Lloyd could have won a lot of races." Seay was shot and killed in 1941 during an argument over an unpaid bill for sugar used in making moonshine.

Bill France, Jr., thought the redneck-moonshine connection was a drag on NASCAR, Pirkle says. He wanted to make NASCAR a major-league sport, and he didn't want any unsavory alliances getting in the way. "He tried to sweep it under the rug. It was bad publicity. Now with all these moonshine shows and festivals, one of these days I want to make heroes out of these outlaws."

And, in a way, Pirkle has accomplished his goal. With his insistent support, the Dawsonville City Council has named eight city streets in Dawsonville in honor of racing champions from the county: drivers Gober Sosebee, Lloyd Seay, Roy Hall, Bernard Long, and Bill Elliott and car owners Raymond Parks, Ted Chester, and Harry Melling.

Pirkle's Dawsonville Pool Room is now located on Bill Elliott Street. "I had nothing to do with that choice," Pirkle says quickly. But he's not complaining. He loves to tell stories of Bill Elliott's victories, and of the wailing siren that celebrated them, and he's grateful for the cornfield story, too. Despite the claims of others, that's where stock car racing really started, he says: in the Etowah River bottoms of moonshine country.

Drive-in Movie Theaters

An American icon, reborn

RUNNING A DRIVE-IN THEATER has never been easy, even back in the days when that was the place to go if a guy wanted to snuggle up with his sweetie with only a slight chance that the warden would shine a flashlight into his car.

The first drive-in theater in America was located in a cow pasture in South Carolina, the late author William Price Fox writes in one of his humorous pieces. Or maybe it was a bean field in North Carolina. In 1921, Claude V. Caver of Comanche, Texas, received a permit from the city to project films downtown. Parked bumper to bumper, folks watched movies from their cars. They saw, but they didn't hear. The movies were silent. The best-documented claim comes from Camden, New Jersey, where chemical company magnate Richard M. Hollingshead, Jr., applied for and received the first patent for an outdoor theater. In 1932, he tested his concept in his own backyard. He nailed a screen to some trees, set up a 1928 Kodak projector on the hood of his car, put a radio behind the screen, and birthed movie watching under the stars. He opened his first "park-in theater" on June 6, 1933. The term "drive-in" came later. So did the term "passion pit," a place for young lovers.

The popularity of the drive-in peaked in 1958, when 4,000 outdoor movie theaters were operating in the United States. In 1982, the number had declined to 3,178, according to Charles Reagan Wilson, one of the writers of the *Encyclopedia of Southern Culture*.

It wasn't easy for a drive-in owner to get his money, because somebody was always trying to sneak in without paying. Then the film would often break right in the middle of a movie, and folks who were truly watching would rudely blow their horns, as though the projectionist didn't know there was a problem. And because this was before the word "environmentalist" had been invented, somebody had to pick up all the empty popcorn boxes strewn around the lot like it was open house at a new landfill.

In family lore, it was via a poker game that Sherryl Major's ancestors ended up with the Tiger property. Her great-grandfather, Jesse Shirley, the story goes, won the land with a good hand in 1816.

Eventually, Louise Cannon Wilson, Sherryl's mother, became one of the landowners. Her subsequent husband, Bill Wilson, had received a scholarship to attend Georgia Tech, but he dropped out after two months to open a skating rink in Commerce, Georgia, where he was raised. After they married, the Wilsons decided to move to Tiger. "Mama wanted me to be around her folks," Sherryl says, and Mama was commuting to Commerce, where she owned a beauty school. She wanted her husband to have something to do, so they bought the Twin Lakes Motor Court in Tiger from an uncle.

It was in the early 1950s that Wilson, Cousin Larry "Satch" McClure, and Uncle Clyde Cannon got to thinking about building a theater. Drive-in movies were popular in those days, so why not give it a go in Tiger? Local folks, they figured, needed something to do besides go to the square dance in Mountain City. And they were right.

Wilson eventually bought out McClure and Cannon and took ownership of the drive-in outright. In the meantime, Sherryl, about six years old when the theater opened, was learning to cook, sort of. She popped popcorn and made pizzas and hot dogs. A few years later, she was accompanying her daddy to pop more corn at the Sherryl Auto Theater, a drive-in named for her in Hiawassee, Georgia.

Then the government decided to mess with the clocks, approving something called daylight saving time, pushing the time one hour ahead, which meant it didn't get dark enough in the summertime to show a movie until nearly nine thirty, and folks working the third shift at the carpet mill had to be at work at eleven.

Wilson and other drive-in owners went to Atlanta trying to get the state legislature or the governor to kill daylight saving time, but no deal. Of course, it didn't help business that the now-teenage Sherryl was supposed to be selling everybody tickets at the ticket booth but was letting a bunch of people in free.

"Daddy would get so mad," says Sherryl, now Sherryl Major, married for forty-something years to California native Tom Major. "He'd say, 'I used to drive up there, and that place would be packed. And I opened that tackle box up, and there'd be three to four dollars in there.' I'd let the whole football team in free. I wasn't very good at working there."

Well, Sherryl felt sorry for people, she says, and when a driver whined that he had enough money for only one ticket, she'd let his passengers in without tickets. "Daddy fired me."

Even those who didn't take advantage of Sherryl's soft heart sometimes found a way to get in free. Sometimes they didn't make it. Bill Blalock remembers the night that about fifty people had bought tickets, but another seventy-five or so tried to sneak in from the backside of the theater lot. Sheriff Lamon Queen was there to arrest them. "He had two or three deputies with him," Blalock says, "and they were picking up folks right and left."

One night, Blalock himself tried to get two in for the price of one. While he paid at the ticket booth, a friend hunkered down on the passenger's running board of Blalock's 1940 Ford and hung on to the door handle. But as Blalock drove off, someone spotted the other guy and started yelling.

"I jerked that thing down into low gear," Blalock says, "went flying through the lot and out the exit, spinning wheels, with my buddy still holding on. I stopped down the road, and he was white as a sheet. He said, 'You like to kill me.'"

Sherryl Major and Blalock recall the night Lester Flatt and Earl Scruggs, the bluegrass boys who became famous, came to Tiger to perform on top of the refreshments building before the movie started.

"I guess it was summertime, but it was so foggy, you couldn't see them. You could hear them, but you couldn't see them," Blalock says. Scruggs had to retune his banjo several times because the head would get wet and the instrument would wander out of tune.

Bill Wilson, Sherryl Major's father, did make some money, despite efforts to the contrary, and people around town obviously knew it. One night, Tom Major says, a man knocked on Wilson's door at home after the drive-in had closed, claiming his car had broken down. Wilson said he could use the phone, but once inside, the man demanded the cash box from the drive-in. "I've already taken it to the bank," Wilson said. "I'm sorry. But I'll write you a check." Wilson got a couple of broken ribs after that remark; the would-be robber didn't get anything.

When the movie *The Great Locomotive Chase* was being filmed in Rabun County in the mid-1950s, the actors, Fess Parker, Jeffrey Hunter, and Slim Pickens, "came to the drive-in all the time," Sherryl says. In fact, she was in the movie, a young girl sitting at a table with Jeffrey Hunter, with her back to the camera, unfortunately.

As the years passed, one by one, drive-in theaters were shuttering all over Southern Appalachia and across the nation. Finally, in 1984, Bill Wilson got tired of fighting a losing battle and closed the place down.

Tiger Drive-In sat empty and alone for twenty years. The screen rotted and fell in; the ticket booth and the refreshment stand wasted away. All that remained, besides weeds, were entrance and exit roads and the terraces built so that all the movie watchers, even those without cars, could see the screen.

One day more than a dozen years ago, Sherryl Major told her husband pitifully, "I want my theater back."

Instead of buying a new screen, he bought several creosoted power poles, ordered aluminum panels from a company that makes NASCAR fenders, had them painted brown on one side and white on the other, attached the panels to treated lumber and steel and then to the poles, and, using a cherry picker, erected a new screen. Instead of sixty thousand bucks for a ready-made one, he spent eight thousand.

Major built a new ticket booth, and for the refreshments building and projection room, he ordered two portable garages and had them placed end to end. He bought a used film projector, erected a new marquee with a colorful likeness of the drive-in's trademark tiger, and then was ready to show movies and sell "some of the best drive-in food anywhere."

On April 1, 2004, fifty years after Bill Wilson welcomed his first customers with a movie starring Burt Lancaster, his daughter had the drive-in theater back up and running. The grand reopening featured the grandest of all drive-in movies: *Thunder Road*, a movie about moonshining and fast cars, a movie that Bill Wilson had shown several times a year, often to a packed lot.

———

Bill Blalock was there in 1958 when *Thunder Road* flickered onto the Tiger Drive-In screen for the first time. He was fourteen years old and tagging along with a couple of friends who had dates. He has seen the movie Lord knows how many times since then.

Today, Blalock owns a 1950 Ford Custom Deluxe Tudor with a 292 Ford Y block engine, a car just like the one that actor Robert Mitchum drove in the movie. The car is an exact replica, down to the numbers of the Tennessee license plate.

Blalock agrees that the movie is certainly about cars, but the underlying message goes deeper, he says. It's about Southern Appalachia. It's a history and a way of life. The movie was always a crowd-pleaser at the Tiger Drive-In. But when Tom Major was ready to reopen the theater in 2004, he had to pay about two thousand dollars to retrieve the 35 mm film from archives in London.

After its release in 1958, *Thunder Road* kicked off every season at the Tiger Drive-In. For the event, "everybody souped up their cars," Major says, "and when they left the theater, they laid rubber all the way down the road."

Today's drive-in patrons are better behaved, Major says. Tiger Drive-In now appeals largely to a different audience: older people with families who enjoy a nostalgic evening out under the stars with a Coke and maybe a Philly cheesesteak. Those who laid rubber in 1958 are now in their seventies, and they drive cautiously out the exit.

If an R-rated movie is being shown, Major says, he makes it the second part of the double feature, giving people with families a chance to leave after the first one. The projector was upgraded in 2014 from a 35 mm film version to digital, giving Major several possibilities.

Now that the projector is digital, film is not a problem anymore. There is none. Tom Major equipped the place with a satellite dish, allowing him to show Monday Night Football or, as he did one night, feature Jimmy Buffett in a show simulcast from somewhere in Texas. "We packed this place," Major says. "We had people from all over."

The drive-in lot is also available for flea markets, farmers markets, antique-car shows, arts festivals, and other events. Major is big into marketing, using social media to get the word out about upcoming movies. "We tell people to come and bring your dog, bring your friends and family and sit outside."

PLATE 13   Annual MG Convention at the Tiger Drive-In

PLATE 14   Tom Major says business is good, but drive-ins are fading across the nation.

Many people do bring lawn chairs and sit outside—sound for the movie is FM broadcast from six speakers—but some prefer to stay in their vehicles.

If it's raining, well, that's not a good night for the drive-in. But business overall has been good. The theater is open on dry weekends thirty-six weeks a year, from April until Thanksgiving week, and in October 2015, income was forty-eight percent higher than the entire year of 2014, Major says. He credits marketing, word of mouth, a better menu, and good weather.

Drive-in theaters still have their problems, though. For one thing, it's hard to schedule screenings several weeks out because distributors require that some movies be kept longer than they're wanted. Not-so-good movies can be problems, too, and movie distributors demand half of the nights' profits. Perhaps that's why, as of October 2015, there were only 270 drive-ins left, according to Tom Major, four of them in Georgia.

By the way, Tom Major is usually in the ticket booth on movie nights, so the drive-in has a better chance of making a reasonable profit than it did back in Bill Wilson's day, when Sherryl let people in for free. Of course, Major is lenient with a resident of the assisted-living village, which the Majors own next door, who regularly drives her electric wheelchair down the hill to the refreshments building to enjoy a free ice cream.

Come Thanksgiving week, Tiger Drive-In again will close for a few months. It gets cold in mountainous Rabun County in the wintertime, and snuggling isn't what it used to be for folks who grew up fifty years ago. But in the spring, when the sap begins to rise and trees decorate themselves in chartreuse, that old Southern favorite, *Thunder Road*, in glorious black and white, is expected to flicker onto the drive-in's homemade screen one more time. And like the swallows to Capistrano, those now-mature movie fans will return to Tiger Drive-In, some in their restored Fords and Chevys from the 1950s and '60s. They'll sit and watch—and remember their salad days under the stars.

Water Dowsers

The ancient art of finding underground water

MOSES MAY HAVE BEEN the first good water dowser. The Holy Bible's book of Exodus says he could coax water from a rock just by striking it with a stick, and according to Numbers 20, he could simply talk to a rock and bring forth water. But Moses, a hardheaded fellow sometimes, decided to smite the rock again, instead of speaking to it, as God commanded. And God was not pleased.

But the fact is, according to the Bible, Moses struck water both times, albeit with some divine assistance. Locating sufficient underground or under-rock water before you dig or drill is a little more difficult today, but it's not impossible.

Back in 1973, the late Charlie Hammonds Patton of Banks County, Georgia, used a forked stick from a peach tree to find underground water, and he didn't have to smite anything. He just watched for the stick to tilt downward, presumably toward water. He always found what he was looking for, he said in an interview. In that same county, the late Hoyt Duncan made a contraption out of wood with copper tubing attached. And according to his son, Paul Duncan, he too found water.

Hoyt Duncan's great-grandson, Dee Rylee of Banks County, who along with Rickey Hicks of White County, Georgia, owned Northeast Georgia Well Drilling, used L-shaped copper rods to go water hunting all over the region.

PLATE 15   Mr. Patton ready to dowse

But what does the movement of a forked stick or copper rods have to do with finding water? Hicks has one answer. "When you're witching—we call it witching for water—I think actually what it marks is the seam or crack in the rock [underground]. Water can't run through solid rock. So that's where the water is at: in the crack or seam. But, every now and then, you'll run into a dry seam. It won't have water in it. It's got to be some magnetic pull," causing the dowsing device to move.

Does he think witching for water is a gift?

"I think it's more of your body makeup," says Hicks, who has retired from the well business and sold his part to Rylee. "You can call it a gift if you want to. It's the way your body is made up."

Charlie Patton says all you need for successful dowsing is "enough electricity in your body." A retired well digger, he has not heard of the controversy surrounding water witching; many believe that the person holding the divining rod controls its movement. He's never heard the word "rhabdomancy," which is the technical name for divining, or dowsing, with rods or wands. All he knows, he says, is what he was taught by "a feller name a Suggs" in the 1920s. With that knowledge, he brags, he has found water for maybe two hundred people, without a miss.

I ask Patton to demonstrate his dowsing technique: He cuts a forked stick from a peach tree located behind his simple, four-room home and, grasping the prongs, puts the point of the Y-shaped stick into his mouth and positions it straight up.

With his palms turned outward and his eyes focused trancelike on the point, he begins to walk toward the side steps of his home, being careful to hold the stick steady. Just before he reaches the steps, the stick appears to pull itself downward and in a second is pointing toward the ground. Patton then walks toward the steps from another direction, and when he reaches the same spot, the dowsing stick does its thing again.

"There's a vein of water that runs right under them steps," says Patton. "A forked stick from any tree that grows fruit will work in huntin' water."

More than forty years ago, a study showed an estimated twenty-five thousand water diviners still practicing in the United States. Today, that number probably is smaller, says Lee R. Barnes, Jr., of Waynesville, North Carolina, vice president of the Appalachian chapter of the American Society of Dowsers. One indication might be the number of people who attended Barnes's water-dowsing classes at a chapter conference near Asheville, North Carolina, in March 2015. Of the 260 attendees, only about five percent were interested in water dowsing. "Dowsing is more diversified today," says Barnes. "Our local chapter is about forty years old. Originally, it was mostly water dowsers. Now it's more metaphysical people, body energies and other stuff."

Lee Barnes usually isn't dowsing for energy; he's looking for underground water. And he offers a money-back guarantee if he doesn't find it. Now that he's semiretired as a land consultant—he has a PhD in agriculture horticulture—dowsing for water provides his cash flow.

Asked about his success rate, he says it depends a lot on the well driller. "With my best driller, I have a ninety-five percent success rate," he says. "I've had about two hundred wells drilled, and on average, I have a better than ninety percent overall success rate. When I can, I go back and check to see if the driller has drilled straight. And they don't always drill straight."

In western North Carolina, where Barnes lives and works, well drillers normally penetrate crystalline bedrock to get to underground springs. And, like Rickey Hicks, Barnes believes that when dowsing, he senses "the elec-

PLATE 16   Paul Duncan uses his father's dowsing contraption.

tromagnetic differences in the bedrock cracks, and that's where the water is flowing." The depth of the drilling, he says, is normally anywhere from two hundred to four or five hundred feet, sometimes more.

Barnes teaches classes on dowsing; in fact, he was named the 2012 Educator of the Year by the American Society of Dowsers. Besides water witching, his students learn how to find old railroad routes, whose tracks have been gone for ninety years. In those cases, he says, the ground was probably magnetized by the physical wear of steel wheels on steel rails. So the dowsing rod reacts to the magnetization. In dowsing for old gravesites, which he also has done, he believes the divining rod detects changes in electromagnetic properties resulting from the digging and refilling of the grave. "Some of this I can explain scientifically," he says. "Other things are more difficult."

Charlie Patton and Hoyt Duncan didn't have such scientific explanations. They just knew that their dowsing devices worked. Duncan's dowsing instrument was a contraption he made from the back of a child's chair with copper rods attached. When over a vein of water, two of the rods would turn around and around, his son, Paul Duncan, says. "If it turned one way, the water was under rock; if it turned the other way, it was above rock."

Hoyt Duncan found 150-something wells for a driller in Lavonia, Georgia, his son says. He found water in Rabun, Towns, White, and Hart Counties in Georgia. One small town hired two professionals and one water dowser to find water and ended up with three wells. But Hoyt Duncan came in and "found enough water to furnish the town with one," his son says. Duncan never charged for his services, although he would accept a chew of tobacco if it was offered. He was afraid he'd lose his abilities if he took money, Paul Duncan explains.

When he was ninety-nine years old, Papa Hoyt checked himself in at a nursing home, where he spent his last four years. When one of his nurses asked if he could find water for her, Duncan responded, "Yeah, but you'll have to lay down on the floor."

Can anyone learn to dowse for water? "I think so," Barnes says. "I have taught close to eight hundred or nine hundred people in an hour, two-hour or longer classes. How to do it over a water hose and then over a culvert and then over a completely hidden site. I had maybe five or six people who did not get a response. I think it was because they were in fear or were blocking themselves somehow."

It was Papa Hoyt who taught Dee Rylee and Rickey Hicks how to dowse for water. They both use L-shaped copper rods.

Rylee compared his dowsing method to techniques used by hydrogeologists. "In talking to them," he says, "they put ohm probes down in the ground, just like an ohmmeter, and then take resistance readings. What they're hunting is voids in the rock. Everybody says you're hunting for water, but you're hunting for cracks. You've got to have cracks to flow through because we're in granite."

The origin of the divining rod is lost in antiquity. The "rod" is mentioned many times in the Bible connected to miraculous performances, especially in the books of Moses. If you believe that Moses was a water dowser, as passages in Exodus and Numbers imply, then, dowsing goes back more than seven thousand years. Though it is certain that rods or wands of some kind were in use among ancient peoples for forecasting events and searching for lost objects, little is known about how they were used or what relation, if any, they may have to the modern device.

But does the divining rod really work? In controlled tests, researchers failed to find a correlation between the rod's actions and the locating of

PLATE 17   Rickey Hicks uses metal rods for dowsing.

underground water. But don't try to tell that to people who still practice, or believe in, the art of dowsing for water.

Asked what he tells skeptics, Dee Rylee says: "I tell them God put it down there, we just got to find it. My theory is, it's not foolproof, but it helps better than anything else we've got." People might spend two to three thousand dollars to get hydrogeologists to hunt for water, he says, "and I've had friends who'll have flags all over the yard, and the hydrogeologists will tell you which flags to drill first. Not much water. And then you witch it and that well will be good. And it's not one of the flags."

Says Lee Barnes: "I can show a lot of wells that were unsuccessful or dry, and I found good water within twenty, thirty, forty feet of them. That convinces me that I am sensing something that does lead to water." Charlie Patton says flatly that he never missed finding adequate water.

Did Hoyt Duncan ever fail to find water? "Not that I know of," his son says. "Maybe not enough as needed." Rylee says that during a drought about fifteen years ago, several vein pockets turned out to be dry.

Rickey Hicks recalls a chicken grower who wanted a well drilled in a certain spot, one convenient to his broiler houses. That's where he and Rylee drilled. "We never did hit water," Hicks says. "Then we went up on top of a hill and marked it where we wanted to drill, went three hundred and twenty feet and got twenty-something gallons a minute."

Outhouses

An interview with "priviologist" Mary Frazier Long

AT FIRST, the soft, sweet, Southern voice of Mary Frazier Long might deceive her listeners. She comes across as a stereotypical teacher of the old-school variety: prim, proper, polite, persnickety. But then her mischievous wit breaks through as she gets into the subject of her chosen expertise. Mary Long is a priviologist.

That's a made-up word, of course, but it is descriptive. It means that this lovely lady has the scoop on privies. You might call them outhouses, earth closets, water closets (although there's usually no water), johnny houses, or other names a bit too colorful to list.

Whatever the name, Long knows her stuff. She can speak from experience; like most people in their eighties who grew up in Southern Appalachia, she has walked the walk. Or she can speak from her vast studies of one-, two-, three-, or more-holers.

Years ago, Long put together a little pamphlet that featured photographs of outdoor thrones in Georgia, most of them accompanied by a thoughtful quotation such as: "Let all your things have their places; let each part of your business have its time." She has sold or given away about ten thousand copies as she travels the state giving lectures, between two and three hundred of them on her "Privial Pursuit," as she calls it.

"That just goes to show that people don't have much taste," she said. "This pamphlet makes a good golden-wedding-anniversary gift. It's got gold on the cover. By the time you have a golden wedding anniversary, you don't need anything anyhow."

So why did Long become an orator on outhouses?

Here's how it started: She and a United Methodist minister, Don Herndon, were named to a scholarship committee for the Georgia Retired Teachers Association. "I thought all we had to do was choose people to get the scholarships," she said. "But then we found out we were responsible for getting up money for scholarships. That threw a whole new light on the matter."

What are we going to do, Don? she asked Herndon, a school guidance counselor. Said Herndon, "Well, I'm a preacher, and I can raise money by getting honorariums for preaching at different churches. But you're a Baptist, and you can't even dance."

Then Long realized that "not a lot of people are going around giving lectures on privies, and I thought I'd try it," she said. She spoke in churches and elsewhere on the history and usefulness of outhouses, and earned money to contribute to the association's scholarship fund.

One day, a local librarian telephoned Long and asked if she knew she'd been included in a book called *Weird Georgia*. No, she didn't, she said, relieved that the call wasn't about overdue books.

But there's nothing weird about her field, Long maintains. After all, Deuteronomy 23:13 explains plainly what people are supposed to do after relieving themselves. So she has a biblical basis for her lectures.

Judy Johnson, mayor of Lawrenceville, proclaimed September 4, 2013, "Mary Long Day" in Lawrenceville. "She's our local historian," Johnson explained. "She has authored several books [five, to be exact] and articles on Lawrenceville. In the past few years, she has participated in a trolley tour. Residents get on a trolley and ride around the city, and Mary gives the historical aspects, all the interesting facts, some true, some not true. You know, Mary has a sense of humor."

When Long lectures, she displays her privy photos on poster boards. She shuns electronic media, she said, because old people tend to go to sleep when you dim the lights to show slides.

Long knows a lot of outhouse jokes and pranks, but sometimes reality is even better. For example, she had kinfolks, Uncle Henry and Aunt Lizzie, who had a rooster that controlled both his roost and the couple's. "They'd

PLATE 18   An outhouse

get about halfway to the outhouse," she said, "and that rooster would chase them the rest of the way. They never had a can of Metamucil or anything in the house. Because of that rooster, you had to go when you got there."

One of her favorite stories involves a young preacher in Bostwick, Georgia, who invited her to speak and then found out on the day of the lecture what she was going to talk about.

"Just before I was to speak, the preacher said, 'Now, Mrs. Long, I'm going to introduce you, so what do you want me to say?' I said, 'Just tell them I'm going to talk about privies.'" Her program, remember, is called "Privial Pursuit."

"I thought you said 'Trivial Pursuit,'" the preacher told her, terrified of his congregation's reaction. "Just promise me it's not vulgar," he pleaded. "I felt sorry for the little fellow," Long said.

One time, Long's reputation as a funny lady reached all the way to the nationally televised *Ellen DeGeneres Show*. "Are you still able to travel?" a staff member of the show asked her by phone. "Well," she said, "I can manage to get up in the morning and brush my teeth." She had to turn down the invitation, though, because she had committed to speaking to a group of local teachers at the same time.

PLATE 19   Mary Long

Long, by the way, is versatile in her presentations. When talking to a bank group, she cracked jokes about making deposits, and for an event for public-housing employees, she referred frequently to "the relief office." She embraces anyone with a sense of humor. "If you don't have a sense of humor," she's been known to say, "you don't have any sense at all."

Long has cut down her number of lectures because of her husband's health problems. He often accompanied her to speaking events and always supported her however he could, even when she was sneaking into people's yards to take photographs.

Long has been a member in good standing of the National Privy Diggers Association, although she's never dug a privy. She prefers digging up nostalgia instead. People enjoy remembering the days of the early-morning treks to the little house located away from the residence, but no one has expressed an interest in returning to them.

Thanks to Mary Long, however, a lot of people in Southern Appalachia are more aware of how far they've come since the days of "unplumbed households," to use the government term. In her lectures, she tells the history of bathrooms and a few things about Sir John Harington, an English writer and ambitious courtier credited with inventing the first flush toilet in the late 1500s. Seeking favor from Queen Elizabeth, his godmother, he installed a flusher in her palace, but she found it too noisy and Harington's satirical writings too crude for comfort.

Times have changed considerably. There was a time when the city of Lawrenceville was loaded with outhouses. It was an era when a person's quiet time was more predictable, and visible. "You knew not to go to see certain people at certain times," Long recalled, "because that's when they were in the outhouse. You could look out and see when they were going."

Mary Long loves history, whether it's about presidents of her country, the city of her birth, the denomination of her Christian faith, or the outhouse of her youth. And when the history and stories are about outhouses, the subject goes pretty deep. Perhaps it's because material for her lectures goes back to the beginning of time. As she said, "People have been going to the bathroom since Adam and Eve."

Appalachia on Television

The story of Heartland

WHEN WILEY OAKLEY GOT MARRIED in East Tennessee in the early 1900s, he and his bride decided to honeymoon way back in the mountains. To get to their cabin, they had to crawl over logs while carrying their suitcases, along with some wild honey Oakley's daddy had given them.

"Of course, we was on our honeymoon, you know, so we just had honey and *more* honey," Oakley said.

"After three or four weeks or a month or so, I don't know just how long, but anyway, she said something that didn't sound very good, and I said, 'If you're going to talk that way to me, I'll just get my hat and I'll go to Dad's down in Gatlinburg. You can go wherever you want to.'

"I started out the door, and I looked back and she smiled and said, 'You ought to give me a lock of your hair before you leave me up in these wild mountains.'"

Well, that comment angered him even more, so he walked on. After a few steps, he had to go past a cow barn, and he said to himself, "That's a mighty few words to leave that girl up here in these wild mountains. Up here among the bears and the bobcats, and so on. Maybe I better see her out." He hid behind the cow barn.

"I waited for a half hour, or you might say something like an hour, and I decided to walk around and peek around the corner to see if she was making any effort to come out. When I looked around, why, she had her head stuck out the door and said, 'I guess you better come back.' And I said, 'I don't care if I do.'"

Oakley walked back to the cabin. The couple never parted again. "So, these young people," Wiley Oakley said, winding up his story, "when they get married, shouldn't ever pass up the cow barn. If they ain't got a barn, it might pay 'em to build one. Save a lot of trouble."

Knoxville, Tennessee, television station WBIR was well into its Heartland Series when a recording of Wiley Oakley's story turned up. This was story-telling at its best. But Jim Hart, the station's general manager, already knew about storytellers in the Great Smoky Mountains. They were people who could spin a yarn without cracking a grin, even if the story was somewhat embellished; people who knew the hills and hollows like moss knows a tree, people who cared deeply about the traditions and heritage of their region.

The Heartland Series began in 1984 as Hart's brainchild. A hiker and supporter of the Great Smoky Mountains National Park, he envisioned some sort of short, regular feature to commemorate the fiftieth anniversary of the park, whose official birthday was June 15, 1934. He turned to Steve Dean, marketing and promotions director at the station, to make it work.

Assuming they could find a sponsor, the series of five-minute vignettes might last six months. That was the plan anyway.

To everyone's surprise, the series ran not for six months, not for a year, but for twenty-five years, thirty, if you count the fifteen or so one-hour specials that followed, from 2009 to 2015.

"The show was a huge hit," Dean said, "because it wasn't something you normally see on TV. So after six months, we thought we were going to shut down, and the public just said, 'We want it to continue.'" Viewers wrote letters, made phone calls, showed up in person to say, *This is too good. Let's keep it going.*

Hart carved out a spot in three local newscasts—morning, noon, and late night—to feature two different Heartland stories fifteen times every week, three times each weekday. Each segment was to run three minutes, forty seconds, with a commercial and introduction pushing it to five minutes.

"Foxfire was a huge influence on deciding what it would be like," said Dean, who wrote scripts for most of the early stories. He had read several books published through the Foxfire program, but Dean himself, Hart said,

PLATE 20   Steve Dean

PLATE 21   Steve Dean's grandfather
Sylvester Patton "Major" Dean
never learned to drive a car.

also "had an ancestral voice inside of him that picked up on the nuances of what it was like to live in those times."

Sylvester Patton "Major" Dean, Steve Dean's grandfather, for instance, rode a horse everywhere he went until he was ninety years old. "He kept falling off it, and we said, 'You've got to stop,'" Dean said, smiling. "My father tried to teach him to drive in the 1940s. He ended up in a creek, and he never got back into the driver's seat again."

Dean knew about killing hogs, about the make-do attitude of the mountain people, about their ability to make something from nothing. He also knew how to tell stories—that's what television was all about—and he wanted a special person to tell them. Shying away from news reporters, he opted for a local actor, Bill Landry, who for years performed a one-man play about Albert Einstein called *Einstein the Man*. Landry had traveled thirty-eight states and two provinces in Canada, portraying this man of extraordinary wisdom. Now, as narrator of the Heartland Series, he would present the wisdom of the Southern Appalachian people.

Doug Mills had been with the station for about three years when the Heartland Series began, and he was chosen as third-string videographer, which meant he "drew the hikes and riding horseback and stuff like that," he said. But after the first year, he moved up to first-string, shooting nearly all the segments.

The Heartland Series kicked off with two pilot programs, one on Lucinda

PLATE 22   Bill Landry

Oakley Ogle, "the queen of Gatlinburg," Landry called her, and daughter of Wiley Oakley; and another on William Bartram, the flower hunter for whom the Bartram Trail is named. Jim Hart took the tapes to Martin Marietta, which later merged with the Lockheed Corporation to form Lockheed Martin, an aerospace, energy, and technology company. The corporation agreed to a six-month sponsorship. Even the governor of Tennessee at that time, Lamar Alexander, cut a couple of public-service announcements promoting the series.

"The first year," Dean said, "we were centered in the park and the movement to create a park and the people who were displaced. Bill Landry did a great job of finding genuine people." But then the series expanded its boundaries, interviewing Southern Appalachians even in neighboring states.

Heartland never ran out of material. Once the series caught on, viewers often called in with suggestions: *There's a whittler over here you ought to interview; we know a great storyteller you should meet; my granddaddy knows about moonshine because he made it.*

"Some of them were so powerful and the characters so interesting and colorful," Hart said. "Now they're all gone, but we were recording some of the great history of the area, people who never would have been recorded. Many of them grew up even without a high school education. On the other end of the spectrum, we had PhDs from University of Tennessee."

Wiley Oakley was one of those powerful, interesting, colorful characters. Landry called him a "mountain guide with the soul of a poet." He was also a musician, humorist, author, folklorist, yodeler, artist, homespun philosopher, and friend of big shots like John D. Rockefeller and Henry Ford.

The Heartland team discovered Oakley's cow barn story on a recording he made of two tales. On one side of the 45 rpm record was "The Cow Barn," the mountaineer's message to young married couples; on the flip side was a tale called "How Wiley Caught the Bear."

Landry wrote about Oakley and dozens of others in his book, *Appalachian Tales & Heartland Adventures: Stories from twenty-five years of the most successful local TV show in the region's history.*

Oakley was such a great storyteller, the Heartland folks decided to use his own words with no script, only a short introduction from Landry. A couple from the TV station reenacted the story, pantomiming Oakley's story of hiding behind the cow barn, waiting for his wife to appear in the doorway of the cabin.

"All of it made a wonderful piece," Dean said. "That influenced the way we told stories from then on. You don't have to be complicated to tell a story."

Oakley's stories would fill a fifty-five-gallon oil drum if they were all recorded, and many of them involve ingenious pranks he pulled off with straight-faced aplomb.

Famous for his one-liners, when asked if he ever got lost in the Great Smoky Mountains, Oakley responded: "I twern't never lost, but I been mighty bothered."

Some Heartland stories were found accidentally. Early in the life of the series, while it was still finding its identity, Bill Landry and Doug Mills were on their way to shoot one of Landry's introductions for another story when they spotted two men fishing in Little River near Townsend, Tennessee. Mills got some shots of them fishing, and Landry interviewed them.

"One was tall and lanky," Landry wrote in his book. "He wore hip boots. He didn't have on full body waders that fancy trout fishermen wear. Not this tall drink of water. He was a lean mountain man and wore old-school black hip boots that tied to his belt."

That was Walter Bohanan. The other fellow, shorter and a little heavier, was his brother, A.D. The interview, Landry admitted, was rather awkward. The Bohanans weren't sure what these television guys wanted, and the television guys weren't too sure themselves. But they took their tapes back to the studio, and Steve Dean, the executive producer, watched them. Several times. Finally, it hit him. "Here's the show," he said. "Listen to what they're saying. They're telling you what it was like to grow up in the Great Smoky Mountains. They're as good as any man, and they know it. Listen to how they talk, like they're sons of the mountains, and they know them."

It wasn't what the men said, but how they said it. So, Dean wrote a brief introduction for Landry, and the crew put together a piece called "Fishin'." They aired the interview, and just as they did later with Wiley Oakley, they let their subjects tell their own story. More Bohanan stories would follow.

If you ask videographer Doug Mills about his most memorable Heartland shoots, he might have a hard time narrowing them down. He loved his work. "I was extremely lucky to see all the sights we got to see and a lot of the beautiful countryside that I'd never taken the time to see," he said. "The main thing, though, was the people. They were so inviting and welcoming. Everybody was. I think that was because we weren't really news. Once people knew us and we had a little of the history, everybody knew we weren't going to do anything negative."

Over the years, the Heartland team visited Harlan, Kentucky, seven times. That's where Mills grew up and where his father was a coal miner for forty-something years. But the closest this cameraman ever got to mining was cutting weeds outside a mine during a couple of summers. He didn't know how scary a coal mine could be until the day he filmed a process the miners call "robbing the coal." That happens when the miners are on their way out of a mine, getting as much coal as possible as they leave.

"When they'd get to a section," Mills said, "they would purposely let the section they'd just left fall in, so it would relieve the pressure on where they were working." He wasn't afraid at first. The coal will stop here, the miners assured him, pointing to a particular spot. But then, suddenly, they all started running past him while he stood there holding a camera.

"They knew it *should* stop at this certain point," Mills said, "but sometimes once it starts, it doesn't stop. They didn't tell us that until it was over."

Mills names other memorable segments: the one on Joe "the Mule Man" Long from the Clinton, Tennessee, area; the story of a ferry boat that no longer operates; the time he filmed a fawn running to its mama while Mills's young daughter lay asleep in the front seat of his truck parked in Cade's Cove, a beautiful, fertile area of the national park.

The Heartland folks couldn't resist tongue-in-cheek segments, of course, when April Fools' Day rolled around. They ran twenty of them in all, including pieces on "electric trees," trees in the national park equipped with electrical outlets; ten-thousand-year-old water skis found in an archaeological dig indicating that Paleo-Indians were way ahead of their time; and the introduction of elves, not elk, into the national park.

After the Heartland Series ended in 2009, the television station decided to hold a reunion at the Museum of Appalachia, just outside Knoxville. Except for about fifteen one-hour specials that Steve Dean produced occasionally for the next six years, the series had run its course. But officials at WBIR, sold in 1995 to the Gannett Company, wanted to celebrate its legacy with whoever wanted to come.

About ten thousand people, many more than expected, showed up for what was called "A Gathering of Friends." Most everyone who worked on the series was there, including Jim Hart, the man who first decided that something needed to be done to celebrate the national park's fiftieth anniversary. He left the station in the mid-1990s. Since 2002, he has been president of Friends of the Great Smoky Mountains National Park, a fund-raising organization.

Steve Dean was there, the series' executive producer for several years who came up with a format that fit the station's needs. He left in 2004 to start his own video production company.

Bill Landry was there. He was the face of the series, "East Tennessee's favorite uncle," someone called him, the actor with the down-home, friendly voice who wrote many of the scripts.

Doug Mills was there, body, video camera, and special memories still intact. He was there to record the events of the day, to summarize twenty-five years of the Heartland Series, and to say thanks to viewers and to everyone who participated and helped out.

"This was the first local television that had seriously dealt with the Appalachian culture and did it in a manner that was truthful and respectful," Dean said. Over the years, seventeen or eighteen people worked on the show and left their mark in some way. Obviously, they did a good job. Otherwise, it wouldn't have taken twenty-five years for a six-month series to finally say good-bye.

Georgia: First in Flight!

The story of Micajah Clark Dyer

by Jessica Phillips

AS THE CAR TURNED onto a dark paved road, the trees began to become bigger and fuller. To the left was a large field. To the right was access to Rattlesnake Mountain, from the peak of which Mr. Dyer flew his "flying machine." Continuing down the road, we drove across a wooden bridge that was built over a crystalline creek. The trickling sound of the creek was calm and soothing. Just past the bridge, we saw Mrs. Sylvia Turnage's house peeking through the trees.

As soon as I opened the door, Sylvia approached me with a smiling face and a welcome. Her house was filled with books, a testament to how much she valued knowledge. As we started the interview, you could immediately see her excitement about her great-great-grandfather, Micajah Clark Dyer.

Mrs. Sylvia Dyer Turnage is a local author who loves to record the heritage of Blairsville, Georgia. She started out writing poems, and she has now written several nonfiction publications. One thing that seems to stand out in most of her books is her great-great-grandfather's story. Micajah Clark Dyer was the first to come up with the idea of what we now call the airplane. This fact shocks most people. I know what you're thinking, "Didn't the Wright brothers invent the first plane?" That is correct in that they invented the

PLATE 23   The monument at Micajah Clark Dyer's grave

first gas-engine plane. But in the late 1800s, Clark's ideas were so advanced, people thought he was crazy. Everyone said, "Why would humans need and want to fly?"

Clark's "flying machine" was somewhat different from planes we see today. It was made of wood in the shape of an oval. On the sides of the machine were protrusions that looked like oars on a ship. Attached to the top was a balloon that made it look something like a blimp. Sylvia believes her great-great-grandfather did not use this until later in his flying career.

"He was one of the pioneers that came over with his family when he was eleven years old, and they settled here in Choestoe. That was in 1832 or 1833. He is my great-great-grandfather. He was a farmer, of course. He was very much an inventor. He was always inventing things, even when he was very young. Of course, his greatest invention was his flying machine," says Sylvia.

She goes on to say, "Kenny Akins, my nephew, teamed up with a guy name Bob Davis. They went all around and interviewed the old-timers. Several of the old-timers said, 'Oh yeah, of course he did [build the first airplane].' Kenny said, 'Well, do you have anything written about it?' The old-timers said, 'No, nothing written.'" There were only three people who knew the story firsthand. Kenny said, "You know, I'm more convinced than ever that it happened." He added, "Those people's stories were consistent. They didn't know we interviewed the other. It just has to be true."

PLATE 24   Mrs. Turnage telling Jessica Phillips about Micajah Clark Dyer

Sylvia wrote her first book about her great-great-grandfather "primarily because I said this story is going to be lost. The next few generations are not going to even know about it. That was like in 1994, I believe. Then, in 2006, my book was published. A lot of people saw it. A lot of the family was interested in the story after reading it. About twelve years later, I was sitting in church, and a distant cousin of mine and her husband were sitting beside me. He leaned over and said something about the patent for the flying machine." She and her family had been looking for the patent for years with no luck, but her relative was insistent.

" 'No. I'm telling you they found it. They found it,' he repeated. I tell everybody you can guess how much I got out of the sermon that morning!" recalls Sylvia.

It turned out, she'd been looking for the wrong thing. "When Kenny and Bob were searching, they were searching for 'airplane,' 'flying machine,' " but "of course, there was no such word as 'airplane,' " she explains. Instead, it was patented as an "apparatus for navigating the air."

After discovering the patents, Sylvia remembers, "We got to sayin', 'Well, we've got to have a model [of the airplane].' I mean everybody was sayin', 'Well, what did it look like? What did it look like?' Well, we had no pictures." Sylvia says, "I was speaking to the Georgia Mountain Writers Club telling them about it. When I finished, a retired nurse who was just a pink lady at the hospital, that volunteers, came up to me. She wanted to buy one of the books. She said, 'You know, I've got a neighbor who worked for Delta.' She said, 'He was a machinist there. He is just amazing and has done all kinds of models, especially of airplanes.' She said, 'Would you mind if I tell him?' I said, 'I would just be pleased. Tell him if he has any interest at all to call me.' So she took her book over and left it with him and said, 'This lady is looking for someone to build this machine.'"

The man called and asked what Sylvia had in mind. "What I would really like to see would be a model that was built to scale from his patent," she told him. "He said, 'Well, let's get together and look at 'em.' So, we did. I took the patent, and he sat down and looked at it. He said, 'Let me think about it.' In about two weeks, he said, 'Let's sit down again and talk about this.'" The man's name was Jack Allen. Billy, Sylvia's husband, asked how much it would cost to make a model of the plane. "I'm not going to charge you anything to do it," replied Jack. "That is the most interesting thing I've come across lately.

"*Georgia's Pioneer Aviator Micajah Clark Dyer* was finished and put in a display case. They have an exhibit in the old Union County Court House. Around the square in Blairsville, the historical society has a nice museum. I'm really pleased that they've got a real nice display for him. Our son-in-law did the first one, carved it by hand. So, the new model replaced his at the museum. We just moved that one and set up an exhibit in the Union County Public Library. Micajah Clark Dyer now has two places where a model of his plane is exhibited. You can also go online to www.micajahclarkdyer.org and look through the models and other things."

PLATE 25   The model of Micajah Clark Dyer's flying machine
(from micajahclarkdyer.org)

"It was many years after his 1874 patent that the Wright brothers got their patent. I don't think what he did in any way diminishes what they did, but it was a different era. They had a gasoline engine. If he had had a gasoline engine, I guarantee he would have been flying up and down the pastures," says Sylvia.

"The flying machine did not have power, except he had paddles which he could catch wind with. What he would try to do was catch the updraft. He needed to get enough speed to come off the mountain and catch a draft, which would lift him."

Dyer was evidently quite a character. "Everybody says his yard was just strewn with things that he was working on. He was always inventing something, lots of little things, you know. He ran water in his house, which nobody had running water in those days. There's a spring up here, which we used also to supply water to our house for a long time. He hollowed out logs and piped the water into his house, so he was just always doing stuff that no one else was doing.

"There were eyewitnesses that saw Clark fly his flying machine, one whose grandmother saw the machine. She's the last one I know of that has sort of at least a secondhand story. Her grandmother told her of coming up here, and he had a workshop that he kept locked. She looked through the gaps between the log walls and saw the machine.

"People made fun of the man, something terrible," says Sylvia. "They thought he was crazy. Not everybody did, because he was also known as the genius. There was a bunch that called him a genius, but a lot of them said, 'No, he is just crazy.' Those ideas were just too far-out for his generation."

But Dyer's flights were observed by at least three of his friends: Johnny Wimpy, Hershel Dyer, and James Washington Lance. "They were the three that said, 'Yes, we saw him fly it.' It was their relatives, though, who passed the story down.

"I think that what he did was so important, the story needs to continue for generations to come," says Sylvia. "It is important for the state, too, because North Carolina has all the credit. Like I say, it doesn't diminish what [the Wrights] did, but they built on this. Some of the people we have talked to at the Smithsonian and the guy who was patent attorney there says it is important. I mean everybody who knows about such things say that it was a very important part of flying history.

"I think he could control it, which was what the whole purpose of the patent [was]," Sylvia continues. "They had the hot air balloons, but they didn't have any control over them. The wind would crash them into things. So, he did this thing, and it was steerable."

For years, Sylvia didn't believe that any photos of her great-grandfather existed. "This lady called me up. She had read the book, and she said, 'Do you have any pictures of Micajah Clark Dyer?' I said, 'No. I have looked everywhere for a picture.' She said, 'Well, you know I have a picture that has been hanging in my house. First it was in my grandmother's house, then in my parents' home, and I've got it hanging in my home now that is Micajah and Morena [his wife].'"

Sylvia is keen to see the local Blairsville airport renamed the Micajah Clark Dyer Airport. "I mean, they really should," she argues. "I went forth before the mayor and the city council meeting, told them why they should name it that, sang the song for them, and they told me they were definitely going to do something for him at the airport. I don't want just 'something done.' I want it named for him. They can do something. I mainly want them to name it for him.

"It is just a shame that there were no newspapers or cameras to record all of this," she laments. "One of the guys who interviewed me said, 'Oh, I don't know. Then Clark wouldn't have needed a great-great-granddaughter.'

"I would have probably climbed right in the flying machine with him and flew in it."

ARTS AND HERBS

Doctoring with Herbs

The story of Eve Miranda, Medicine Woman

A PERSON CAN LEARN A LOT riding with Eve Miranda down the two-lane roads of western North Carolina, zipping through three counties in less than three hours.

We were late—blame it on me—and Miranda was in a hurry to get to her son's home in Macon County, then to Graham County to visit with two friends, and then back to Cherokee County before suppertime. She wasn't speeding, she said—"I never get over sixty"—but she was steering her 1994 Ford Escort barely right of the centerline, maybe to smooth out the ride. "I like to drive in the middle of the road when nothing's coming," she said casually.

Miranda has been stopped by the law only one time, she said, but not for speeding. She never found out why the state patrolman pulled her over, because he left immediately after approaching her car. "Oh my god, ramps," he said, obviously repulsed, as he spun around on his heels, got into his patrol car, and drove off.

She had been gathering ramps most of that spring day, leaving her and her car smelling like, well, ramps, which smell much like garlic. "People either love ramps or they hate them," she said. The patrolman must've hated them.

Diminutive and dark-haired, Evelyn Martha Thompson Miranda, seventy-one years old, is a medicine woman. She goes to the woods and gathers herbs that are said to be useful in treating certain ailments and dis-

PLATE 26   Eve Miranda in her "sometimes" home

eases. In the spring, she collects ramps, along with bloodroot, hepatica, and galm of Gilead. In the summer, she'll look for mullein, joe-pye weed, pleurisy root, yarrow, and other herbs. In the fall, she climbs to higher elevations to dig ginseng, careful not to harvest the roots prematurely.

On the way to her son's home, we talked about many things: herbs, of course, but also God, doctors, our purposes in life, serving people, her mother and father, her grandmother. Miranda even sang part of a favorite song, "Wayfaring Stranger," at the insistence of her passenger.

Eve Miranda is not one for earthly possessions. She does not even have a house. You might say she's homeless, although she prefers "without a permanent home." She house-sits and pet-sits for people in or near her county. When she's not looking after someone's home, she sometimes stays at an old, two-story house just off the main street in Andrews, North Carolina. The house is being completely remodeled inside, and the owner often is out of town.

When she gets tired of being around people, or when she feels "used up," she goes to meditate on a rock in the middle of a river and sleeps in her car for a night or two.

"When you're a medicine person, sometimes you care so much about a person, it takes your strength," she said later, following our ride through the countryside. "It takes your spirit, if you want to call it that. It's like sitting at the bedside of someone you love. Eventually, you get used up."

People around Andrews know Miranda is a medicine woman, and they come to her for advice. Sometimes they'll see her car parked at McDonald's and drop in to talk. But Miranda is careful how she doles out medical advice. She doesn't want to be accused of practicing medicine without a license. So after hearing about a person's ailments, she is likely to preface her response with "My grandmother would have done this."

It was her grandmother, Florence Thompson, who lived in Quitman, Georgia, who taught Miranda the healing properties of certain herbs, starting when she was only six years old. Miranda's parents owned a large farm in nearby Monticello, Florida, and her grandmother stayed with them a lot of the time. Now it's time to pass on her knowledge of herbs to someone else. Miranda chose her daughter-in-law, Tracey Milton.

"A medicine woman," she said, "has the opportunity to choose whom she passes the information on to. She has to feel something between her and that person, and that person has to be willing to be taught."

Miranda has written numerous newspaper columns and magazine articles and published books on flowers, herbs, and Civil War recipes. She earns a little money speaking at seminars about herbs, gardens, edible plants, and trees, you name it. She sells plants she has gathered, but she gives away her concoctions and her advice because that's what a medicine woman is supposed to do.

Miranda founded the Appalachian Heritage Alliance, an organization dedicated to the documentation and preservation of Appalachian history and culture, traditional and modern uses of native plants, and wild crafting. She has worked closely with the Revitalization of Traditional Cherokee Artisan Resources, gathering bloodroot for basket makers and teaching programs on dye plants.

The Bent Creek Institute, a research group for crop growers and botanical medicine developers and processors, dubbed her one of the most knowledgeable people in medicinal plants and featured her in its promotional video "Plants to People." The list of honors, speaking engagements, and community involvement goes on.

———

PLATE 27   Dan and Tracey Milton
in front of the home they built

And yet this woman is homeless. How could someone with such credentials end up without a permanent home? It happened suddenly. Miranda and her mother, Gladys Thompson, moved to Cherokee County permanently in 1995, following the death of Miranda's father, Roy Thompson. Their first home was in Topton, on property that Miranda owned. But after a few years, she "bartered off the home" so that her son and daughter-in-law, Dan and Tracey Milton, could have land for a house. Miranda and her mother moved to Andrews and lived in the back of a store, which Miranda operated, selling watercolors, quilts, homemade soup, and "other stuff appropriate to the Appalachian way of life." She wanted to be in town in case her mother needed a real doctor. But she never did, her daughter said. She wasn't sick, "just wore out."

After Miranda closed the shop, she and her mother rented a small house and lived there until Gladys Thompson died at the age of 105. That was in 2013.

"My mother died July tenth," Miranda said, "and when I went to pay the rent on August third, they said they were going to have to double [it]." She refused to pay the new rate. "I was going to stand on principle," she said, and decided she could live in her car for two or three months, until cold weather arrived.

Miranda admits she felt sorry for herself, at least for a while. "I took care of my husband. He died. I took care of my father. He died. My mother moved in, and I took care of her for twenty-one years. And she died. And I said, 'Lord, I've been a good daughter and a good wife. I've tried to help my community, and I end up with nothing. How come I'm homeless?'"

One day, she drove to the Nantahala River and waded out to a large boulder. She just sat there. "A Bible verse that I had learned as a child kept coming to mind: 'Be still and know that I am God.' But I said, 'Lord, speak to me in a voice I can understand and let me know what I am to do now. Show me.'

"Suddenly a fish jumped close enough to me to spray icy cold water against my face, and it was a wake-up call. I gazed at the river running past me. I had been coming to that same spot in the river for many years, as had my mother and grandmother, and it dawned on me that for twenty-four hours a day, month after month, year after year, decades after decades, centuries after centuries, thousands of years, that river had been running by that rock without my help, and everything began to fall in place."

As Miranda saw it, God was telling her that everything has its time and place on earth, she said, and it was up to her to do something with hers. She gave thanks for the people in her life who quoted scripture to her, hoping that she would follow in their footsteps and go about doing good. Half of all healing, her grandmother had told her, was "being of good cheer, sharing and caring, showing compassion, not taking illness into your heart and soul, and not being a selfish speck."

Her purpose in life, she figured, was not just to gather and prepare her medicines, but also to share her knowledge with others.

"Eve is unique," said Judy Johnson of Andrews, who has known Miranda for nine or ten years and accompanied her on forays into the woods to photograph plants and herbs. "She is one of the most caring people I've ever come across. She tries to help people in different ways. She's good at networking and putting people together who can help each other. That was one of the first things that I noticed about her. She's very community minded."

As an example, Johnson mentioned Miranda's work at the community center in Topton that she kept going, where she helped older people stay busy and useful. She's always willing to help, but don't assume that she will march to anybody else's drumbeat, Johnson said. She has found her own.

PLATE 28   Eve Miranda and daughter-in-law Tracey Milton
show off a crop of mullein growing in the Miltons' yard.

By the time we arrived at her son's home in Macon County, Dan Milton
had closed the gate that protects his place, located on a little hill in the Nantahala Community. "Dan knows I'm never late for anything," Miranda said.

We stayed only a few minutes, long enough to take several photographs
and to listen to Milton talk about how a wad of wet yarrow had stopped his
bleeding after a hay thatcher punctured his arm all the way through. His
wife, Tracey, posed for photos with Miranda, both holding different herbs
growing in the Miltons' yard.

For the past fifteen years, Tracey has been helping her mother-in-law
research the usefulness of herbs, try out new concoctions, and compile data.
She's also been reading and studying herbs on her own. Miranda said she'll
be a good medicine woman.

Soon it was time to mount Miranda's Ford Escort and head off across
the ridge to Pinhook Road in Graham County, near Robbinsville, where
we met Bob and Carol Lawson at their home. They had fled a hurried and
harried life in California and settled down in picturesque North Carolina.

To no one's surprise, the Lawsons have herbs and interesting plants grow-

PLATE 29   Bob and Carol Lawson with a pawpaw tree

ing on their property, including the service berry, or sarvis berry, as it's sometimes called in the mountains. "When it bloomed," Miranda explained, "it
meant the ground was no longer going to freeze hard, and you could bury
your dead."

Standing stately in a neat row at the Lawsons' place are several pawpaw
trees, which produce a fruit used in jellies and pies and even for making
wine. Before he moved here, though, everything Bob Lawson knew about
pawpaws came from the children's song that goes, "Pickin' up pawpaws, put
'em in a basket."

The Lawsons, along with Miranda, were instrumental in starting the
Smoky Mountain Native Plants Association, and Miranda also helped form
the Cherokee Native Plant Association. The three of them helped to produce what Miranda calls "the only ramps product in the US." It's a locally
grown and ground corn made into meal and infused with dried, powdered
ramps. The state patrolman who pulled Miranda over probably wouldn't
like it.

After taking a few photographs at the Lawson place, we were on our way back to Andrews, scheduled to arrive by five thirty. We were on time. "I am never late," Miranda reminded her passenger.

It had been a day of adventure and learning. But one question remained: Where does a person who owns no property gather herbs and plants without breaking the law or getting shot by an angry landowner? Well, some landowners are generous and understanding, Miranda said, and they allow her to gather. She also has friends in forestry and in plant research such as at the Bent Creek Institute, which allows her to gather plants for study.

"The government is making it harder for gatherers," she said. "They say ramps are getting scarce, but they're not. Restrictions play a large part, but if you have a permit or you're on private land, you can still gather." True gatherers, she said, know what they're doing, and they respect the land.

Miranda has no plans to stop. Her grandmother no doubt would have been proud of her. Florence Thompson taught her granddaughter all about herbs: how to identify them, how and when to harvest them, how to use them. To help the child with gathering, Thompson folded up the bottom of one of her large aprons and sewed the sides, closing it off to form a pouch for the herbs. Then she would tie the apron around young Miranda's waist.

For herself, Miranda's grandmother attached a large sash to a croker sack or burlap bag and slung it across her shoulders. They each carried paper sacks with the names of the plants they were looking for. The two set out and gathered first the hard-to-harvest materials, those with deep roots. "If we gathered those later in the day," Miranda said, "it would be much harder, energy wise, to harvest."

Eve Miranda has gone "from rags to riches and back to rags," as she put it, but she wants no pity. "I am perfectly happy," she said. "You don't have to be somebody or have a lot of money to be happy."

She has no earthly home. But she has herbs to gather, workshops and festivals to plan, roads to travel, dances to dance, and songs to sing. She sings somewhere around Andrews practically every Saturday night. She wants to help establish gardens using native plants and pass on her knowledge about herbs to her designated medicine woman. She wants to stay busy.

Today, she's looking at the end of her life, not the beginning. "Okay," she said, referring to herself, "you got ten good years left, fifteen good years left. What are you going to do with your life?"

It appears she's already doing it.

SEVEN IMPORTANT HERBS

Miranda and her grandmother looked for all kinds of herbs, but here we've narrowed the list down to seven that Miranda still harvests, or purchases.

Pleurisy root: "This brightly orange-flowered plant with roots resting in China was the first on the list," one that she created. "It is commonly called butterfly weed because it attracts large swallowtail butterflies. Many times, this root was mixed with other herbs for people with deep-seated wet coughs, lung problems, or pneumonia. It seemed to help get the phlegm up and out. Since harvesting kills the entire plant, I now buy it in bulk from a commercial grower instead of digging it."

Joe-pye weed: "One of my favorite plants to gather was joe-pye weed, or queen of the meadow. While Grandma was digging the roots, I would use the hollow stems to drink water from a nearby creek, or later in the day, when it was hot, I would jump into the creek, into a deep spot, and breathe through it, hiding my body completely under the water. Of course, Grandma just watched for the stem, knowing where I was hiding at any given time.

"We would dry the root, which looked like a person with a bad-hair day, its many parts spangling out in all directions. Then we would dice it up or string it out. And for anyone with gravel or kidney stones, [my grandmother] would make a tea to be drunk until the person found relief."

Yarrow: "One of the most lifesaving and useful of herbs is the yarrow. Just read about Achilles, the great man of war, who insisted that all his soldiers carry a medicine bag filled with yarrow into any battle. He gave away his last amount to a young soldier who had none. [Achilles] was nicked on the heel and bled to death, when, if he had had his usual pouch of yarrow, he could have staunched the flow of blood until his medic arrived. Yarrow also has been used by patients with hepatitis C and those with liver problems."

Bloodroot: "Cancer was not so prevalent in Grandmother's day, but I remember that she used a combination of bloodroot, sheep sorrel, comfrey, and other herbs to treat external cancers. The mixture created a black salve that appeared to draw cancers out by the root."

Wild yam root: "The most called-for these days is wild yam root. I, again, use this root in bulk powder form, filling capsules with the exact amount needed, for folks with acid reflux, babies with colic, and many cold sores and fever-blister cases."

Jewelweed: "For anything that itches, including poison ivy, the jewelweed or touch-me-not is the best there is. The inside of the lush stalk in early summer soothes the rash and seems to stop the eruption in its tracks. We also harvest the seed for making cookies in the fall. They taste a little like walnuts."

Plantain: "This is another plant that is high on any gatherer's list. While tramping through the forests, one is often stung by yellow jackets or wasps or ants, and nothing stops the pain better than your own saliva and plantain. When stung, we just put a wad of plantain in our mouths, chewed it up and put the juice and wad on the bite. Instantly the pain is gone, and usually no swelling occurs."

Wild Ginseng

Interviews with four men who still hunt it the right way

IF YOU DIDN'T KNOW what they were talking about, you might think the Hayes boys were gold prospectors. "To me, it's spiritual," says Bob Hayes. "Spiritual because it's getting harder and harder to find, and when you find it, you thank God it's still around."

Says his son, James Thomas "Tommy" Hayes, "Yeah, it makes you feel really good because you know if you find one, you're going to find others in that area."

"I just sell it," chimes in Isaac Thomas Hayes, Tommy's son and Bob's grandson. The Hayes boys are standing in the kitchen of Bob's home, one he built himself on a hill just outside Mountain City, Georgia. And they're discussing not gold, but the next best thing to a lot of people: wild American ginseng root.

"Here you have three generations of ginseng folks," Bob says. "I taught Tommy, and Tommy taught Isaac." And Bob learned how to recognize and dig wild ginseng from his parents, Arthur and Mary Hayes, whose family lived around the edges of western North Carolina, Tennessee, and Georgia.

In all that moving around, though, Bob learned a lot of things about the woods and how to survive on meager earnings. Wild ginseng was a treasure worth looking for.

"I was about seven years old," he says, "and Mom and Dad would take us up there [on Pack Mountain in Cherokee County, North Carolina]. Mama

PLATE 30   Tommy Hayes and his father, Bob

would always cook a big pot of beans the day before. And that morning of the hunt, she'd cook a pone of cornbread, and she'd take it up on that mountain, put it in a certain spot [in a tree so the critters wouldn't eat it], and tell us to meet back there at lunch. We were usually back before lunch because we were hungry."

That was in the 1950s, when wild ginseng that had been dried would be shipped to New York to be sold there or elsewhere. A pound would bring about seventeen dollars. In 2015, the price had leaped to several hundred dollars.

And why is wild ginseng, or "sang," as they say in the mountains of Southern Appalachia, worth so much money?

Well, it's said to prolong life.

Most of the wild sang dug in Southern Appalachia goes to China. "They pay high dollar for it," Tommy says. "They sell it by the ounce or half ounce. It's very expensive. The Chinese then pulverize it and sell it to the Chinese public. To them, it's an aphrodisiac."

But the root of the wild plant has other, more important benefits, researchers say. The Mayo Clinic Cancer Center conducted a ginseng trial that showed "good results in helping cancer patients with fatigue, when compared with a placebo." And in 2015, researchers at Vanderbilt-Ingram Cancer Center found that ginseng may improve survival and quality of life following a diagnosis of breast cancer.

But researchers warn that the quality of the ginseng is important. Just anything off the pharmacy shelf may not help at all. Which supports what the Hayes boys have been saying all along: You must know what you're looking for when you go into the woods, and if the ginseng is not ready for harvest, don't harvest it.

"We don't dig anything that's small because that's for future digs," Tommy says. "If it's not five years old, it's not marketable. It's not potent. If you dig it and it's small, you judge how old it is, and if it's not old enough, you put it back in the ground." Trouble is, some ginseng hunters don't follow those rules.

"There's too many hunting before the season," Bob Hayes says. "That's the problem. They also dig everything. And that's why sang is going out. I wish they'd catch every one of them."

And, in 2014, the law did catch several men near Highlands, North Carolina, who had spread out in a row to dig young ginseng right and left, a process known as "rowing." They were charged under North Carolina's ginseng-protection laws. Taking ginseng from another's land with intent to sell is a felony.

"Some people go through the mountains like a vacuum cleaner," Tommy says, "but what are you going to do the next year?"

Sometimes, he says, it's not even ginseng that's being dug. "Most beginners dig poison oak like crazy," he says. "And hickory sprouts will fool you. People will truck halfway down a mountain to dig a hickory sprout." Adds Bob: "Especially in the fall of the year because it turns yellow," like ginseng. "And there's a certain briar" that looks like ginseng, too.

Ricky Alexander, a ginseng convert and friend of Bob's, drops in at Bob's home and joins the conversation in the kitchen. He says that walking through the woods looking for sang does wonders for his attitude toward life. "Most of it, I keep for myself," he says. "I haven't harvested enough to sell."

Asked if he feels better when he takes sang, Alexander says, "Yeah, when I get run-down. Like in the summertime, I work seven days a week on the property [apartments next door to Bob], and working for other people." Looking for ginseng in the woods is peaceful, he says, and taking it is beneficial. He takes no store-bought medicines.

PLATE 31   Ricky Alexander,
a ginseng convert and friend of Bob's

PLATE 32   Isaac Hayes,
Tommy's son, enjoys gathering.

Still a novice in ginseng hunting, Alexander says he must be careful where he hunts. He doesn't want to hunt on another person's land without permission, and he doesn't want to dig around someone's home, as someone did at Bob's place.

While hunting and harvesting ginseng is part of hammering out a living for some people, it's more of a hobby for Tommy and Isaac.

Tommy works full-time as a builder; he's pastor of Covenant Baptist Church in Murphy, North Carolina, and the father of four boys. Isaac, a student at Western Carolina University, is the only one interested in digging sang.

"We'll get in maybe six [ginseng] trips a year," he says. "So a good year for us is three dried pounds." It takes three or four pounds of wet ginseng, roots just out of the ground, to make a pound of dried, but that amount depends on the quality of the root.

Bob knows of three types of wild ginseng in this area: five-leaf—the most common in the mountains of Southern Appalachia—three-leaf, and double-decker. He hasn't found any three-leaf ginseng, and he has discovered double-decker in only one place. "Double-decker stands this high," he says, holding his hands at his waist.

Mature wild ginseng bears berries, and sometimes it takes eight years for them to appear, Bob says. But the absence of berries doesn't mean the ginseng is not old enough to harvest; it could be that birds ate the berries, which they sometimes deposit next to logs, a good place to find more ginseng. All ginseng, whatever its type, needs plenty of shade. Store-bought ginseng, along with the stuff found in energy drinks, is often grown commercially with fertilizer, which enhances growth. "It's tame sang," Tommy says. "Tame sang is cheaper, but it doesn't have all the good properties that wild sang has." Tame sang has bigger, whiter, smoother roots. On wild ginseng, the buyer looks for a darker tint on the skin, stretch marks on the roots, and lifelines that indicate the approximate age of the plant.

As a child growing up in western North Carolina, Bob was never sure what the next day would bring. His father made moonshine, and when the law was on his tail, the family often packed up and moved. "Sometimes we'd go to at least three schools a year," he says. "We'd get off the bus and [my parents would] be already packed. Well, it ain't funny on kids. I always said that if I had a kid, he'd go to school, and Tommy went to the same school [his entire childhood]."

Bob's family moved to Murphy after his father became disabled. He and his mother worked at a restaurant, usually eight-hour shifts. "I'd work the third shift and try to get on in to school," he says, "and I'd go to sleep in school." At sixteen years old, he dropped out and began working in chicken houses to help care for his parents. When a deadly influenza hit the area in the late 1950s, "Mama kept us all alive," he says. "She was an herbalist, and she could make some of the strangest-tasting tea you've ever drunk in your life."

But through it all, Bob learned how to survive by developing many skills—logging, construction, plumbing, electrical work—and getting jobs wherever he could find them. Even after he married and moved into his own home, life was not easy.

"Around Murphy," Tommy says, "there wasn't much work for Mom and Dad. They found work where they could. So in the summer, we'd sell lizards. We'd go up in the mountains and creeks, finding lizards. And then we would scatter out and dig ginseng back down the mountain. We did that about every weekend. We also picked up night crawlers. All the money went into one kitty to pay the bills. We sold everything."

Tommy learned that ginseng could be beneficial, but he also learned what not to eat from his father. One day, his dad cut off part of an Indian turnip and handed it to his young son. He ate it. About thirty seconds later, the pain hit. "It's not hot," Tommy remembers. "It's like needles. It's like taking a bunch of needles and throwing 'em in your mouth and crunching down on them. I took off running, and it was probably a half a mile to the next spring, and I drunk that spring dry and it didn't help a bit."

As a pastor, Tommy feels good about digging ginseng if he and his son do it right, the way Bob showed them. "God put everything we need here," he says. "[The Bible] does not identify ginseng, but it does say that God put all this stuff here for man's use. It's up to man to figure out what's good and what ain't. How you learn that is usually trial and error."

Tommy and Isaac enjoy hunting ginseng, not just for the extra money, but because of the opportunity it affords them to spend time together, walking around enjoying nature.

Bob Hayes doesn't get out much now because of a breathing problem. He enjoys staying inside his cozy home on the hill, where he reads constantly. But he can take satisfaction in knowing that his son, grandson, and friend Ricky are following his lead, hunting ginseng on Pack Mountain. A family tradition lives on.

How to Turn Junk into Art

An interview with Jane Taylor

JANE TAYLOR is a folk artist. She finds sad, useless pieces of iron and other metals and welds them together to create whatever that overactive, artistic mind of hers can envision. If she somehow sees a cow in a rusty piece of iron, it will be an iron cow when she's done. If it's a philodendron, those farm-tractor seats she's working with will soon become the hardy leaves of a philodendron. And Taylor is multitalented. She paints. She does interior and landscape designs. But, she says, "I think I will always work with metal."

This petite woman with the pixie cut and perky personality looks like anything but a welder of dirty, rusty, unusable pieces of iron. Still, the evidence is there, some of it standing tall and imposing, some of it "itty-bitty," as she puts it. She welds when it's ninety-plus degrees; she welds when it's freezing outside.

Taylor says she loves art. "I breathe it," she says. But it hasn't always been that way. Her passion only came after many unsatisfying years in more commonplace lines of work.

Jane Elizabeth Taylor—no, she wasn't named after the actress Elizabeth Taylor—was born on June 8, 1961, in Gainesville, Georgia, to Nesta and J. Verlon "Bo" Taylor. Jane's father was a dentist, a man serious about his work and equally serious about everything else. That's the way he wanted his

PLATE 33   Jane Taylor, artist at heart

PLATE 34   The cottage

young daughter to be, serious. So, after high school, Taylor worked in her father's dental office, then in a physician's office, and in a clothing store in Macon, Georgia. "I was very serious most of my life," she says. "Very serious. I was brought up that way. You don't play. I was good at what I did, but I never really enjoyed it."

One day, with enough money saved to carry her for six months, Taylor quit her job and set out to find her calling, or at least something more fulfilling. A friend talked her into getting into the antiques business with him. She went to auctions, bought antiques, and put them in the store. Within a week, they had sold. She filled up her space the next week, and everything sold again. The antiques partnership lasted about a year. But she didn't like not knowing the people who were buying from her. She wanted her own shop.

"So then this place became available," she says, referring to her present cottage and property, which, at one time, had been used to store tractors for a farm-equipment dealership next door.

By 1997, Jane Taylor was in business for herself, owner of a small house and display area on Cleveland Highway, about two miles from downtown Gainesville. But babysitting antiques wasn't her thing either. "I got bored selling antiques very quickly," she says.

But while looking for new stock, "I would go to auctions and see gorgeous iron, broken, sad, beautiful," she says. "It was all hand-forged. But no one bought these pieces, so I bought them, anything that was interesting. At that moment, I fell in love with iron."

At first, she enlisted professional welders to execute her vision, but nothing came back exactly the way she envisioned it. The welders would add their own little touches.

One day, her father, the man who was known for his seriousness, said to her, "Why don't you do it yourself?" Why not? If she did her own welding, she could create exactly what she wanted. Just go to Lowe's, buy a welder, and start welding. What could possibly go wrong?

For one thing, self-taught welders burn themselves a lot, even after they've read the directions carefully. Finally, though, Taylor started to catch on.

"Then," she says, smiling, "the artistic side of me came out. I'd wake up in the morning: 'I must build the Statue of Liberty *today*.'" Of course, she didn't build her scrap metal reproduction of the Statue of Liberty in a day, but in her mind, it was a finished piece, even if it took six months to com-

PLATE 35   *Statue of Liberty*

plete. Once built, her Statue of Liberty stood about fifteen feet tall, solidly constructed out of sheet metal, stove parts, cobbler's shoe molds, shovel heads, and, for the torch, a discarded light fixture illuminated by a dusk-to-dawn solar-powered tiki light.

"I think every artist has a muse, somebody that comes to you and tells you what to do next, tells you what direction to go," says Anne Brodie Hill, a painter and a friend who gets inspiration for her own art every time she visits Taylor's place. "I don't know what kind of muse she has, but a lot of the things she does, like her paintings she's doing now, I don't know where that comes from. She's either got a new muse, or the old one got tired of working with rusty stuff."

Taylor's old muse is still there, ready to nudge her along when she's ready. It's just that right now, for the last few weeks, she's wanted to paint, and she's been turning out abstracts and paintings of cats and other characters.

"The other night," she says, "the person I painted, I painted over it because she looked so sad. You can't hide your feelings in your art." If you ask Taylor about her favorite pieces, she says quickly, "Oh, gosh, they're all my favorites. Then when it's placed in a home, it becomes special. It stands in a perfect spot."

"The figures probably are favorites," she says, "because they develop a personality."

Everything at Taylor's studio is for sale, everything except the seven-foot-tall angel *Marguerite*, named for her grandmother, Marguerite Marie Hine, which stands on the cottage's roof, directly over the office; and an old cash register on her desk that came from a traveling side show. She found that in her dad's garage.

Even the pieces she has taken home for her own enjoyment can be bought, but she admits that she creates art more for her pleasure than for money, not always a good idea if you're trying to make a living. Taylor says she doesn't promote herself as well as she should. "The more arty I have become, the less businesslike I have become," she says. "It trumps that side of my brain. I should be online and have a website, but I have a Facebook page. It must be something about my insecurity as a person. A lot of artists are like that. That's why we're all broke. We don't market ourselves because we'd rather make our art."

Still, Jane Taylor is one of the top-selling exhibitors at the

PLATE 36 Jane with her angel wings

Quinlan Visual Arts Center in Gainesville. Amanda McClure, the executive director, says, "She looks at the world with a perspective all her own, and we are fortunate that she shares this with us."

Making art, after all, is both Taylor's vocation and her avocation. She turns out whimsical works that coax a smile or even a laugh from visitors. She makes refined pieces, such as towering doors and wings and candelabras. And then there are the just plain interesting items that might require a little imagination from the viewer.

Commissioned by an anonymous donor, she built a pair of angel wings to adorn the North Tower entrance to the Northeast Georgia Medical Center in Gainesville. The wings, nearly twelve feet tall, are made of found and sheet metal.

Taylor sees beauty and possibility in some of the strangest objects. Her cramped office offers perfect specimens. There's a spiraling, tapering piece of metal that was used to stir grain in a silo. There's a wheel spacer from a tractor trailer and a set of scales for weighing cotton. There's a chain designed to move feed along in a chicken house. All of these are just waiting to be transformed, like the pipe cutter she turned into a lamp and the angel gleaned from a four-legged Victorian table.

"I just love her angels," says Valerie Kirves, a friend, who has three of them in her home. "I saw those, and I couldn't let them go anywhere else."

Kirves owns a furniture/art business that specializes in iron and metals, and she sometimes takes broken pieces of iron and other metals to Taylor. "I'd be so excited to go back and see what she had created from the broken pieces," she says. "I can't even imagine putting stuff together like she does. She is just so tremendously talented. She's just a really good, bighearted person, and all of her work comes from her heart."

Besides metal that people donate, Taylor regularly scouts around for "strays," as she calls them. While her other strays—three cats—are allowed to hang around the shop, stray metal is transformed into art and eventually moves on. And to Taylor, it's all play, no work.

"My mother is aghast at what I do," she says. "She's proud of me, but she's amazed. She doesn't know where it came from. But she looks at my little hands and cries." Taylor says her hands are marred by calluses, burns, and cuts, and she holds them out to prove it.

Taylor is unpretentious and honest, humble, in fact. For years, she drove

PLATE 37   Jane dressed for work

a 1973 Ford Ranger she called Zelda, which she equipped with wrought iron cemetery fencing for its truck-bed railing. She refuses to copy others' art. "If I can't think of something myself," she says, "I shouldn't be doing this." In describing her folk art, she eschews fancy terms. "I mean, I'm in vogue now," she says a bit sarcastically. "I was doing this twenty years ago, and now it's repurposing. The new one is upcycling. I'm just a recycler."

Whatever you call it, Taylor makes it work. She can turn a dome that covered food in an upscale restaurant into a lovely chandelier, and tarnished cream pitchers into shades for light bulbs. She welds and hatches a bigger-than-life bird from stray parts. She makes three-dimensional Christmas ornaments from sardine cans and trinkets.

Behind her cottage and display yard is a fenced-off area that contains hundreds of metal pieces of all shapes and sizes, along with a shed that houses Taylor's welding station. She's now trying to incorporate paint into her metalwork. "I'm not sure how that will work," she says, but she'll give it a try. And when she succeeds, which is often, she inspires other artists.

"Every time I go over there, I see something I want to paint," says Anne Brodie Hill. "I want to take a photograph of what she has set up, and I want to do a painting of it because it's just so cool. As an artist, I'm kind of an

PLATE 38   Junk for future art

abstract realist, if there is such a thing. I like to do layered paintings of the kind of stuff that she makes. She and I did a collaboration one time, and I've never had so much fun, because of her inspiration. She made me look at old, rusty junk differently." Exhibiting together, Brodie and Taylor called themselves "the Twisted Sisters," taking their cue from the heavy metal band Twisted Sister.

There was once something twisted, Taylor says, about the cottage where she set up shop twenty years ago. The back-left room was, well, a little strange. Taylor and her father painted the room white, perhaps subconsciously trying to sanitize the space. All the pieces Taylor chose for the room were also white. But nothing sold. Nothing. "People would go in the room, and they'd walk right back out," she says.

Taylor had a morning routine for every room in the cottage. She would turn on the lights and a fan and move to the next room. But the lights in the back-left room would flicker off, and the fan would turn itself off. Taylor and her dad avoided the room as much as possible. "Dad didn't like that room."

One day, "this very bohemian woman comes in," Taylor says, "and she's

PLATE 39   Jane with an unfinished project

looking around. And she tears out of the store. I went out on the porch and said, 'Are you okay?' And she said, 'You're going to think I'm strange, but I see auras, I see energy, and that back-left room has a big ball of pulsating evil.'" The woman told Taylor what to do to get rid of the evil. You'll have to do it yourself, the woman said, because it's your space.

Jane Taylor felt a little silly, but she prepared to do exactly what the woman instructed. "It was all kind of comical to me," she remembers. "I took it all with a grain of salt. But there was a little part of me that believed, you know?"

The woman gave Taylor a small sage brush tied with hemp and

explained the ritual. On a night when the moon was full, Taylor placed a small candle on a table in the center of the room. She lit the sage with a match, extinguished the blaze, and then smudged the room's walls with the smoky brush. She stepped into the doorway and prayed, "This is my space. In the name of Jesus, please leave this house."

Suddenly, she recalls, the flame shot up from the candle and splayed on the ceiling. "I dropped everything, the sage brush, and ran out of the room," Taylor says, her voice lowering. "Whew! It was a terrifying experience." The woman came back later to see what had happened. She walked into the back-left room, and when she came out, she said, "You did a good job." "I haven't seen the woman since," Taylor says.

She did hear that several decades ago, five men wanted by the law had holed up in the house, and one or two of them died in a shoot-out with officers. It all made sense, she says.

PLATE 40   Tractor seats become flowers.

A couple of days earlier, Taylor's mother, the coolest mom in the world, her daughter says, texted her about the interview for this story. "Does he understand you?" she asked, referring to me, the interviewer. "Are you projecting what you want him to see?"

Taylor texted back: "I don't know, Mom. I am a work in progress, and I

PLATE 41   Jane's art

learn something new every day. My biggest delight is making people happy. And hopefully I will evolve into an artist who is at peace with her work, finally. It's a battle I go through every day."

Her friends and customers will tell you that Jane Taylor should be at peace with her work. Whether she realizes it, she is an artist in the truest sense of the word.

PLATE 42   Jane's first abstract

PLATE 43   *Picasso's Bull*

Artist, Flint Knapper, Fiddle and Banjo Player, and Naturalist

An interview with Joseph "Doc" Johnson

DOC JOHNSON likes to walk along shorelines, wade in rivers, and wander in fields looking for rocks that talk to him. Rocks that tell him stories about what life was like thousands of years ago, back when Native Americans had this land all to themselves.

Sitting at the kitchen table of his Northeast Georgia home, Johnson holds up a tiny piece of chiseled flint. "This little bitty scraper," he says reverently, "would have been used for scraping fine hides like on a muskrat or a rabbit, something with real thin skin. It would have been used to line the inside of shoes, maybe for adults, but especially for children. It just added comfort for walking around in those shoes in cold weather."

Johnson's goal is to reveal the complexity of Native American culture. He speaks at history, college, and nature events in several places, especially in Northeast Georgia, where he has lived since moving in 1984. If someone will listen, he'll talk and demonstrate.

"He has a broad knowledge of archaeology and prehistoric stone technology—primitive technology in general," says Dr. Max White, professor of anthropology at Piedmont College in Demorest, Georgia.

That's why White invites Johnson to speak to his classes once or twice a year. It's cool, his students say, sitting in a classroom hearing about the stone technology of American Indians. But even more fun is going outside and learning to throw spears using an atlatl, a type of lever Native Americans

PLATE 44   Johnson works with students throwing atlatl.

used to improve speed and accuracy. "They enjoy that so much," White says. So does Johnson.

So who is this man who speaks for voices frequently ignored? Joseph Lloyd "Doc" Johnson is a sixtysomething-year-old of Native American heritage, with longish gray hair and beard, a leftover from the hippie generation but never really a bona fide hippie.

He is nicknamed Doc because his father lost a poker game to a doctor friend from World War II. Dad said he'd name his son after the doctor if he didn't win the next hand. He didn't win. The doctor's name was Delmus. Not surprisingly, the Johnsons settled on Doc.

When he was eleven years old, Doc Johnson was exposed to a number of amateur archaeologists in the country, one of them his Scout leader, Bob Lester. "I loved archaeology instantly," he says.

As a kid, he worked in tobacco fields, a great place for a budding archaeologist because practically every plowed field in hilly Kentucky, where he grew up, revealed artifacts of some kind. In high school, he learned more about archaeology from his track coach, Carl Yahnig, and from friends Hugh Dossett and Sonny Thompson. He accompanied Dossett as he squeezed through cave openings to look for interesting pieces from the past. Dossett liked digging, but "I'm too ADD for digging," Johnson says.

Besides being an amateur archaeologist and defender of the American

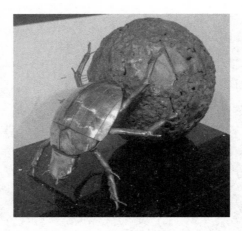

PLATE 45   Johnson's dung-beetle art

Indian, Johnson is many other things: a flint knapper, a fiddle and banjo maker, a musician, a naturalist, an art welder, a speaker and teacher of archaeology, a philosopher, a long-rifle maker, and a sculptor who can turn trash and tin cans into treasured art. He even transformed an image of an ugly dung beetle into a fine copper sculpture that any art collector with a sense of humor would value.

Johnson's route to practically everything has been a bit circuitous; there has been little logical order, few straight lines in this man's career.

Even in high school in Kentucky, Johnson did not completely fit the mold. He played fullback in high school.

"Let me proudly clarify that," he adds. "I played *third-string* fullback, which means that whenever somebody had broken their helmet or face mask, and they needed one, I always volunteered mine, because I didn't want to play. I loved that bench. I knew that the only way I was going to get hurt on the bench was when somebody ran into me sitting there." His goal was to become a fourth-string fullback, but he was too good.

He did have to play on one occasion. "But I hated it," he recalls. "I played the last ten seconds of a game my senior year. I tried breathing real hard to look like I'd just come out, but that didn't work that day. I couldn't get out of it."

After high school, he was offered scholarships to Ole Miss, Ohio State, and Vanderbilt. Not for football, of course, but pole vaulting. "I could do that by myself and nobody ran into me and got me hurt." His vault of thirteen feet, three inches still stands, fifty years later, as his high school's record.

Why didn't he accept the scholarship? "Because I was stupid," he says flatly. He was in love, and his girlfriend was planning to attend Western Kentucky University. But they broke up in 1970.

At the age of twenty-one, this quasi-hippie cut his hair and became a rookie cop in Hopkinsville, but he didn't stop believing in the freedom of lifestyle. Unlike some of the policemen he worked with, Johnson thought a man or woman should be able to dress and wear their hair the way he or she wanted to, as an expression of First Amendment rights.

PLATE 46   Johnson's ID card when he was a cop in Kentucky

"The early 1970s," he says, "was a time when there was a big wall of separation of values, especially with male hippies with long hair. It was nothing for a cop to stop somebody and grab him by the hair and tell him, 'Get your hair cut or get out of town.'"

Three years later, Johnson had been promoted to the detective division of the police department, and one night, he was assigned Elvis duty. It was not unusual for Elvis Presley to fly in his private plane from Memphis to Hopkinsville at about three o'clock in the morning—he didn't want to be mobbed by crowds—and Johnson would pick him up at the airport, take him to an ophthalmologist's office, where Elvis presumably got his eyes checked, and eventually return him to the airport for his flight home. "He was a nice fellow," Johnson says of Elvis. "He wanted to buy my revolver, but I didn't sell it to him."

In the mid-1970s, Johnson gave up law enforcement and finally got serious about college. He earned a bachelor's degree in literature and chemistry from Austin Peay State University in Clarksville, Tennessee, and then moved to Carrollton, Georgia, where he attended graduate school at West Georgia State University. He paid his way making Kentucky long rifles in his dorm room.

Not satisfied with run-of-the-mill courses, Johnson got permission from a professor to design one of his own, called "Psychology of Changing Lifestyle."

"I figured my lifestyle was changing so drastically that I ought to benefit from this, so I designed a course," he explains.

Johnson studied author John Steinbeck's literature on transient and migrant people and decided to become one, with his professor's blessing, of course. He set out for Montana, where he knew nobody, had no job, had no connections to society at all. He didn't make it to Montana. He had bought a 1968 Oldsmobile Cutlass for a dollar—the dollar was for the title, not the car—and it broke down in Springfield, Missouri. Soon afterward, he began working as an apprentice on an organic farm in Arkansas and as a model for the art department of Southwest Missouri State University in Springfield.

He also got a job with the Springfield city school system, working with low-achieving students, and, in his free time, sat in an antiques store. All this time, he was writing letters to his professor, telling him about loneliness and isolation, working and living from hand to mouth. He came out of the course believing he could survive anywhere if he had to. "I lived from day to day," he says. "I got food for the day each day. I wanted to understand prehistoric people, who got food to eat that day and nothing more. I didn't have a problem with that." He received twenty hours' credit for his self-made course.

At WGSU, he also met history professor Newton Leroy "Newt" Gingrich, who later became a congressman from Georgia's Sixth District, Speaker of the US House, and a candidate for the Republican Party presidential nomination. "I was long-haired then like I am now," Johnson says. "And I told Newt: 'You know, the main difference in us is you don't have a bit of hippie in you, and I don't have a bit of bureaucrat in me.'"

Other than that, he says, they were the same, he and Gingrich. "We pursue our passions. To have a passion for something reduces the world to a manageable size. The grand essentials of our pursuit of happiness are these:

something to do, something to love, and something to hope for. All else is only fluff and trimming."

He also met Julia Turnipseed in graduate school. They married in 1977. With Doc equipped with a master's degree in psychology and Julia with a degree for teaching, they moved to Wayne County, Kentucky, where Doc became a counselor at a camp for boys with psychological problems, and Julia taught in a mountain school. For eight years, he counseled sixteen-to-eighteen-year-olds with serious emotional disorders and problems with criminal activities.

They moved to Gainesville, Georgia, in 1984 so that their daughter, Jennifer, could grow up near her grandparents, Julia's parents. One of the positions Johnson took in Gainesville was working as a teaching naturalist at Elachee Nature Science Center, where volunteers and staff had been trying to do some archaeological work on the property to learn its history. "Doc stepped out and, unbeknownst to us, had quite a bit of knowledge in that area," says Andrea Timpone, president and CEO of the nonprofit center. "And he himself found a site that was used by the Native Americans to craft stone tools." He also found quartz artifacts.

Max White was the first professional archaeologist to identify the site

PLATE 47   Doc and artifacts

as being seven to nine thousand years old, and then a nationally renowned archaeologist, Dr. Michael Gramly, visited the center and confirmed Johnson was right: the site had been used by prehistoric Native Americans. Johnson named the site "Hummingbird Hill," in honor of Timpone, whom he called "the Hummingbird." Native people, he says, "believed the hummingbird protected the environment, just as Andrea protects the environment."

Even today, years after his working days at the center, Johnson is ready to share his knowledge with visitors. Says Timpone, "He gets them excited about archaeology and the impact that the Native Americans had on this land, how they used it and what their lifestyle was like."

He does the same thing for Max White's students at Piedmont College, especially when he talks about the stone technology of American Indians. Johnson, after all, has been searching for Indian artifacts since he was eight years old, rambling around creeks and rivers in Kentucky. And now, living in Northeast Georgia, he's even more serious about finding new sites.

The Johnson home is filled with Stone Age artifacts collected from private property in Northeast Georgia and Christian County, Kentucky. These include stone knives, points, arrowheads, and tools for daily activities used among the first people of both regions during the Paleo through Woodland archaeological periods. Johnson can spot similarities and differences between artisans from each area.

"He looks at something and tries to figure out, 'Now, how could that have been used?'" White says. "And he experiments and gives a perspective that's different from what other people would have."

White and Johnson are concerned that this country in general, and certain states in particular, have not respected sacred Indian sites as they should have. "We've made some progress," White says. "We now have laws protecting Indian burial sites and archaeological sites in general from destruction, after we have destroyed most of them, I would say, at least the most important ones. That's some progress. But then you have total disregard in other respects."

As an example, White cites the fight between the Apaches and the government over an area known as Oak Flat in Arizona's Tonto National Forest. It's a section the Apaches have used for generations of young women's coming-of-age ceremonies. In 1955, President Dwight Eisenhower removed the area from consideration for mining activities. But that changed in December 2014, when Senators John McCain and Jeff Flake, both of Arizona, added a rider to a bill that opened the land to mining companies. "McCain sneaked that into a bill as an attachment, and it was approved," White says. "And he got very angry when somebody at a meeting asked him about it."

"We say Indians don't matter," Johnson says. "They were savages anyway. Our ancestors were not the first ones here. It was the Indians."

But this nation has washed their blood from its hands. The US Supreme Court justified the way colonial powers laid claim to lands, ruling that titles lay with the government of those who traveled and occupied it, a concept known as the "Doctrine of Discovery."

"The Doctrine of Discovery was meant to cleanse us of our sins for doing this," Johnson says. "If we discover a people who don't believe the same as us, we have the right to kill them. But we don't like to talk about it in our history books. You want to be proud of your country, but we have committed atrocities against everybody that was here when we got here."

Doc Johnson is also an artist and sculptor, one who often donates his talents. A mother bought lessons for her teenage son as a Christmas present, but Johnson gave the money to a young Eastern Band Cherokee woman with health problems.

Johnson often has an ethical or political issue in mind when he sculpts his own pieces. He titled his dung-beetle art, for example, *Copious Pecuniaria, Trickle Down*. Billionaire Warren Buffet says the "trickle-down theory is the greatest fraud ever perpetrated against the American taxpayers," according to Johnson.

Of course, Johnson continues to look for artifacts, which he says should be used in schools to tell the story of Native Americans. "He's always looking down," says his wife, who retired from teaching in 2011. "I have even caught him digging in my flower beds at three o'clock in the morning."

The Johnsons still travel to Kentucky occasionally to check out the streams and shores. And they're breaking in a new dog, Cayce, a Havanese poodle. The most famous Johnson family dog was Mudbone, an Irish terrier that wandered with Johnson for nine years. He himself became a "barkaeologist" because he found one of Johnson's favorite pieces, a multipurpose basket-making tool. On a rock-hunting expedition in Kentucky, Mudbone lay down with the artifact right between his front legs and waited for Johnson to come check it out. "I think he knew what I was looking for," Johnson says. "It was a perfect match for one I had found there a year earlier."

During another hunt for artifacts, this one on a hot summer day on Lake Lanier in Hall County, Georgia, Johnson became dehydrated and dizzy and passed out, falling off a rock and onto the sandy beach. "Mudbone went into the water and drenched himself," he says, "and he came and stood over me to drip water onto my face to wake me up. He saved my life."

Johnson has located an important archaeological site in Hall County that he estimates is twelve thousand years old. He hopes to get professional archaeologists to certify his find as authentic and to get the state government to take it over for protection from recreation. If he has his way, it will be called the Mudbone Site. "We spent many hours there sometimes," he says, "napping under a shade tree, with Mudbone as a pillow."

In the meantime, Johnson continues to weld and craft his sculptures, to make his copper wildflowers, his knives and tomahawks and fiddles and banjos, or "canjos," as he calls instruments made from tin cans. And he keeps walking along rivers and lakes and fields with his head down, hoping to find another stone that will talk to him.

It's too late to undo the damage done to Native Americans when this country was settled by European colonists. But it's not too late to respect the lands they consider sacred. Legislation helps, but archaeologists like Johnson say this country mostly needs to show a little respect for those who lived here first. And, if asked, Joseph "Doc" Johnson is ready to speak out on their behalf.

FOOD FIT TO EAT

Dishin' Up Love

Interview with Lazell Vinson

by Jessica Phillips

MY GRANDMOTHER, LAZELL VINSON, was born and raised in Scaly Mountain, North Carolina, and has been cooking ever since she can recall. She learned this skill from her mother, who was also an outstanding cook, and has watched the Dillard House, once a tiny family boardinghouse, change and evolve into a family-owned business that is famous for its Southern cuisine. Granny started cooking professionally at the Best Western in Dillard, Georgia, where she worked for several years until it was sold and the owner transferred her to the Dillard House restaurant. She has cooked many outstanding foods that have set customers drooling with excitement.

Her most famous dish would be her seasonal fruitcakes. She spent many hours and late nights preparing these cakes for thousands of people. Granny has received awards for her recipes and her mama's recipes that were passed down to her. Her cabbage casserole, which was originally her mama's recipe, won a blue ribbon at the fair, and it was featured in *The Dillard House Cookbook*.

Granny has passed down her love of feeding a family to her daughters and granddaughters. It is not just about food. It's about creating a feeling of unity and a time when the family joins in conversation and shares moments of joy and sorrow. The saying "I made it with love" still applies. God willing, one day I will get to pass these unique skills down to my children to continue the legacy.

PLATE 48   Jessica Phillips, Lazell Vinson, and Joy Phillips—three generations

My grandmother started cooking when she was just a little girl. "I was about twelve years old. I did not start cooking because I had to. I started cooking because I wanted to," she recalls. "Me, Evelyn, Haze, and Mama all get in there in the kitchen, and we'd have supper ready. Evelyn and Hazel were my sisters. We cooked beans, potatoes, cabbages, and slaw. We cooked whatever we had for that evening. She'd give one of us a job, and we'd do it. The other girls would do something else to help. We'd have supper ready in just a few minutes."

Lazell Vinson on her early cooking experiences:

"When I was a little girl, we cooked on a woodstove. We would have to put wood in it to heat it up. I liked cooking on the woodstove, because you could cook several things at one time. There wasn't anything better than bread baked in a woodstove. There was no way to gauge how hot the stove got. You could tell when it got hot enough to cook, and you kept wood in it to keep it going. . . .

"My mama was one of the best cooks around. She worked at the Edwards Hotel in Highlands. She ran the hotel for a while, I think. She also worked at Trasmill Inn up there. . . . She worked at the hotel we lived at when I got married. I guess you could say I come by it honestly. Mama could cook anything. Daddy could cook, too. He didn't cook for anyone else except us. If

Mama wasn't there, he'd fix us a meal. He was a good cook. He learned how to cook from his mother.

"My mother's mom was also a good cook. She never worked for the public like Mama did. Mama worked in all the restaurants up in Highlands."

On becoming a cook at Best Western:

"I did get married at a young age, but that didn't stop me from cooking! I cooked all the time. I shocked [my husband's] mama, because I could make pies and stuff. I was only fifteen when I got married. She didn't think that I could cook, but I did. Boy, she'd let me cook, though.

"I didn't start cooking for the public until Jesse [her husband] died. Then, I went down there, and John Dillard was standing out there on the street. I stopped and asked him if he needed any help. He hired me on the spot. . . . John told me to come back, and he'd start me out at so much an hour. He hired me because he heard I was a good cook.

"I went to work at Best Western about five in the morning. I started breakfast as soon as I got there. I could cook it all, but I didn't. They had short-order cooks in the room there by us. I made the biscuits and the gravy. They cooked the sausage, eggs, and stuff like that. I helped cook dinner and supper, too. At dinner, I'd help fix the vegetables and make the homemade yeast rolls. I made the cakes. I made the pies, too. I also cooked the Brunswick stew.

"I liked John a lot. I told him just what I thought, and he told me just what he thought. John took me out to the dining room quite often. Different people would ask about the cook, and John would just take me out there to talk to some of them. He wanted me out in the dining room, so everyone would know who was cooking, and that it was home-cooked and clean."

On cooking at the Dillard House:

"I stayed at Best Western for about ten years or more. I stayed there until John sold it. Then, he brought me up to the Dillard House. I did the same things at the Dillard House I did at Best Western. I helped cook the vegetables and made sure they were seasoned right. I started out making the bread, and I made all of the pies and cakes. I had little books that I took to work with me every day.

"I met several people. I met Senator Sam Nunn. He wanted to know who did the cookin', so John brought me out there. He would always take back a bunch of fruitcakes. I met Waylon Jennings, the music man. He came as one of their guests, and I got to meet him. There were lots of people who would come in to meet the cook.

"I didn't do too much cookin' during fruitcake season. When it came fruitcake season, I took over the cake bakin' for a while. We cooked for parties, and I catered to parties. I've got no idea how many people we fed a day, but I know that there were hundreds. . . .

"I stayed at the Dillard House until I moved to South Carolina. I worked at the Dillard House for about thirteen years. Altogether, I worked at both Best Western and the Dillard House for about twenty-one years. I really liked working at the Dillard House. I just enjoyed cooking. I knew a lot of people, and we all got along good. John treated me fairly, and he paid me good. It was long hours, especially during the fruitcake season. I worked weekends and on holidays, but I would do it all over again. Out of all the jobs I've had my whole life, I would say workin' at the Dillard House was the best. I liked seeing people enjoy the food I had cooked. A lot of times people would come and ask for the recipe. That flattered me the most.

"If my granddaughters went to work as a cook, I'd tell them to go cook for the Dillard House, and work for Little John [Dillard]. But, my grand-children have got to do their own thing. I taught my daughters how to cook, just like Mama taught me how to cook. They are all very good cooks."

Lazell Vinson's Award-Winning Cabbage Casserole

Ingredients
   1 large head of cabbage
   1 teaspoon salt
   ½ stick margarine or butter
   3 cups Basic White Sauce (below)
   2 cups grated cheddar cheese
   1-½ cups buttered bread crumbs

Directions: Preheat oven to 300 degrees. Shred cabbage and cook it
   on the stove top 5–8 minutes in boiling water with 1 teaspoon

of salt (cabbage should remain crisp). Drain well. Layer half of the cabbage into a buttered 2-quart casserole dish. Pour half of the White Sauce over the cabbage to cover it. Then, add a second layer with the remaining cabbage, covered with the remaining sauce. Next, spread the cheese evenly over the second layer. Top with the bread crumbs. Bake in the oven for 15–20 minutes. This will feed about 8 people.

Basic White Sauce

Ingredients
1 cup margarine
3 tablespoons all-purpose flour
Salt and pepper to taste
1 quart milk

Directions: Melt margarine in a sauce pot. Add the flour, salt, and pepper to make a paste. Add milk and cook until thick, stirring constantly.

Joseph Dabney

Winning the James Beard Cookbook of the Year Award

JOE DABNEY didn't know a lot about moonshine whiskey—he was a good Baptist teetotaler, after all—but he wrote three books on the subject. He didn't know much about the traditional foods of Southern Appalachia either; he only knew how to eat them. But he wrote a prize-winning cookbook on the subject, nonetheless.

Dabney has been able to turn near-ignorance into expertise for several reasons: He's curious, he's a great reporter and writer, he's an intrepid researcher, he has an ear for the language, and he's a sentimentalist who loves folklore and the people of the Southern Appalachians. So, no one was surprised, except perhaps his wife, Susanne, who says he wasn't much of a cook, when Dabney started appearing at food festivals and talking on National Public Radio about the kinds of food that raised him from a puppy in South Carolina to a grown man of literary accomplishments.

But when his 1998 cookbook, *Smokehouse Ham, Spoon Bread & Scuppernong Wine: The Folklore and Art of Southern Appalachian Cooking*, won the James Beard Foundation Award for Cookbook of the Year, no one was more surprised than Dabney himself. He was sitting in the back of the Beard awards banquet in New York, thinking about leaving early but remembering the big party and wonderful food that would be served later. "So I said I'd better hang around. So, I did. Lo and behold, toward the end of the program, they said, 'And the winner of the James Beard Award for Cookbook of the Year goes to *Smokehouse Ham, Spoon Bread and Scoopernong Wine*, by Joseph Dabney.'"

Dabney, totally flabbergasted, didn't care that the KitchenAid executive had mispronounced the word "scuppernong." All he could think was, "Lord, have mercy on my soul." He practically galloped to the stage, "like running down to the creek to go swimming." He knew he'd have fifteen seconds to make a speech and wondered what he'd say. Famous French chef Jacques Pépin hung the Beard medal around his neck, and the man who admits he's neither a chef nor even an accomplished cook stepped up to the microphone and expressed his appreciation to sixteen hundred gammed-up chefs and food professionals.

He thanked the people who opened their hearts, home, recipes, and memories to him, and quoted one of his mountain sources, Chris Boatwright of Holly Creek in North Georgia: "After my interview one day, Chris asked me, 'Joe, have I learned you anything?' I just want to thank him and other people, and they did learn me a lot."

Following the ceremony, "as I was walking around with that big medallion swinging around my neck," he said, "someone yelled out, 'Congratulations, just what is a *scoopernong* anyway?' I thought to myself, 'Just what you'd expect from a Yankee.'"

The idea for this cookbook, a term that doesn't do the tome justice, came from a feature story Dabney had written for *The Atlanta Journal-Constitution* but that got lost as the *AJC* shuffled to cover the 1996 Summer Olympics in Atlanta. The idea, however, was still there; he'd been researching the food of the region for several years, way before *Smokehouse Ham* was even conceived. The itch to write was growing; gasoline was in the car; Dabney was retired from Lockheed-Georgia Company, where he worked for twenty-four years as a public relations executive; if nothing else, he'd continue researching and write a memoir for his five children. He hit the road, intensifying his research for the next three years.

About ten thousand miles and sixty cassettes of interviews later, Dabney had turned out a colorful account of the folklore and art of Southern Appalachian cooking and loved every minute of it. He worked from his home in Brookhaven, Georgia, a new suburban city north of Atlanta, and sometimes from his cabin in Euharlee in Bartow County, Georgia. Near his desk in Brookhaven sits one of two miniature moonshine stills his friend Thee King made for him, and on his back deck is displayed a thirty-five-gallon (nonoperating) still he bought from ex-moonshiner Peg Fields in Jasper, Georgia. Not surprisingly, Dabney's desk is surrounded by photos, files, books, tape recorders, and all the jumbled mess of supplies of a writer at work.

In 2005, Dabney received the Jack Daniel Lifetime Achievement Award from the Southern Foodways Alliance, which Director John T. Edge said pays "homage to the grand men and women of the Southern food world, the people who have told stories of our region on the national stage." Five years later, Dabney published his companion cookbook, *The Food, Folklore, and Art of Lowcountry Cooking*. He had become, as one writer put it, "the grand old man of Southern food writing."

Joseph Earl Dabney was born January 29, 1929, in Kershaw, South Carolina, the youngest of seven children; one died as a child. His father, Wade V. Dabney, an overgenerous man, ran a grocery store/service station in the little town, and two of his sons, Connie and Herman, made deliveries in a T-Model converted into a pickup truck. Most of the townspeople earned a meager living at the Springs Cotton Mill, located across the street from the store. But when the stock market crashed, those jobs were gone. The mill closed down and so, eventually, did Wade Dabney's store, bankrupt because customers couldn't pay off their tabs. To survive the Great Depression that followed, the Dabney family loaded up and moved 150 miles to a farm northeast of Greenville, in the Blue Ridge foothills. There they rode out the hard years that followed.

"My brother Arthur, twelve at the time and ten years my senior," Joe Dabney wrote, "felt the reason Dad took such a drastic step, hauling his brood to what seemed to be the other end of the universe, was to get the family near our oldest sibling, Geneva, then in nurse's training at Greenville's General Hospital." "Or perhaps to be near Uncle Gilmore, a Greenville insurance man," said brother Connie.

Whatever the case, renting the Spart Dill Farm in the shadow of Paris Mountain saved the Dabneys. Wade and his sons, who ranged up to eighteen years in age, produced a bale of cotton to an acre on the rolling red clay hills and harvested bumper crops of corn and hay. They grew roast'n'ear corn, raised pigs for meat to fill the smokehouse, and killed rabbits and squirrels in the nearby woods and fields.

Their mother, Wincey, tended a garden that yielded fresh vegetables galore—cabbage, tomatoes, and beans—and prayed daily that the family would be all right. They would be. As farm children of that era often say, the Depression was going on, but they didn't know it. The Dabneys had plenty to eat, always with biscuits, and little need to buy anything but salt, most of it for hog-killing time, and sugar. The family eventually moved back to Kershaw, where Joe finished high school.

Unlike most graduates of the school, Dabney, along with his cousin Ben Lucas, went on to college. They chose Berry College in Rome, Georgia, after a teacher recommended it. Dabney majored in English and journalism. After graduating in 1949, he immediately went to work for the Cartersville (Georgia) *Daily Tribune News*, where he started off at a salary of thirty dollars a week, which was soon raised to thirty-five.

"I made it okay," he said, "because I lived in Mrs. Donahue's boarding-house for twelve dollars a week, and got a big breakfast and big supper." After enjoying a fifteen-cent lunch every day, he had money left over. But soon he would be lured away to Columbus, Georgia, which had a bigger, more profitable newspaper, the *Columbus Ledger*, and a more exciting city next door, Phenix City, Alabama, a place loaded with juke joints and organized crime. "On occasions," Dabney said, "I visited the joints along Fourteenth Street in the evening and on Sunday sang in the choir at the local Baptist church."

But in 1950, the US Army offered him a deal he couldn't refuse. A short time after he wrote a story about men his age going off to the Korean War, Dabney was invited to join them. He was drafted. But because he had a college degree and experience in writing, after training, he flew with eight other people from Fort Riley to Tokyo in May 1951. He was assigned to write broadcast news and commentary in both Korea and Japan as part of an effort called psychological warfare, or Psy War.

Dabney's father died in January 1951, while he was in Korea, but Dabney didn't know it until after the funeral. "Sorry you weren't here," a sister-in-law wrote him. "Your dad died." She wrote the note on funeral home stationery.

After the war, Dabney came home and found reporting and editing jobs at three newspapers: first, *The Daily Times* in Gainesville, Georgia, then the South Carolina *Florence Morning News*, and finally at *The Atlanta Journal*.

Still searching for the right job, Dabney left newspapers in the mid-sixties

PLATE 49   Joe Dabney with moonshiner
Simmie Free of Tiger, Georgia (photo was taken in 1975)

to join the Lockheed aircraft company. But he wasn't satisfied writing just for Lockheed. He was looking for a book idea. He found it in Dawsonville, Georgia.

"We were on vacation and had taken a trip to Northeast Georgia and came back through Dawsonville," he recalled. "We saw a sign that said, 'Visit the world's only moonshine museum, Fred Goswick's Museum.' Goswick got to telling us about the Scotch-Irish coming down to the mountains and the whiskey lore and all that kind of stuff, and Susanne said, 'There's your book.' I said, 'I believe it is.'"

Dabney said he "researched the devil out of that book." He even got locked up one night while doing research in the old Carnegie Library in downtown Atlanta. "I was down in the catacombs of the library until nine o'clock one night, closing time, and they shut the doors and cut the lights out on me. And I said, 'Lord, have mercy on my soul.' I went upstairs and found a telephone, and I knew one of the people on the board. I called and told him my predicament, and about an hour later, the janitor came in and let me out."

Dabney used his weekends, holidays, and vacations to roam the hills and valleys of Southern Appalachia, mostly in North Georgia, western North Carolina, and East Tennessee. He was looking for former moonshiners, trippers or runners, bootleggers, and revenue agents willing to tell their stories for print.

Joe Dabney doesn't look down on anybody. He comes across as warm and honest, much as he does in his writing, and he's gregarious, quick to laugh, and enjoys a good story. He found that moonshine whiskey making, though illegal, was a Southern way of life facing extinction. He respected the people he interviewed and never wrote condescendingly.

His first book, *Mountain Spirits*, originally published by Scribner's, came out in 1974. *Time* magazine called it "a splendid and often hilarious history of mountain folkways." Dabney ended up on NBC's *Today* show chatting with critic and interviewer Gene Shalit, who inscribed a photo from the show: "To the most spirited man in the mountains." Dabney's follow-up books include *The Corn Whiskey Recipe Book*, 1977; *More Mountain Spirits*, 1980; and *HERK: Hero of the Skies*, 1979, about the twenty-fifth anniversary of the C-130 troop transport and cargo plane, the *Hercules,* which his former employer, Lockheed Martin, manufactured.

But it wasn't until Dabney ventured into the kitchen that he received national acclaim. He already had several contacts in the mountains, people he'd met researching his moonshine books, and friends at Lockheed introduced him to other families. Folks invited him into their homes to share their stories and their recipes. Recipes for squirrel dumplings, apple stack pies, pickled kraut, hominy and cracklin's, Cherokee yellow jacket soup, mule ears (peach fried pies), and all the other scrumptious fare the region is known for.

Dabney didn't produce one of those slick, full-color cookbooks whose photos are usually more appetizing than the dishes themselves. He took Instamatic-style, black-and-white photos and borrowed others from the people he interviewed. He told stories; he wrote history, filled with anecdotes from the mountains. "I'm more of a folklorist than a cook," he said. One writer tagged him a "fork-lorist."

The original title of the book ended with "Strawberry Wine," but he changed it to "Scuppernong Wine" to give it a little more pizzazz.

Sitting in his cluttered office at home, Dabney occasionally recalled a special person he interviewed, turned to a page in the cookbook, and started reading:

" 'I can see my mother now. She had a rack in her fireplace and she'd have her kettle a-cookin' beans, 'specially shuck beans and green beans.' Nina

PLATE 50   Curtis Underwood displays a
Dutch oven used for slow fireplace cooking
in Southern Appalachia.

Garrett, now ninety and living in her family's elegant old tin-roofed homeplace near Cartecay, Georgia, remembers the mountain manner of hill country cooking in earlier days, right in the fireplace.

"For centuries, old settlers depended on their fireplaces for the cooking of their foods. That is up until the end of the Civil War and the advent of the cast-iron and modern-day stoves.

"As we sat and rocked and talked on Miss Nina's front porch, she reminisced that the food tasted better back then, around the turn of the century when she was a young woman. Food had a full-bodied flavor because the meats and vegetables were cooked more slowly. It didn't hurt the flavor any that a nice chunk of fatback always shared the pot with the beans and stews. And biscuits had a generous amount of lard."

Susanne Dabney shares her husband's love of history, having researched ten generations of her family through thousands of letters. She often accompanied Dabney on his journeys into the mountains. On one trip, she met Maude Thacker of Pickens County, Georgia, who possessed "a personality and yodeling mountain voice equal to her wines," Dabney wrote in *Smokehouse*. "You know, Susanne was a teetotaler," he joked, "until she drank some of Maude Thacker's elderberry wine."

For *Lowcountry*, Dabney covered the coastal areas of the Carolinas and Georgia and wrote about foods with funny names—she crab soup, hoppin' john, Benne Seed Biscuits, and, of course, purloo, a rice-based dish. "The best meals I had were chicken purloo," he said. "I've eaten it all my life. Chicken purloo, you just can't beat it, if you cook it right."

"He is as patient as Job," said Ed Heys, Dabney's friend and Sunday school teacher. "Now he's worked on this new book," *Cherokee: Valley So*

Wild, a novel Dabney has researched off and on for thirty years. "He's just a very committed guy, and loyal as the day is long."

Joe Dabney, Heys said, has had some health problems, but he's a bulldog about completing his books. "He gets hold of something—and look out." And when it comes to food—whether he can cook it or not—he certainly knows how to write about it.

For that, all of us—even the sixteen hundred chefs and food professionals who watched this unknown walk off in 1999 with the Best Cookbook of the Year award—have multiple reasons to thank the good Lord and Joe Dabney for stories about good food from God's country, the mountains and valleys of Southern Appalachia.

PLATE 51   Joe Dabney
portrait wall at home

Joe Dabney died just a few days after this story was written. After his death, his family completed what Dabney was not around to do. They published his novel, Cherokee: Valley So Wild.

These recipes are taken, with permission, from Joseph E. Dabney's *Smokehouse Ham, Spoon Bread & Scuppernong Wine: The Folklore and Art of Southern Appalachian Cooking.*

Aunt Martha's Buttermilk Cornbread

"Berry College's founder, the late Martha Berry, had a beloved cook at her ancestral home on the Oostanaula River in the Appalachian foothills near Rome, Georgia—'Aunt Martha' Freeman. Long deceased, Aunt Martha was a legend in the area for her cooking wizardry.

Although she never wrote down her recipes, some of Berry's friends did. Here is Aunt Martha's basic buttermilk cornbread recipe as preserved by the Daughters of Berry, with my personal thanks to Lillian Farmer, assistant director of the Martha Berry Oak Hill Museum. Her recipe calls for a wee three tablespoons of flour, which admittedly is a mountain no-no. But Martha Berry, a belle of the mountains in her day, gave the recipe high marks."

Ingredients

3 tablespoons flour
1-¼ cups cornmeal
1 teaspoon salt
¾ teaspoon baking powder
1 cup buttermilk
2 small eggs
2 tablespoons shortening
½ teaspoon soda

Directions

Mix flour, cornmeal, salt, and baking powder. Add buttermilk to beaten eggs. Melt shortening. Cut into dry ingredients. Add soda dissolved in a little water. Pour in hot greased skillet or pan and bake at 425 degrees until done. *Yields six servings*

Sue's Apple Fritters

"Over the years, apple fritters have been a great mountain dish," Dabney wrote. "My friend John LaRowe, who for many years ran the famed Mark of the Potter shop on North Georgia's picturesque Soque River, obtained this recipe for fritters in a collection he published and that is still being published by the pottery's present owner, Jay Bucek. This recipe was offered by Sue Tharpe of Glenmeadow":

Ingredients

1 cup plain flour
Pinch of salt
2 egg yolks, plus 1 egg white

1 tablespoon cooking oil
5 fluid ounces milk
1 pound North Georgia cooking apples
Juice from one lemon
Sugar
½ cup butter or cooking oil

Directions

Sift flour and salt into medium-sized mixing bowl. Make a well in the center and add eggs and oil. With wooden spoon, mix eggs and oil slowly into flour, gradually adding milk. Beat well, then cover and keep in cool place for thirty minutes. Peel and core apples; slice into rings ¼-inch think. Sprinkle with lemon juice and sugar. Dip apples into batter and fry in the hot butter. Drain and serve immediately.

Linda's Corn Pudding

"Stewed corn and creamed corn were frequently taken a step further in the cooking of fresh corn pudding. Throughout the Appalachian and Blue Ridge country, people enjoyed eating what many called 'a big bait' of corn pudding to celebrate the arrival of summer. For this recipe, we thank Linda Arnold, who with her husband, Stan, owns the Grandview Lodge in Waynesville, North Carolina. Their tables during the summer and fall reflect the season's bounty from neighboring gardens and local farmers' markets."

Ingredients

2 eggs
½ cup granulated sugar
2 tablespoons all-purpose flour
4 cups fresh sweet corn kernels (about 6 ears)
½ cup milk
½ cup butter or margarine, melted

Directions

Preheat oven to 325 degrees. In a medium mixing bowl, beat eggs with sugar and flour. Add corn and milk and then stir in the melted butter or margarine. Pour into greased 1-½ quart soufflé dish. Bake for 55 minutes or until pudding is set and browned on top.

A further refinement of this dish was one that mountain folk called "green corn pie," baked in a casserole dish and containing most of the ingredients listed in the pudding above. Some additions were a couple of tomatoes, two cups of crumbled cornbread, one and one half cups of grated sharp cheese, plus five slices of crisp bacon. The procedure was to line the casserole dish with the slices of bacon, sprinkle over with bread crumbs, followed by slices of tomatoes plus the corn mix above, followed by another layer of crumbs and tomatoes and corn. The topping would consist of the grated cheese plus leftover crumbs.

Mother Wincey Dabney's Banana Pudding

Dabney wrote: "Bananas became popular through the Appalachian South in the late 1800s when railroads began shipping in the tropical fruit. They reached most of our Carolina upcountry through the port of Charleston. Fulton, Kentucky, became the banana distribution point for that region when the Illinois Central Railroad in 1880 began shipping bananas out of New Orleans in their new 'icebox cars.' The Appalachian diet has never been the same since. Bananas became a great hit everywhere, particularly for those Sunday puddings. Every September, townspeople in Fulton, Kentucky, cook up the world's largest banana pudding—a one-ton monster loaded with three thousand bananas—at their big banana festival.

"As I said, banana pudding was such a wonderful dish in my preteen years that I overate one Sunday and had to lay off bananas for a week or two. But not for long.

"With the help of two of my sisters-in-law, Lib and Jeanette Dabney, I here attempt to re-create my mother's banana pudding recipe."

Ingredients
    4 eggs (separated)
    4 cups milk
    ½ cup sugar

4 teaspoons flour

7 to 8 bananas

Vanilla wafers

⅔ cup powdered sugar

Directions

In a large saucepan combine the egg yolks, milk, sugar, and flour. Mix thoroughly and bring to a boil, stirring constantly. Set aside and allow to cool. Into a greased casserole, place sliced bananas and wafers in alternating layers, pouring the mix into each layer and on top. For the topping, beat the egg whites and add powdered sugar. Bake at 300 degrees until lightly brown. Chill before serving. *Yields 8 servings*

Lavender Mountain Spoon Bread

Ingredients

2 cups milk

¾ cup sifted meal

1 teaspoon salt

3 tablespoons butter

3 eggs (separated)

Directions

Heat milk in double boiler until steaming. Add meal slowly. Stir and cook until thick, like thick white sauce. Add salt and butter. Beat egg yolks and stir into cornmeal mixture. Then fold in stiffly beaten egg whites. Pour into buttered baking dish and bake in moderate oven for 30 minutes.

BARBECUE

Dabney wrote: "Barbecue, my esteemed friend and Blue Ridge mountaineer Carl Dodd has informed me, 'is the product of a piece of pork that has been carefully and lovingly juxtaposed to just the right amount of heat, just the right amount of smoke, for just the right amount of time. Then, sliced or chipped, enhanced with just the right amount of just-right sauce and placed between two slices of perfectly toasted Piggly Wiggly white bread.'" And, as Dabney's cookbook notes, recipes for those just-right sauces vary from state to state and even from family to family. Dabney's book offers recipes from three states: North Carolina, Tennessee, and Kentucky. Here are those recipes. First from North Carolina:

Tar Heel Barbecue Sauce

1 cup apple cider vinegar

½ cup water

1 bay leaf

2 tablespoons peanut oil

½ teaspoon salt

1 teaspoon black pepper

1-½ teaspoons red pepper flakes

1 teaspoon sugar

1 garlic clove, crushed

⅔ teaspoon thyme

1 cup minced onion

2-½ teaspoons dry mustard

5 teaspoons cold water

Directions

Mix all ingredients except mustard and water in a saucepan. Bring to a quick boil, then simmer 5 minutes. Remove from heat. Dissolve the mustard in the cold water, then thin with some of the hot vinegar sauce. Mix the mustard into sauce. Let cool, and store in the refrigerator.

Tennessee

Joe Dabney wrote: "Martha McCullough-Williams wrote one of the wittiest books on Southern cooking in 1913, *Dishes and Beverages of the Old*

South. The book fortuitously has been brought back to print by the University of Tennessee Press. Born in 1848, northwest of Clarkesville near the Tennessee-Kentucky border, Martha was named Martha Ann Collins, but she took on the more elegant name after moving to New York City, where she became a famed magazine writer. Here, in Martha's own words, is the recipe she obtained from her father, William Collins, of Tennessee's Montgomery County":

Tennessee Mopping Sauce

Daddy made it thus: Two pounds sweet lard, melted in a brass kettle, with one pound beaten, not ground, black pepper, a pint of small fiery red peppers, nubbed and stewed soft in water to barely cover, a spoonful of herbs in powder—he would never tell what they were—and a quart and a pint of the strongest apple vinegar, with a little salt. These were simmered together for half an hour, as the barbecue was getting done. Then a fresh, clean mop was dabbed slightly in the mixture, and was lightly smeared over the upper sides of the carcasses. Not a drop was permitted to fall on the coals—it would have sent up smoke, and films of light ashes. Then, tables being set, the meat was laid, hissing hot, within clean, tight wood trays, deeply gashed upon the side that had been next to the fire, and deluged with the sauce, which the mop-man smeared fully over it. Hot! After eating it one wanted to lie down at the springside and let the water of it flow down the mouth. But of a flavor, a savor, a tastiness, nothing else earthly approaches.

Kentucky Barbecue Sauce

"For this final recipe," Dabney wrote, *"I am indebted to Irene Hayes, author of* What's Cooking in Kentucky. *This nice recipe (the adaption therefrom) came from Mrs. Robert D. Daniels of Paintsville, in eastern Kentucky":*

Ingredients

    2-½ cups water
    2 tablespoons butter
    2-½ teaspoons salt

¼ cup vinegar

2 teaspoons chili sauce

¼ onion, chopped

1 bud garlic (or less, depending on taste)

1 tablespoon sugar

½ teaspoon hot sauce

½ teaspoon red pepper

2-½ teaspoons black pepper

1 teaspoon powdered mustard

1-½ tablespoons Worcestershire sauce

Directions

Combine well and bring to a rolling boil. Let stand overnight or marinate 4 to 6 hours. Keep sauce hot during basting.

Peach Grower Dori Sanders of South Carolina

Recipes from her cookbook

THE TELEPHONE RINGS just as peach farmer Dori Sanders and I sit down for an interview. It's Katherine Stoyer calling. "It's serendipitous that you should call," Sanders says in her delightful singsong voice. "You're asking about cooking, and that's what we're talking about. "You're making vegetable beef stew right now. Well, tell me what you're doing.

"You're slicing the beef. When you slice it, my dear, you're going to slice it across the grain. Take that sharp knife, my darling, and you will see how that grain is running. Please slice and cube across. Okay, what else?

"The *water* is on the stove? You didn't start the soup in *stock*? But you don't start beef stew or soup in water, darling. Always save stock for that. I know you're kind of Northern, but never ever, if you can, never start soup in water." The conversation bounces back and forth for a few more minutes. Sanders tells Stoyer which vegetables to put in early, which ones late. "Now the tomatoes can go in very early. The longer they cook, the more intense the fla-a-a-a-vor." She draws out the word for emphasis.

And then, at the end: "Love you, too. And make sure you always have a little container of stock next time, my darling. That makes it robust. All right, thanks for the call. Love you, too. Bye."

Katherine Stoyer of Providence, North Carolina, has just received a free cooking lesson from the woman who wrote the book on delectable soups, buttermilk-marinated wild turkey, chicken and dumplings, cornhusk-grilled catfish, and, of course, easy peach cobbler. Dori Sanders knows rural Southern cooking because she grew up on a peach farm in York County, South Carolina, and when she wasn't picking peaches or gathering okra or digging sweet potatoes, she was at the farm stand selling or at home cooking for her parents and brothers and sisters.

Decades after she made her first biscuits, she decided to write a cookbook. She'd already turned out two best-selling novels, *Clover*, which was made into a television movie, and *Her Own Place*. So why not a cookbook, something to help people "remember forgotten smells and tastes of old-fashioned cooking" while offering a slice of rural Southern life? The result was *Dori Sanders' Country Cooking: Recipes & Stories from the Family Farm Stand*. It's a book, the publisher says, that "reads as good as it cooks." And it does so because Sanders is a master at mixing stories with recipes. She's also a speaker in demand. She even spoke in Oxford, Mississippi, at the seventh annual symposium of the Southern Foodways Alliance, which awarded her the 2011 Craig Claiborne Lifetime Achievement Award. Her speech, titled "Promise Land: A Farmer Remembers," coincided with the fortieth anniversary of the Civil Rights Act of 1964.

Sanders has been honored in many ways, but readers don't want to know stuff like that, she says, when asked to be specific about her awards and speaking engagements. Tell them something that piques their interest, she

PLATE 52   Dori Sanders with her longtime friend
Katherine Stoyer and Stoyer's daughter, Rainer

insists. Perhaps this will: In the summer of 2017, Epicurious, a website that offers information on food, wine, and restaurants, named Sanders one of the "100 Greatest Home Cooks of All Time."

"A fourth-generation South Carolina farmer, Sanders grows peaches that are nearly as nuanced and sweet as her novels and cookbooks," the article on the website says. "The joys of 'make-do' cooking that she grew up with only intensify when you try them out in your kitchen, connecting you to the scarcity and abundance that drove the creation of many of the world's most delicious recipes."

The cookbook, published in 1995, is not for the hoity-toity person who wants fancy cuisine for every meal. But if you grew up cooking in the country, as Sanders did, you'll no doubt agree with some of her methods. Working on the farm leaves little time for anything but simple cooking, and Sanders still cooks the "simple survival foods, dishes that brought us through the Great Depression and the hard times of failed crops and lean harvests."

By simple cooking, she means quick and easy—not boring—dishes whipped together almost automatically. "Like most farm-family cooks," she writes, "I don't measure or fuss too much with details. How much of an ingredient? Enough for one good mess, a couple of handfuls or so. What size pan? Whatever I have handy. If it's too small, I just cut down on the amount I'm going to cook. If it's too big, I end up with something cooked for tomorrow as well."

But cookbooks, even country cookbooks, require specific ingredients and directions. So Sanders and her sister Virginia picked, prepared, and tested everything from the first page to the very last. The cookbook, appropriately, is dedicated to Virginia.

They already knew, of course, how to cook turtles, or cooters, as Dori Sanders calls them. She had eaten so many cooters, she says tongue in cheek, her backyard looked like a hard-hat factory. "Cooter legs have the taste of forty different kinds of meat," she says, quoting her brother Orestus. "You fry them boogers and make brown gravy."

"I can still turn to the farming life for roots, for those influences and traditions that have remained basically the same through the years," she writes in the introduction of her cookbook. "Today we farmers still subsist mostly off the fruit of the land, living from harvest to harvest just as in earlier times.

And unlike what so many people think, we Southern farmers don't—and never did—eat our food swimming in sugar and fat."

One chapter in Sanders's cookbook is titled "Cooking for Northerners." "So how do I cook for Northerners?" she writes. "I'll let you in on a little secret: I cook the same foods I've cooked for years, only I change the presentation, or the name, or the herbs. For example, when I make a vinegar pie with fresh fruit sauce, an old family favorite, I might strain the sauce through a sieve and call it a 'coulis.' When I fry up some okra, I'll use olive oil instead of vegetable oil and call it a 'sauté.' When I cook collard greens, I call them 'winter greens.' And if pressed for an exact name, I *never* say 'karlards.' Instead, I say 'cawl-erds,' all fancy like. Can you believe that I've even started adding Parmesan to my black pepper cornbread, and sometimes to biscuits? I also cut down, way down, on the sugar for my Northern friends. Fresh minted sugarless iced tea always goes over big."

Sometimes Sanders improvised to keep a customer happy and coming back to her peach stand for fresh produce. This was the case with her best customer, someone who bought a peck of okra every Thursday during season to cook on the weekend. One Thursday, though, the woman arrived at the stand and announced, "No okra today." She said her family was tired of stewed okra, or okra in any form.

Sanders was disappointed, of course, but then she noticed in an open newspaper on a chair a recipe for eggplant parmigiana. She looked at her customer and asked, "But have you ever served them okra parmigiana?" The woman had never heard of okra parmigiana. Neither had Sanders. "Well, I don't have the recipe with me right now," she said, "but if you stop by here tomorrow, I'll have it." Sanders spent most of the night creating a recipe for okra parmigiana. The woman dropped by the stand the next day, got the recipe, bought some okra, and went home to surprise her family with a brand-new dish. That recipe became so popular that it spawned other similar ones: fried green tomato parmigiana; vegetarian okra lasagna; a salad of okra, tomatoes, and corn—the list goes on.

Some things have changed for the Sanders family. The original family home no longer stands. The old wood-burning stove has rusted away. The teas served in silver that her folks enjoyed on their front porch are gone. "But precious recipes are still intact," Sanders writes, "and the tastes and smells of the foods of my childhood let me know that I can go back again." And *Dori Sanders' Country Cookbook* takes the reader along with her.

A SAMPLING OF DORI'S RECIPES

These recipes were taken, with permission, from *Dori Sanders' Country Cooking: Recipes & Stories from the Family Farm Stand*.

"No Regrets" Apple Bread Pudding

This recipe got its name because you will have no regrets for either the calories or the labor involved in making it.

Ingredients

    5-½ tablespoons unsalted butter, softened

    2 Granny Smith or other tart cooking apples

    The juice of half a lemon

    ¼ teaspoon ground nutmeg

    ¼ teaspoon ground cinnamon

    1 tablespoon plus 1 cup sugar

    5 slices of good-quality white bread, each slice about ⅓ inch thick

    2 tablespoons dark raisins, soaked in boiling water for
        10 minutes, then drained

    ¼ cup roughly chopped walnuts or pecans

    2 whole eggs plus 2 egg yolks

    2 cups light cream

    A pinch of salt

    1 teaspoon lemon extract

    ½ teaspoon vanilla extract

Directions

1. Smear ½ tablespoon of softened butter on the inside of a 10" x 7" x 2" baking dish. Set aside.

2. Preheat oven to 350 degrees Fahrenheit.

3. Peel and core the apples, cut into very thin slices, and toss in the lemon juice. In a heavy skillet, melt 2 tablespoons of butter over moderate heat, add the apples, and sauté until just tender, about 10 to 12 minutes, stirring occasionally. Remove

skillet from heat, stir in the nutmeg, cinnamon, and 1 table-spoon of sugar, and set aside.

4. Remove the crusts from the bread. Spread the remaining 3 tablespoons of softened butter evenly over the bread. Arrange bread in a single layer on the bottom of the buttered baking dish, overlapping the edges of the bread slightly. Over the bread scatter the raisins, nuts, and sautéed apples with the pan juices.

5. In a small bowl, beat together the whole eggs and the yolks. Beat the remaining 1 cup sugar into the eggs.

6. In a heavy saucepan, combine the cream and salt and scald over moderate heat. When tiny bubbles form around the edges of the cream, remove from heat and strain by small amounts into the egg mixture, stirring to combine after each addition. Stir in the lemon and vanilla extracts. Strain this mixture over the bread and apples, pushing down the edges of the bread to cover completely with the egg-cream mixture.

7. Place the baking dish in a large roasting pan and fill the roasting pan with enough hot water to come a third of the way up the baking dish. Bake in the preheated oven for 40 to 45 minutes or until a knife inserted in the center of the pudding comes out clean. Place on a wire rack to cool and serve warm or cold.

Batter-Fried Corn on the Cob

Serves 6

Before we had a freezer, we used to can all our favorite vegetables, including corn still on the cob. Wide-mouthed half-gallon Ball Mason jars were used, and it was surprising how many ears of corn we could squeeze into them. A good thing, too, because this dish was a must for corn-shucking suppers, and with the canned ears, we always had enough to go around.

Ingredients

6 ears fresh corn, shucked, silked, and cut in half crosswise
(thawed frozen ears can also be used)

¾ cup yellow cornmeal

⅓ cup all-purpose flour

½ teaspoon garlic salt (optional)

¾ cup milk

2 tablespoons plus 1 cup vegetable oil

1 large egg

1 cup cornflake crumbs

Directions

1. In a medium bowl, combine the cornmeal, flour, garlic salt (if desired), milk, 2 tablespoons oil, and the egg. Mix well.
2. Place the cornflake crumbs in a shallow dish. Dip the halved ears of corn into the cornmeal batter to coat, then roll them in the cornflake crumbs.
3. In a deep fryer or heavy skillet, heat 1 cup oil over medium-high heat until hot but not smoking.
4. Fry the coated corn in the hot oil for 2 to 3 minutes or until light golden brown. Place on heavy brown paper or paper towels to drain. Serve as soon as they are drained.

Buttermilk Pie with Raspberry Sauce

Serves 6

This is a simple pie, but it is as delicate and delicious as any complicated dessert you'd find in a fancy restaurant. The raspberries cut the richness of the butter and sugar just a bit, so if you can't find raspberries, substitute another berry with some tartness, like blueberries or blackberries, rather than a sweeter berry, like strawberries.

Ingredients

4 tablespoons unsalted butter, softened

1 cup sugar

3 large eggs, lightly beaten

3 tablespoons all-purpose flour

1 teaspoon vanilla extract

2 tablespoons fresh lemon juice

1 cup buttermilk

A pinch of baking soda

1 unbaked 9-inch pie crust

1 cup fresh raspberries or other tart berries

¼ cup black currant or other fruit liqueur

Directions

1. Preheat oven to 350 degrees Fahrenheit.
2. In a medium bowl, combine the butter and sugar and beat until fluffy. Add the eggs one at a time, mixing well after each addition. Add the flour, vanilla, lemon juice, buttermilk, and baking soda and stir until well combined. Pour the mixture into the unbaked pastry shell.
3. Bake in the preheated oven for 15 minutes. Reduce heat to 300 degrees Fahrenheit and bake for 1 hour or more or until the custard is set and the top lightly browned. Remove from oven and place on a wire rack to cool.
4. Toss the raspberries with the black currant liqueur in a small bowl.
5. When the pie is cool enough to eat, cut it into slices and serve each slice topped with a generous spoonful of the raspberries.

Okra Parmigiana

Serves 6

I may not be a mama Italiana, *but I am a Southerner, and I want taste in my tomato sauce, too, so I make my own. I use home-canned tomatoes, but store-bought canned tomatoes are fine as well. Be sure to get whole tomatoes, though, so you can chop them in big pieces and get a nice, chunky sauce. Make sure you use fresh-picked okra, too. Served with a hearty salad and hot garlic bread, this delicious dish makes a satisfying summer meal.*

Ingredients

About 4 tablespoons olive oil

¾ cup chopped onion

¾ cup chopped celery

¼ cup chopped fresh parsley

2 cloves garlic, minced

One 14-ounce can whole tomatoes, undrained, roughly
chopped

One 6-ounce can tomato paste

Salt and freshly ground black pepper to taste

1 pound fresh okra pods, each about 3 inches long, washed

2 eggs, lightly beaten

1 cup seasoned bread crumbs

½ cup freshly grated Parmesan cheese

Directions

1. Preheat oven to 350 degrees Fahrenheit.

2. In a large, heavy skillet, heat 1 tablespoon of the olive oil over medium-high heat until hot, but not smoking. Add onion, celery, parsley, and garlic and cook, stirring occasionally, until tender, about 5 to 7 minutes.

3. Stir in tomatoes and tomato paste and season to taste with salt and pepper. Reduce heat to low, cover, and simmer for 45 minutes, stirring occasionally.

4. Remove the caps from the okra pods and slice the pods in half lengthwise. Dip into the egg and then roll in the bread crumbs to coat. Heat 2 tablespoons of the olive oil in the skillet over medium-high heat until hot but not smoking. Add a single layer of okra slices and brown on both sides, about 3 minutes per side. Remove, drain on paper towels, and set aside. Repeat with remaining okra slices, adding more oil if necessary.

5. Layer half the okra in a lightly greased 13" x 9" x 2" baking dish. Spoon half of the tomato sauce over the okra slices. Repeat the two layers. Top with Parmesan cheese and bake in the preheated oven for 45 to 50 minutes or until bubbly and browned.

Smothered Chicken

Serves 4

Some people object to the sour cream in traditionally prepared smoth-
ered chicken, so for them I have devised an alternative that uses fresh
peaches instead. To make it, prepare the dish as directed through step
4 in this recipe. Then add two tablespoons of water, cover the skillet
tightly, and simmer over low heat for twenty-five minutes. At that
point, add a cup and a half of chopped fresh peaches, cook for another
ten minutes, and then remove the cover and cook ten minutes more to
crisp the skin lightly. But if sour cream is what you like, just proceed with
the recipe as written.

Ingredients

8 pieces of chicken (legs, thighs, or breasts, with or
    without skin)
1 cup all-purpose flour
Salt and freshly ground black pepper to taste
¼ teaspoon garlic powder (optional)
¼ teaspoon onion powder
1 teaspoon paprika
About 1 cup vegetable oil
2 medium onions, sliced thin
¾ cup sour cream
¼ cup chicken stock
¼ cup chopped green onions (including green part)
2 tablespoons water

Directions

1. Preheat oven to 350 degrees Fahrenheit.
2. Wash chicken pieces and dry well. In a clean plastic or brown
    paper bag, combine the flour, salt, pepper, garlic powder (if
    desired), onion powder, and paprika. Shake a few times to
    mix. Place 2 to 3 pieces of chicken in the bag, shake to coat
    evenly, remove, and shake off excess coating. Repeat with
    remaining pieces of chicken.
3. In a large ovenproof skillet, heat ¼ inch of vegetable oil over
    medium heat until hot but not smoking. Add the chicken

pieces and brown well, about 3 minutes per side. Remove from pan and set aside.

4. Pour excess oil out of the skillet, leaving just a thin layer. Add the onions and sauté, stirring occasionally, until they are translucent, about 5 to 7 minutes.

5. In a medium bowl, combine the sour cream, chicken stock, green onions, and water and mix well.

6. Place the browned chicken on top of the onions in the skillet and pour the sour cream mixture over the top. Cover lightly with foil and bake in the preheated oven for 40 to 45 minutes or until the chicken is tender and shows no trace of pink near the bone. Serve at once.

Sweet Potato Rolls

Makes 1-½ dozen

These little rolls taste best when served hot from the oven. My sister Virginia sometimes adds one small, thinly sliced, mildly hot banana pepper to turn them into hot-pepper rolls. You can also substitute white potatoes for the sweet potatoes if you wish.

Ingredients

¼ cup warm water

3 tablespoons sugar

1 tablespoon active dry yeast

2 eggs

⅓ cup milk

¼ cup plus 1 tablespoon unsalted butter, melted and cooled

1 teaspoon salt

¾ cup cooked, mashed, and sieved sweet potato (about 1 large or 2 small potatoes)

3-½ cups all-purpose flour

2 tablespoons unsalted butter, not melted

Directions

1. In a small bowl, combine the warm water with 1 tablespoon of the sugar. Sprinkle the yeast over this mixture and allow to proof for 5 minutes or until foamy.

2. In a large bowl, whisk together the proofed yeast mixture, remaining 2 tablespoons sugar, and the eggs, milk, ¼ cup melted butter, salt, and potatoes until well combined. Stir in 3 cups of the flour, 1 cup at a time.

3. Turn the dough out onto a floured surface and knead, using some of the remaining flour to keep it from sticking, until smooth and elastic. Shape into a ball, place in a large bowl that has been coated with the 2 tablespoons of butter, and turn to coat with the butter. Cover with plastic wrap and let rise in a warm place until doubled in size, about 1 hour.

4. Preheat oven to 400 degrees Fahrenheit. Cut or pinch off walnut-size pieces of dough and form into balls. Put three balls of dough into each buttered muffin-tin cup, brush the tops with the reserved tablespoon of melted butter, and allow to rise, covered loosely, in a warm place until almost double in size, 30 to 45 minutes.

5. Bake in the preheated oven until golden, about 12 to 15 minutes. Serve immediately.

A SENSE OF COMMUNITY

On Artistry, Ancestry, and African Americans

An interview with Ann Miller Woodford

ANN MILLER WOODFORD has a vision: Her world in western North Carolina is a beautiful place where all of God's children get together and celebrate. There's no racial prejudice, no harsh words spoken, no hatred at all. And everybody is treated equally and is equally visible.

Unfortunately, in the real world, that is not the case. In fact, Woodford agrees with Edward J. Cabbell, an African American scholar and former civil rights activist in West Virginia. He bemoaned the "black invisibility" that plagued studies of the Appalachian South. African Americans, he said, were a "neglected minority within a neglected minority," the latter referring to Southern Highlanders in general.

So Woodford decided to do something about that invisibility. She spent more than seven years gathering information from church records, old letters, diaries, factories, cemeteries, family histories, and hundreds of interviews. The result is a book, more than six hundred pages long, titled *When All God's Children Get Together: A Celebration of the Lives and Music of African American People in Far Western North Carolina.*

Woodford's father, Purel Miller, was her inspiration for the book. "Your daddy was *somebody*," one man in town told her decades ago, and she knew he was right. Her daddy really was *somebody*, a man respected by blacks and whites alike, a man people listened to when he spoke. And he knew stories to tell. Lordy, he knew stories.

PLATE 53   Barbara McRae and Ann Woodford

"My father was a living, walking history book," Woodford writes in her book. "He had worked in so many places and heard his own father talk about his adventures over the years when they sat around their old pot-bellied stove at night in the wintertime."

"He told me his stories all the time," she says, "and I wasn't listening for years. Suddenly one day, I woke up and said 'this man has a story to tell.' I wish he could've lived to see the book." Purel Miller died of pneumonia in 2013. The book was published in 2015.

On this warm spring day, Ann Woodford has driven from Andrews to Franklin, North Carolina, and is sitting in the home of Barbara McRae, retired editor of *The Franklin Press*, a twice-a-week newspaper in town. McRae designed Woodford's book, battling cancer at the same time. There's so much to talk about—the book, Woodford's family, her neighbors, the struggles and successes of black people in her region—but the author takes a couple of minutes to praise the beauty of the western North Carolina mountains.

As she was driving over, she wondered, *Have I been here before?* "I know I have, a thousand times," she says. "But everything is so beautiful: the tree limbs and the way the light shines through them. I lived in New York City; I lived in Atlanta for six or seven months; I lived in California for nine years.

But there is nothing in any of those places that is as beautiful as it is right here."

Woodford sounds like she works for the chamber of commerce, her smile almost fixed as she talks. But the reality is that she genuinely loves her mountains, and the smile is natural. So, it isn't altogether surprising when she briefly breaks into John Denver's "Take Me Home, Country Roads." The song may be about West Virginia, not western North Carolina, but they're still mountains. And she adores them.

That's one reason she came home from California in 1992. Andrews is a beautiful hometown, lovelier than any place she'd been. After the two businesses she launched on the West Coast folded, and to be closer to her mother, Margaret Ann Wykle Miller, Woodford moved back to the Great Smoky Mountains of Andrews, North Carolina, where she was born and raised during the days of segregation.

Her grandfather, William Cleveland "Cleve" Miller, she says, built the first house in the Andrews black community, a place that became known as Happytop. He had packed up and left Forsyth County, Georgia, where he was born, after a black man, twenty-four years old, was murdered for allegedly raping and killing an eighteen-year-old white woman in that county. It happened on September 10, 1912. The young man was lynched by the "North Georgia White Caps," Woodford says, and hundreds of African Americans abandoned their homes and fled the area along with her grandfather. Some of them ended up in Andrews, located in Cherokee County, and in other far western counties of North Carolina. Woodford says she has found descendants of the Forsyth County "cleansing" throughout the region.

Life in Andrews was not without racial discrimination, but, unlike other places that African Americans years ago referred to as "sundown towns"— don't let the sun set on you in this town, was the warning—Andrews was never that way, Woodford says.

Ann Miller was born on January 31, 1947, not a good day for her mother's ride to the hospital. A thick snow covered the ground, maybe eighteen inches deep, her father remembered.

With his wife in labor, Purel Miller frantically ran down to the home of Buck Holland, a white man who drove a taxi. Holland was happy to help. He started driving toward the Miller home, but the snow was too deep. The

PLATE 54   Ann's best black-and-white photo of her mom and dad

car got stuck. "Daddy all a sudden thought, and he ran to the neighbors', and all the men came and picked up the car and carried it up to Mama and Daddy's house, put Mama in the car, carried it back to the road, and Holland took her to the hospital."

Ann was the first baby born in the new Rodda–Van Gorder Clinic in downtown Andrews. The attending physician was Dr. Charles O. Van Gorder, who was featured in Tom Brokaw's book *The Greatest Generation*. Both Van Gorder and his partner, Dr. John S. Rodda, were decorated for their service in the US Army during World War II. Coincidentally, taxi driver Buck Holland's daughter was the second baby born in the clinic. The Hollands named their girl Margaret Ann, after Margaret Ann Miller.

As a little girl, Ann was very shy (she's not anymore), and it was her sister, Mary Alice, two years younger, who protected her from bullies at school.

"We called her 'yellow jacket.' She was light-complexioned, we call it, and she had sandy-colored hair. But you know that yellow jacket, that littlest bee tears you up, boy. She wouldn't put up with anybody messing with her older sister," Woodford says of Mary Alice. She proved it one day by chasing down a boy who had drawn a nasty picture of Ann on the blackboard and written the word 'pickaninny' under it. Little Mary Alice Miller took care of the situation after school, and the boy never taunted her sister again.

Purel Miller always wanted a boy, but he ended up with three girls: Ann,

Mary Alice, and Nina. So Ann tried to be the boy her father never had. If he went to the field to work, she went along with her broken-handle hoe, even though Daddy didn't believe little girls should do such things. But Ann persisted and even helped her father build a barn. She also built a barbecue pit using bricks from an old building her father tore down and a refrigerator rack for the grill. One day, her grandfather, Cleve Miller, said, *Ann can do anything*, "and that encouraged me," she says. "I couldn't do anything, but he said it and I believed he meant it."

Ann attended Andrews Colored School, later called Andrews Negro School, where there was one room and one teacher. From the second grade forward, she was the only child in her grade, "so I graduated valedictorian," she says with a hearty laugh.

Ann was born to be an artist. She was always drawing pictures and making artsy objects.

The elementary school teacher had children from eight grades, and she was happy when a child concentrated on something she liked to do that wasn't disturbing other students. Ann concentrated on art. She used clay to create a farm with cows and horses, and a couple of years later, her farm sculptures covered half of the classroom's study table.

After elementary school, she set her sights on Allen High School in Asheville, North Carolina, the school that Purel Miller's two younger sisters had attended. Allen was a boarding school established in the late nineteenth century for local African American girls and later directed by the Woman's Missionary Society of the Methodist Episcopal School.

"They told me I wouldn't make it because kids there came from New York and everywhere," she says, "and I'm coming from a little ol' school in Andrews."

Her first semester at Allen in 1961, she made a C in Algebra, but an A in World History, a course she took with juniors and seniors. As it was with her father, who quit school after the third grade and could not read or write, history was her passion. The older kids liked her—they even chose her as their little mascot—and she was on the school's honor roll from then on.

Ann's talent in art boosted her popularity with her teachers. One of them, Jacqueline "Jackie" King, would take her out of class every quarter to design bulletin boards. Julia Titus, principal of the school, paid for her to attend art classes in Asheville, and the librarian, Josephine Litchfield, drove her over and picked her up.

PLATE 55   Ann Miller Woodford displays one of her paintings, *My Sister, Myself.*

One day, Ann asked Miss Litchfield how she could repay her for her kindness. "And she said, 'Honey, you can't repay me. You'll just have to remember
what you've gotten out of this and do for other people.' And I never forgot
that. So, I do my best, even to this day, to do for other people."

Ann graduated fourth in her high school class of fifty-five students. Confidence in herself and her abilities was higher than it had ever been.

Encouraged by her teachers, her mother, and others, to attend college, Ann applied to Ohio University in Athens, Ohio, and was accepted. She borrowed six hundred dollars for her first year there, but grants and scholarships paid for everything the rest of her time in college. She graduated cum laude with a fine arts degree in interior design and was named a member of the Mortar Board National Honor Society, the only black honoree in 1969, the year she graduated. The society recognizes college seniors for their exemplary scholarship, leadership, and service.

Ann's work history ran the gamut, from working for a nonprofit project in Pittsburgh, Pennsylvania, to serving as a stewardess for American Airlines while based in New York City. She also worked as a teacher in a public school, in sales in California, and as a planner for Cherokee County. She even painted houses with her father after her marriage dissolved and she moved back to Andrews for about four years. She left for California in 1982 and worked in sales with her sister Nina and Nina's husband, Otis Moses, before venturing into business for herself.

Several years after the mountains of North Carolina lured her home again, it finally dawned on Woodford: There's a book out there about her parents that needs to be written, a book telling the history of African Americans in far western North Carolina. She'd already made tape recordings of her mama and daddy talking about their earlier years. But writing a whole book? How much work would that entail?

She was about to find out.

A retelling of her daddy's stories, the ones she failed to listen to closely when she was young, would be a good way to start. In fact, her father encouraged her to write the book, to save the old tales and songs that were part of the black culture of the region. Some stories her father told in detail. On others, he didn't elaborate, because he didn't like to dwell on the negative. That's when Woodford had to find out more from both black and white people alike.

One year—this would've been in the late sixties or early seventies, Woodford estimates—Purel Miller heard that the Ku Klux Klan was planning to march through Murphy, the county seat of Cherokee, and Andrews, a quiet little town where most folks minded their own business and avoided trouble. Several black people in the community started stocking up on ammunition. "Daddy went downtown and walked from store to store and told the white people, 'You don't want this trouble,' and he suggested they close

PLATE 56   Purel Miller,
Father's Day 2010

their stores when the Klan marched through. Ingles even closed, which was really something because they don't even close for Christmas most of the time."

Woodford received added inspiration for the book from her father's habit of preaching sermons and recording memories into his tape recorder, just for his own pleasure. He took his little machine from place to place and recorded how things used to be. One day, he visited the site of the old Andrews Tannery and Extract company. The tannery had closed years before, prompting many African Americans to leave town in search of new jobs, but remnants of concrete vats remained. "He went down there and was walking around talking into this tape recorder. He didn't hear any voices himself. He was recording his own voice. He came home and said, 'I want y'all to listen to my talk.' We got to listening to it, and we could hear voices in the background, all kinds of voices. It brought tears to his eyes. I don't understand it, not to this day."

Woodford says she and her sisters called their daddy an alien, "because he went places no other black person would go, some places where the N word was used regularly, but people would have him come inside the house and eat with them when he was wearing bloody overalls from killing their hog."

To cover some of the expenses of researching her book, traveling around and taking photographs, Woodford received a grant from the Blue Ridge National Heritage Area. Later, she received publishing support from One Dozen Who Care, Inc., an African American–led community development organization she founded in the late 1990s. Among other projects, the group sponsors a Multicultural Women's Development Conference, along with a 10-10-10 program that teaches ten major life skills to ten young people over a period of ten months. In 1998, it hosted a huge gospel singing, called "When All God's Children Get Together," which was the catalyst for Woodford's book.

The book devotes a full chapter to One Dozen Who Care and its benefits to the community.

Woodford recalls old traditions such as lined hymn singing, coded song lyrics, shouting in the spirit, and call-and-response singing. The book features stories that few people knew. One is about Woodford's maternal great-grandfather, Deacon Christenberry "Berry" Howell, who drove turkeys, horses, and other animals over trails from Swain County, North Carolina, and into Tennessee. "They say his turkeys would follow him like he was the Pied Piper," Woodford writes. "They would fly up into the trees at night, while he slept, and dutifully follow him on their way the next morning."

There are tales of Texana McClelland, the first black woman to move into a settlement eventually named Texana in her honor and located high on a mountain about a mile from Murphy; of ministers and their preach-

PLATE 57   *Grandpa Cleve Miller*—oil painting by Ann M. Woodford

PLATE 58   Andrews Colored (later Negro) School building

ing styles; of the town of Marble, once a thriving place where the sidewalks were made of blue marble. There are tales of decades-old superstitions and traditions that manage to live on, along with stories about churches, sports figures, veterans, and teachers who served the community.

Woodford writes of the black experience, going back to slavery days. Some of the stories were submitted by others, and "getting information" was the most challenging part of producing the book, she says. But she managed to gather hundreds of photographs that had never been published before.

Says the book's designer, Barbara McRae: "This monumental work reveals the powerful story of a people who have been largely invisible in their own homeland. Ann Miller Woodford opens a door to the homes, churches, and daily lives of the African American people of far western North Carolina. She unflinchingly captures the horrors imposed under Jim Crow, but also the kindness and decency of the mountain people, who offered friendship and a helping hand to their black neighbors."

Many of the stories, McRae says, could have been about families of any race. "There were so many commonalities, the foods, the whole lifestyle of the mountain is the same. And any home you went to in the country, you would recognize the same elements."

To Ann Woodford, the title of the book, *When All God's Children*

Get Together, says it all: "I believe in that," she says. "We're all going to get together, and when we do, this is going to be a wholly different world. I loved writing [the book] to make sure that the history of these people that did so much for our region will never be forgotten."

Response from readers, she says, "has been absolutely wonderful." And if Purel Miller were still around, he might get out his little machine and record them all.

Keeping the Land and the History

Stories from Wayne County, Kentucky

IT'S A WARM, RAINY AFTERNOON in early May, close to suppertime, and Carl Foster isn't expecting company. He doesn't have email or a telephone, so I couldn't contact him about an interview. I just took a chance that Foster would be willing to sit down and talk, and popped in.

Foster lives about seven miles down Freedom Road, which starts a few miles from Monticello, Kentucky, and fades from blacktop to dirt and gravel. The road meanders through Denney's Gap, crosses a little bridge over a creek, and winds up in the Freedom Community. Freedom Church is just down the road, maybe two hundred yards from the Foster place, and the old Freedom School, when it existed, was about a mile away.

Foster is dressed in a T-shirt and blue pajama bottoms covered with University of Kentucky Wildcats logos. Laid-back and friendly, he sits at his kitchen table and talks as though he's known me all his life.

His dogs, Rusty and Frank, are eating on the front porch. They're brothers and a three-way cross: a quarter beagle, a quarter Australian shepherd, and half cur.

Foster has hunted ever since he was big enough to carry a rifle or shotgun, and he still hunts today. But now he usually drives a Gator four-wheeler, following Rusty's and Frank's barks in their search for quarry.

"I'm doing pretty good to be as old as I am," says Carl, who was born April 23, 1948. He has a little trouble with diabetes, and something that

PLATE 59   Rusty and Frank, Carl's dogs of
questionable heritage, eat well while the master's around.

broke loose in one of his eyes is "floating around like a fly in Jell-O. Doctor said he couldn't do a thing for it."

While we are talking at the kitchen table, a young man drops by to return a set of chains he borrowed to pull a Jeep that had broken down near the Little South Fork of the Cumberland River, on down Freedom Road a piece. He wanted to use Foster's phone to call for help but settled for the chains. Foster doesn't have a phone, because he didn't make but a couple of calls a month, he says, "and I'm not going to pay them thirty-six dollars a month for two phone calls. Other people would call me, but now they can't. If something happened, like a doctor wanted to raise my insulin, now he'll have to send me a postcard." He laughs.

Foster voluntarily repeated the eighth grade at Freedom School because state law said he couldn't drop out until he was sixteen. He reached the required age and quit. High school was just too far to walk. "You had to get up, say, at four o'clock and walk four miles to catch the bus to Monticello," he says.

Besides farming, Foster has done a little of everything to make money. He worked for a Monticello plant that made wood parts for cabinets; he was a night watchman for a coal company; he even went to Indiana to work

for a while, first in a rock quarry and then at a factory that made televisions.

"I never liked Indiana," he says, a frown replacing his friendly smile. "You can't see nothin'. You could see as far as you could, but you couldn't see nothin'."

A coal company official tried to persuade him to come to Perry County, Kentucky, to work in a deep mine. "No way am I going underground," Foster told him.

Foster has lived alone since his mother died. He never married. "No, I never thought about it," he says. "I had too many bosses the way it was: Dad and Mom and then at work, and the older brothers would tell you what to do when you went out to the farm. I didn't need another boss."

These days, he says, he mainly piddles around the farm. He feeds the heifers that are calving, and he turns the chickens out to let them scratch around freely. He keeps them put up at night to prevent the coyotes from killing them. He'll bust wood for his stove for about two hours, take a nap, and get up and make supper. Then it's time to sit back and read or watch television.

Foster's needs are few, and he's content, you can tell, as he walks around in his yard, stopping occasionally to talk about Freedom Community or to pose for a photograph in front of his small, white frame house with an American flag attached to the fascia board waving in a rainy breeze. Foster and each of his seven siblings were born in that little house.

Behind the Foster home is some of the prettiest Kentucky pastureland in the region, along with a cave where family members kept their perishable foods before electricity made its way into the remote community. This land has been in the Foster family since 1915, when grandfather Allen Foster bought about 165 acres from Henry Phillips. He built the present house in 1927, and Carl's daddy, Raymond, remodeled it in 1975.

It's later in the evening, and the rain has stopped. The temperature is pleasant enough for sitting out on the front porch at Carl's brother Boyd's place, situated on about seventy-five acres, four miles or so from Carl and the old homestead. Boyd; his wife, Helen; and son Gerald, just like Carl, are friendly and welcoming, and they invite me to sit a spell.

Carl and Boyd purchased their siblings' parts of the Foster land after their parents died: their father in 1987 and mother in 2008. "If you put land up or a homeplace up in a public auction," Boyd Foster says in a later conversation, "you don't know if somebody is going to outbid you." Together, they own 182 acres in one tract around the old Foster home. And with adjoining land that they own with Boyd's sons, the Fosters can claim about 382 acres in the Freedom Community.

PLATE 61   Boyd Foster sits inside the cave where family kept perishable food.

Keeping land in the family is important not only to the Fosters, but to others in Wayne County. Members of another family in the county even intermarried, marrying cousins, to keep their land.

What makes the Foster land special? Says Boyd: "Well, it's my homeplace, first off. I was born and raised out there. The only time I left this country was when I pulled a tour in the United States Marine Corps and went to Vietnam. We've lived here and never had any trouble with people bothering any of our stuff. And that's something to be thankful for."

Boyd was drafted into the Army and went first to Louisville, Kentucky. But the Marine Corps sent word that it needed two good men to fill out a platoon. He was one of those two good men. "First letter we got," Carl says, "he was in the dang Marine Corps over in South Carolina." Brother Hayden spent twenty-two and a half years in the Army.

"There'd have to be something drastic," Boyd says, before he or Carl

PLATE 62   Barn on Foster farm

would sell any of their land. "It'll be handed down to my children and grand-children." He and Helen have two sons and a daughter: Gerald is a machin-ist; brother, Mark, a civil engineer; and their sister, Sandra, a pharmacist.

Adding to the attractiveness of the Foster land is the closeness of the Lit-tle South Fork of the Cumberland River. The 688-mile-long Cumberland River runs through Kentucky and Tennessee. The Fosters own property that abuts land the government bought before impounding the river to build pic-turesque Lake Cumberland for flood control and to generate hydroelectric power.

Land is important, Boyd Foster says, "but family is more important, more

important than money." He and his siblings were taught to always look out for one another, of course, but also to help their neighbors.

"Back years ago," he says, "people would help each other. If you went to visit someone, whatever they were doing, putting up corn, gathering hay, cutting firewood, whatever, if you was big enough, you'd work with them just like you was at home. If they come to visit you, they done the same thing."

That's what a community, a true community, is all about. And their community, the Fosters believe, is the best. Just consider its name: Freedom.

Boyd thinks the community got the name because so many in that area fought for the freedom of America. "I've been told that," he says, "and I couldn't prove that one way or the other, but it makes sense to me."

Many of the early settlers and members of the Kentucky Militia fought in the American Revolutionary War, and when the Civil War broke out, Kentucky, being a border state between the Northern and Southern forces, sided with the Union. Well, most Kentuckians did. The Confederacy also had its sympathizers in Kentucky, and some of them lived in Wayne County.

On August 30, 1861, a countywide meeting was held at the Wayne County Courthouse in Monticello, and a respected Baptist preacher, W. A. Cooper, spoke for two hours and twenty minutes before a resolution was offered to ease tensions between the two factions. The resolution, which passed almost unanimously, said, among other things, that "we the people of Wayne County should remain loyal citizens, and that we organize home guards as the law directs and that we arm and equip ourselves for self-defense alone."

In other words, the people of Wayne County wanted to forget political divisions and live in peace. The county's residents even voted to hoist a white flag with the inscription "Peace is the motto of Wayne County," and to give other such proofs to "convince the world that we are for peace."

Today, Monticello is often called "The Houseboat Capital of the World" because of the large number of houseboat manufacturers in the city. The health of the local economy depends greatly on recreational and tourist traffic to Lake Cumberland.

In the early part of the twentieth century, however, black gold became the moneymaker when huge pools of oil were discovered in the strata of Wayne County. Entrepreneurs seeking their fortune swelled the town's population from 413 residents in 1890 to more than 1,300 by 1910. Coal was also mined in the area, but "most people didn't object," Boyd Foster says, "because a lot of them got a lot of money out of that." The county lies in both the Mississippian plateau and the Eastern Kentucky coal fields.

People in Wayne County and Monticello are serious about preserving stories of their past, of which they have no shortage. David H. Smith, executive director and curator of the Wayne County Museum, shares a few.

Take, for example, the unusual way Monticello got its name.

PLATE 63   David Smith knows the history of the area.

"When they were trying to come up with a name of the town," Smith says, going back to about 1801, when the town was created, "there was this prominent family whose last name was Jones. They wanted to name the town Jonesboro. The rest of the squires, or whatever they were called, didn't want that name, and this sixteen-year-old boy offers the name Monticello as a compromise. And they jumped on it, more or less to outvote the Joneses."

That boy's name was Micah Taul, and he served as the county's first court clerk, perhaps because he could read and write, which at the time was uncommon. Taul went on to become a lawyer, a leader in the War of 1812, and a congressman.

And then there are the stories of a Cherokee Indian the white people called Chief Doublehead. But the Cherokee disagreed about his name. They called him Chief Chuqualatague, a leader of the Cherokee people of the Cumberland River. The chief is said to have had a son, Tuckahoe, and a daughter named Cornblossom, whom the white fur traders called "Princess Cornblossom" because of her beauty.

The local story says that Cornblossom took part in the vengeance killing of a stranger. The stranger reportedly bribed a young Indian to swap a chunk of silver for a rifle, Smith says, and the Indian died in the process. Cornblossom and some of her young braves caught up with the culprit and shot him. This incident was described as "Vengeance at the Turtle Neck Ford," according to local legend.

"People will come to the museum and say, if they're from here, 'We go back to Princess Cornblossom,' who supposedly married a white fur trader,"

Smith says. "Some people don't even believe she ever existed. It's possible that she did exist. It makes a pretty good story that way. Sometimes the story is better than the truth."

Whether the chief was really from Wayne County is debatable, Smith says. He moved around quite a bit. But it is a fact that he made deals with the government concerning land cessions, and that may have led to his undoing. When land was given up for trade goods, it seems the chief got first pick. In 1808, he was either murdered or executed for treason after negotiating a land cession without the consent of the Cherokee National Council.

It is also a fact, Smith says, that Chief Doublehead, or Chuqualatague, took part in approving the Holston Treaty in 1791, and met with George Washington and his representatives in 1794. The treaty established terms of relations between the United States and the Cherokee, assuring the tribes that they would fall under protection of the government.

Wayne County even has its own Daniel Boone story. Boone apparently joined other long hunters—eighteenth-century explorers and hunters who conducted expeditions into the frontier wilderness for long periods of time—in the Meadow Creek area of the county in the 1770s.

But, contrary to popular belief, Smith says, there is no evidence Boone owned land in the county. However, another Daniel Boone, or Boon, was in the county by 1813 and did purchase Wayne County property, records at the courthouse show. That Daniel was the great-nephew of the famous one.

And then there's a musical twist to Wayne County's history. Richard "Dick" Burnett was born on October 8, 1883, in an area near Elk Springs, about seven miles north of Monticello. You may not have heard of Burnett, but if you saw the movie *O Brother, Where Art Thou?*, you heard his song "Man of Constant Sorrow." Many in the music business credit Burnett with writing that song around 1913, about six years after he lost his eyesight when a robber shot him in the face. Blindness forced him to quit his job in the oil fields, but his boss encouraged him to make music his livelihood.

Burnett was proficient on the banjo, dulcimer, and fiddle, and had been since he was thirteen. In time, he met Leonard Rutherford, a fourteen-year-old orphan who, as Burnett's student, became "one of the smoothest fiddle players around," Smith says. "They would play their music anywhere they could, often setting up on courthouse lawns or on the street. Dick would strap a tin cup on his knee for donations. They became very popular locally, and future fiddle and banjo players would mimic their style of playing."

Burnett was a prolific songwriter. He picked up on tunes such as "Pearl Bryan," "A Short Life of Trouble," "Weeping Willow Tree," and "Little Streams of Whiskey," all songs he helped preserve or may have written, according to Smith.

But did he really write "Man of Constant Sorrow"? If he did, he gave it a different title: "Farewell Song." In 1928, Emry Arthur recorded the song under the better-known title. That title stuck and it was recorded in the 1950s by the Stanley Brothers and in the 1960s by Bob Dylan. Smith says that when Burnett was asked about the song late in life, he replied, "No, I think I got that ballad from somebody, I dunno, it may be my song."

Burnett died at ninety-three on January 23, 1977, "without really realizing the influence he had on old-time Appalachian music," Smith says.

Like most people in Wayne County, the Fosters enjoy the local history stories and legends. But they're more intrigued by stories handed down by their parents and grandparents. Boyd Foster tells about his grandfather Allen Foster cutting trees in the autumn months and putting his brand on each log. Then, in the wintertime, when the water level was up, he'd remove the scotches, allowing the logs to roll downhill and into the river. Foster and other loggers would walk the river banks, using hooks to guide the logs to Burnside, where a huge boom picked them up and deposited them at a sawmill. Each man was paid according to how many logs he turned in.

Carl Foster treasures memories of his family. Pictures of family members line the walls of his home, reminders of how things used to be.

These are the stories that matter. And these are the memories of home, in a community called Freedom.

Forming the Great Smoky Mountains National Park

The story of Glenn Cardwell of Pittman Center, Tennessee

GLENN CARDWELL says he's like an old oak tree planted beside the river. He cannot be moved, at least not very far. Today, he could throw a rock from his front yard and ripple the Middle Prong of the Little Pigeon River, which also stays close to home, seemingly reluctant to flow outside of Sevier County in East Tennessee.

It was on the chilly Christmas Eve of 1930 that Roy Glenn Cardwell was born at home, a three-room house situated on Indian Creek inside a forest that would become part of the Great Smoky Mountains National Park. He and his family moved that year to get out of the park's way. Some families moved to other states, several to Virginia, but the Cardwells ended up in a three-room frame house near what is today the Greenbrier entrance to the park. They were forced to move again in 1947. But they didn't go far, just downstream to Pittman Center, on the border of the park, never again to lose their home to the government.

Glenn Cardwell, the eighth of the nine children of Bill and Pearlie Cardwell, was a child of nature, carefree and happy. While his father and siblings gathered with neighbors on the front porch to pick and sing, he was out with his mother roaming the ancient, hilly, remote forest of Greenbrier Cove, looking for herbs, bark, roots, and twigs, anything she could use to make teas or tonics or poultices for doctoring a sick child.

He could hear the music in the distance, and he appreciated good mountain music, but he appreciated God's creation even more.

Known for the diversity of its plant and animal life, the forest was his first school-room where, without knowing it, he was planting the seeds for a career.

Bill and Pearlie Cardwell were a study in contrasts. "I could sit with my mother all day," Glenn Cardwell says, "and she wouldn't give you a spoonful of words. She was a quiet, calm individual, but she was quick and swift to give advice, admonition, and discipline when needed. She always

PLATE 64   Glenn in third grade

had her kids and other kids there." If you asked her how she put up with a house full of children day after day, she would say, "Well, you just learn to tolerate certain things."

Bill Cardwell, Glenn's father, was a Bradley, on his mother's side, and "they say the Bradleys are 99.9 percent mouth," Glenn says. But he was who he was. "My father wouldn't turn around twice to impress you. If you didn't like him, that was your problem. 'I like myself' was his attitude."

Glenn Cardwell says his father was an excellent musician and made his own instruments. He remembers a banjo his father made from the hide of a groundhog. When a cat chewed on it, he killed the cat and used its hide as a replacement. The sound, he decided, was just as good.

The average Greenbrier family didn't need much money during those Depression years. People grew most of what they ate, and they could eat rabbit meat during any month spelled with an "r." From the river came fish and turtles for the dinner table. The Cardwells always kept a couple of hogs, which they'd kill and put away with salt in the smokehouse, and they kept chickens in the spring and summer. Fried chicken was for Sunday when the preacher came over.

Trapping for hides brought in some money, but moonshine brought a better price. Herbs foraged from the forest were used for bartering. The Cardwells had a magazine explaining which herbs to gather, and once they

PLATE 65   Cardwell in the Navy

had enough to trade, they'd take them to a local store, which in turn took them to Knoxville.

Glenn Cardwell knew in the first grade the girl he wanted to marry. Her name was Edith Faye Huskey. In the fifth grade, he knew the kind of job he wanted. He wanted to be a teacher. He didn't know that a man could be a teacher until the fifth grade, where he had a male instructor. He was inspired.

Glenn was the only one of the Cardwell clan to attend college. After high school, he started classes at East Tennessee State University, but with the Korean War beginning, he joined the Navy in 1951 to avoid the draft. He received an honorable discharge four years later, in September 1955. But he didn't wait four years to marry his sweetheart. He and Faye were wed on June 1, 1953, the very day she graduated from Berea College in Berea, Kentucky.

After his Navy stint ended, Glenn Cardwell went back to college, this time to the University of Tennessee in Knoxville, where he majored in business education. In 1958, he would become a teacher of accounting and history at Pittman Center, a position he kept for three years. He remembers well his first day of teaching. He got to the school early, and so did his most memorable student, a lad named Clarence.

"The thing is," Clarence said, "since I'm having to repeat the seventh grade, I don't think I should have to do all of your homework." Cardwell replied, "I'm sorry, Clarence, but apparently you must not have done everything right, or you would not be repeating the seventh grade." Said Clarence, "I can see I'm going to have trouble." And then he added: "The second thing you should know about me is that I have a dad who likes to drink, and when he's drinking, he wants to beat up on my mother. When that happens, I'll be sleepy in class, so stay off my back."

Turned out, the young man stayed awake at night when his father was drinking. He was there to protect his mother. For Christmas one year, Clarence thought his teacher should have a nice gift, so he gave him a pig's tail, all wrapped up in a box. Glenn Cardwell still has it.

Besides teaching, Cardwell also served as the school's guidance counselor. Then he took a federal service exam, which got his name listed on the federal registry for employment. Not long afterward, he received a postcard from the National Park Service: "If you are interested, please give us a call."

At last, the career path that had taken root as he trailed his mother through the Greenbrier Forest, those days learning about herbs and plants in his "heaven on earth," as he calls it, all of it was coming together for the perfect job. Glenn Cardwell was hired as a park ranger and would eventually become supervisor park ranger in charge of interpretation at Sugarlands Visitor Center, located on the doorstep of Gatlinburg, Tennessee. Although the government had twice taken his family's home, he delighted in the work for thirty-four years.

Even his father wasn't bitter about giving up his land to be preserved as a national park, one that sprawls out from East Tennessee to western North Carolina. He was just angry about losing his neighbors. You can buy a farm anywhere, he told his son during a visit to the park, "but you can't buy neighbors back after they're gone."

As the chief interpreter, Glenn Cardwell got paid to tell stories, about the park and its beginnings, about the herbs and plants he gathered as a child, about the streams, about the wildlife, about the Great Smoky Mountains themselves.

"I never envisioned myself as a storyteller," he says, but that's often how he's introduced as a speaker.

And if you sit a spell inside Glenn and Faye Cardwell's comfortable riverside home in Pittman Center, you'll know for sure that he deserves the title and more. In addition to being a storyteller, he's also a fact-checker, an author who has written two books and is working on a third, a historian, an archivist, a leader, and even a humorist.

"Glenn has a scholar's mind, a scientist's technique, and the memory of an elephant," Bill Landry writes in his book *Appalachian Tales & Heartland Adventures*. "We've gone to him for information about everything, from early knowledge of the people of Greenbrier to genealogy, botany, animals, and park trails. You name it, Glenn knows it."

For starters, Cardwell likes to tell how the Great Smoky Mountains National Park came to be. He gives credit to a woman named Anne Davis, who returned home to East Tennessee after visiting a park out west and then asked her husband, "Why can't we have a national park in the Great Smoky Mountains?" "Honey, I didn't know you felt that way," replied her husband, W. P. Davis, an executive of the Knoxville Iron Company.

So in December 1925, Davis called together a group of influential people, including bankers, AAA and chamber of commerce officials, and businessmen. That's when the Great Smoky Mountains Conservation Association was born, an organization that became Tennessee's godparent in establishing the Great Smoky Mountains National Park. North Carolina formed a similar organization.

A bill establishing the park passed Congress in May 1926, according to Cardwell, but purchasing the land, which initially was to be 700,000 acres, was left up to Tennessee and North Carolina. Once the states donated a minimum of 150,000 acres, Congress said, the federal government would accept the project for administrative purposes only. But when 300,000 acres had been acquired and turned over, then Congress would appropriate money for support and development. Several of W. P. Davis's wealthy friends pledged support, but then went bankrupt during the Great Depression. Still, Davis insisted the park would be established. And it was, eventually.

"There's no way under God's heaven that this land could be bought today," Cardwell says. Even the Knoxville City Council pitched in, despite the fact that the initial spot of land, 75,000 acres from the Little River Lumber Company, was in another county, Sevier. "That's illegal," he says. "It would not be feasible to take taxpayers' money in a city and then go out beyond that city limits and do things like they did in the 1920s."

But the city council did just that, promising a third of the money, provided the state of Tennessee came up with the rest. What started as a citizens' movement now had a nucleus, 75,000 acres, and a marketing base on which to build. The Rockefeller family, who had helped with the Grand Teton National Park, offered five million dollars if Tennessee and North Carolina would match the gift with two and a half million each. "They did it," Cardwell says. Even "children donated pennies."

On June 15, 1934, after Tennessee and North Carolina turned over 300,000 acres to the federal government, Congress issued a charter establishing the Great Smoky Mountains National Park. That date is considered the park's birthday, but the official dedication didn't come until 1940, when President F. D. Roosevelt came down from Washington to speak.

Today, the park covers more than 500,000 acres, divided almost evenly between Tennessee and North Carolina. Attracting more than ten million visitors every year, it is one of the country's most popular national parks.

But not every visitor appreciates the beauty and wonder of the park, Cardwell learned over the years. "You mean it's just a bunch of trees?" some people ask, disappointed.

Cardwell says many tourists don't know what to do in the park because they haven't planned out their vacation. "The three greatest words besides 'love,'" he says, "are 'meditation,' 'preparation,' and 'execution.' Many come here to execute their vacation without even knowing what to do."

Since January 1960, Glenn and Faye Cardwell have lived in a brick house that Glenn, his brother Emert, and his father-in-law built alongside the Middle Prong of the Little Pigeon River in an area called Emerts Cove, part of Pittman Center. The Cardwells have one daughter, Sandra Yorke, who retired in 2015 as coordinator of work environment health and safety in Ithaca, New York.

"Most of the Cardwells were carpenters, but I missed out there, too," Glenn Cardwell says. "But I can lay blocks." So that was his job, laying block for his home, and the foundation for a life with Faye.

Practically everywhere Glenn Cardwell has lived, the Little Pigeon River has been there, about a tenth of a mile away from his two homes inside the park and now almost within spitting distance. It's hard to tell if he is following the river or if the river is following him. The Middle Prong of the Little

Pigeon begins inside Greenbrier Cove of the Great Smoky Mountains and joins other streams toward the Gulf of Mexico via the Tennessee, the Ohio, and the Mississippi Rivers.

"To me," he says, "the river is the heart and soul of Emerts Cove and Pittman Center. We're probably the only town in Tennessee that has a river that's been declared one hundred percent pure by the Tennessee water quality people."

Cardwell retired from the park service on September 30, 1995, but not because he was tired of the work. "Golly, yeah, I enjoyed the job," he says. The park service offered him a buyout three times, and he finally accepted the third offer.

He was the last person born inside the park who ended up working for it. He never had to transfer, even though the man who hired him made it clear the National Park Service wanted supervisory employees to move out eventually and on to another assignment. "And he asked me if I would be willing to do that," Cardwell says.

"I think you said the fastest no in history," his former supervisor recalled years later. But there is virtue in continuity, the boss realized, and Glenn Cardwell was as continuous as they come.

So what does Cardwell do to stay busy, now that he has retired? He

PLATE 66   Glenn at home

needed a project, and found one in politics. In 1998, he was elected mayor of Pittman Center, a town of 502 people, according to the 2010 census. "I didn't intend to get into politics," he says, "but that's what happened."

"This is the best little town in the Smokies," Glenn Cardwell says proudly. And inside its schoolhouse is a museum, the Glenn Cardwell Heritage Museum. "That was the most embarrassing moment of my life," Cardwell says, referring to the museum's being named for him. "I do things because I want to do them, not for recognition."

Modesty aside, the name Glenn Cardwell is a natural fit for the museum. Cardwell is indeed a history buff, one who not only has studied history but has also lived it. One reason he wrote two storytelling books, he says, is that his daughter requested them. "You're going to get old," she told him, "and I won't know those stories, and I want to know them."

It's obvious to anyone who knows him, but Glenn Cardwell says it anyway: "I am a people person." No doubt. Anyone who could put up with thousands of tourists every day, well, he'd either be a people person or, as Pearlie Cardwell said of all those kids who filled her house at suppertime, "you just learn to tolerate certain things." Maybe it's a little of both.

Glenn Cardwell was just a baby when his folks sold their place on Indian Creek to the government and moved for the first time. "They scattered us," he says. His father wanted to move to Virginia with several of his neighbors, but with a newborn in the family, he figured he couldn't travel that far away. So Glenn Cardwell's birth was well-timed. Because of him, the family stayed in Greenbrier.

Glenn and Faye Cardwell couldn't be happier. Like the Smokies themselves, Emerts Cove in Pittman Center is a friendly, inviting place, where peace, like a river, attends the souls of those who live there.

Why would anyone want to leave paradise anyway?

Glenn Cardwell died in November 2016, a few months after he was interviewed at his home. But it wasn't his nature to leave things undone. He had already completed his part of the photo book of Pittman Center.

The Lone Commissioner
of Lumpkin County

The life of J. B. Jones

J. B. JONES has done well for a one-gallus farmer who grew up poor, "I mean p-o-r-e poor," says the man who hadn't been out of Georgia until he was drafted, whose early education was in a one-room school, and whose first brush with politics came in a henhouse.

There's a lot to say about Jones, but first, let's get his name right. Social Security rolls say it's Joseph Benjamin Jones, but his mother always insisted it's plain old J.B. And that's what his birth certificate says: J. B. Jones. That's good enough, he'll tell you.

Jones learned to spend wisely early on because his parents didn't have any money; he easily cleared the US Army's strictest background checks because he'd never been anywhere; he learned the power of communication at tiny Lewis School, which he attended. He wanted to be a farmer with a thousand acres, but he ended up as his county's sole commissioner, a position he held for twenty-four busy years, overseeing 285 square miles.

"Politics is everywhere in the world," he says, talking about his time as commissioner of Northeast Georgia's mountainous Lumpkin County, home of the famous gold rush that started in 1829. "I got a henhouse over here in Frogtown. Ten thousand chickens. Nine thousand hens and one thousand roosters. There's politics in that thing. There's one in there somewhere that's the top rooster. You can walk in, and he'll bump you to let you know he's there."

PLATE 67   George Thompson chats with his friend J. B. Jones at Jones's kitchen table.

J. B. Jones has certainly been the top rooster in his own small world, but he's not above doing a little scratching and working along with the other chickens. And public officials all the way from the Georgia capital to Washington, DC, have noticed. As commissioner, he was known as a hardworking, honest, friendly, *very* persistent, commonsense public servant and storyteller who had a way of getting state and federal money for his county when others left empty-handed.

As a lone commissioner, Jones was close with the county's money. When he took office in 1972, he had to take out a loan to make the first payroll. When he left office in 1996, he says, the county had a surplus of eight million dollars. Explaining his successes, of course, comes with a generous helping of farmhouse logic.

Take, for example, his explanation of how to handle growth and county planning. "It's like back when I was a little boy here," he says, referring to his home in the Frogtown district. "We had an outhouse downwind from the house, a hundred yards away. Rainy and snowy and cold sometimes. You didn't go until you really had to. When you got up and lit your kerosene lantern, well, if you went too fast, you blew your light out. If you went too slow, there was a disaster. That's the way it is with planning. You got to be cautious."

J. B. Jones was born at home on October 25, 1932, the son of Joseph and Rader Armour Jones. His daddy was a farmer, about six feet, four inches tall with brown hair. His mother, part American Indian, was short with black hair. There were six children, four boys and two girls, all born in the same bed in the front room.

The Joneses' mother was "a peculiar person," Jones says, but "the kind of Christian who could pray for a cool breeze and get it." She would've been right at home with the back-to-nature movement today.

Jones attended nearby Lewis School, where all seven elementary grades were crammed into one room. "That was probably some of the best education I could get," he says, "because I listened to all those others that were above me."

An English teacher told Jones that if you can't communicate, you won't amount to much. It was a lesson he took to heart. And that's one thing Jones is known for. "You can put a new cow in with other cows," he says, "and the whole social order turns over."

That's communication farm people can understand. But it also went over well at Harvard University's Kennedy School of Government, where Jones, as county commissioner, was asked *twice* to speak on saving energy. After one of his speeches, a reporter with *Time* magazine told him, "I can't get over that dialect." Says Jones, "I know what you mean. I've been hearing it ever since I've been here."

After getting his diploma from Lumpkin County High School in 1949, Jones was ready for college, but the unexpected death of his father changed everything. Jones was needed to help support the family at home. He took a job at a local sawmill.

As a boy, Jones dreamed of becoming a soldier, and in February 1953, the US Army gave him that opportunity. He was drafted. But the Korean War—Jones calls it "Truman's war"—was winding down, and Jones never went to Korea. He was trained at Fort Jackson, South Carolina, then sent to Fort Bragg, North Carolina, and then to White Sands Proving Grounds in New Mexico. "I hadn't been out of the state of Georgia, and I hadn't been exposed," he says.

Eventually, he was sent to a special-weapons depot in Pirmasens, Germany.

After taking the Army's battery of tests, Jones realized something: "I wasn't dumb. I just hadn't been exposed to what the rest of the world had.

You follow me on that?" He did well on the tests and could've attended Officer Candidate School and become an officer. Instead, thirty-eight months after being drafted, Staff Sergeant J. B. Jones went home to his wife, the former Leslie Meers, whom he married while on leave in February 1955, and joined the Army Reserve. In all, he served thirty-eight years with the Army and the Army Reserve and retired as command sergeant major, the Army's top enlisted grade.

J. B. Jones says his life has been divided into three completely different worlds. The first was growing up as a product of Southern Appalachia; the second was his service in the military; the third was politics.

This third act began in 1972, when Jones decided to run for county commissioner. He was the last of seven men to qualify for the election. "On the way to qualifying," he says, "I asked the Lord not to let me get there in time if this was something I wasn't supposed to do." He got there in time. And he was elected. He now held the rank of top rooster, the decider of crucial decisions, the keeper of the-buck-stops-here sign.

George Thompson, retired manager of an insurance agency in Dahlonega, Georgia, and a native of the county, is sitting with Jones at the former commissioner's kitchen table in Frogtown, where the Joneses and their kin have bedded down for a couple hundred years. The two are reminiscing, telling stories, talking old politics.

"You've got to have political will and common sense" to get things done, Jones says, offering a little philosophy gained from experience. Political will often came into play when Jones was applying for government money. Common sense was needed the rest of the time, especially when applications for grants didn't cover all the money that was needed.

Jones is quick to say that his job wasn't to dictate. His job was to listen, to get people involved, to ask their opinions, to use common sense, and then act. He put a lot of issues on the ballot and let the people decide. "We put on it whether to have a dog catcher or not," he says. "And the voters can feel like they're a part of it," Thompson speaks up from across the kitchen table. "And you were a master at that."

In hindsight, though, Jones says he should have made at least one decision himself, without asking his constituents. That was when money was available to build a regional airport in Lumpkin County. "We could have got that airport built ninety percent federal, five percent state, and all we had to furnish was the land," he says. "And we already had the land." But he had promised the people he'd let them vote on the matter, and he kept his word. The issue failed.

"We could have passed it," he says, "but we didn't have enough time to massage it." The airport would have brought in more industry, "and if I had to do it over, I'd just do it."

His supporters, however, can point to a litany of projects that Jones helped bring to Lumpkin County. They include a hospital, and when the hospital, now Chestatee Regional, was sold, Jones set up a one-million-dollar indigent care trust fund so that the county's needy would have health care. They also include a senior center, a community center, a health department, a Head Start and preschool building (which bears his name), an agricultural service center, and several other centers. A highway bypass was built under his leadership, and he helped the city and county get a permit for a reservoir to ensure residents of enough drinking water. The intersection of Georgia 400 and Highway 60 is named in his honor.

"He was one of the best county commissioners we've ever had," says Charles F. Trammell, who worked for the county after retiring from the Georgia Department of Transportation. "He really got us started into a new era of being a more sophisticated county system. He was an excellent man to work for."

Jones, state and federal officials say, had a knack for getting government and corporate money for Lumpkin County projects. When he served on the board of the Tennessee Valley Authority, George Thompson says, Jones knew that the TVA gave money to counties that had streams flowing into TVA waterways. So he sent someone to walk the mountains in north Lumpkin County. Sure enough, one springhead was located near the Appalachian Trail in Lumpkin, but it flowed northward into a TVA stream. That made Lumpkin a TVA drainage county. The resulting TVA windfall was used to purchase computers for the high school and to help build a welcome center.

When Jones applied for a grant from Housing and Urban Development to build a senior center, he decided to videotape a hearing on the matter. The audience included several senior citizens who had been to Dockery Lake that day, and one woman rose from her seat and said: "I've got a problem.

We were up at Dockery Lake to trout fish—you know how I like to trout fish—and I went to the bathroom, and they ain't no paper in there."

Jones told the woman that the forest service was supposed to furnish toilet paper for Dockery Lake bathrooms. "But I'm going to call my road foreman, and I'm going to send a case of toilet paper right now." "Now, wadn't that sweet of him?" said the woman.

"We sent that video in [to HUD], and the application went through greased," Jones says. "There's nothing wrong with that. We might have gotten it anyway, but that hastened it."

All kinds of J. B. Jones tales were shared when the Dahlonega Sunshine Rotary Club and the Chamber of Commerce roasted the retired commissioner on May 17, 2008. State and national officials showed up to take their turns.

Former Georgia governor Roy Barnes said Jones had an uncanny ability to "pick the pocket of nearly every elected official in the state." Ross King, at that time deputy director of the Association County Commissioners of Georgia, which Jones once served as president, said the commissioner "has been known to take buckets of mud and throw them on the front, back, and sides of [his car] to drive to the Atlanta [state transportation] office and tell them how badly Lumpkin County needed some paving done, and drive home with a back seat full of money."

"I really didn't pour mud on it," Jones says now of his car, "but I never washed it."

Former governor and US senator Zell Miller also took a shot at Jones. "We all looked forward to the days J.B. came down to see us," he began. "We knew we'd hear the most convoluted, make-you-laugh, make-you-cry stories. It was easier just to give him what he wanted than to have him keep coming back over and over again."

The late congressman Ed Jenkins told about the time Jones and the county received $1.2 million to help build Porter Village, a housing development for members of the Fifth Ranger Training Battalion and their families. It was October, Jenkins recalled, when the congressional session was winding down. That's when Jones telephoned. Nothing can be done until next year, Jenkins told him, but the commissioner replied, "That's not good enough."

Jenkins told Jones he'd see what he could do. So he went before the

Armed Forces Committee and made his case. You'll need a survey, someone on the committee said. "I've already got one," Jenkins said. "Well, who did it?" he was asked. "J. B. Jones" was the reply.

You also need a cost estimate. "I've already got one," Jenkins replied. Again, the author was Jones. "Who is this J.B.?" asked a puzzled committee member. Before the end of the session, $1.2 million had been earmarked to build housing for the rangers and their families.

Jones remembers well the time state and federal officials showed up at the Frank D. Merrill Ranger Camp north of Dahlonega to hear complaints from the soldiers' wives about the need for housing. Ben Jones, a congressman at the time and a former actor who played "Cooter" on *Dukes of Hazzard*, was supposed to have been among the visiting officials. Ben Jones wasn't there, but J. B. Jones was present, all six feet, two inches of him, smiling his easy smile and greeting folks. "They thought I was Cooter," Jones says. "So I was signing autographs for those ladies. I guess I signed a dozen autographs. I just signed 'B. Jones.'"

Running a county alone has its advantages and disadvantages, Jones says. The advantages are better efficiency, saving money, and no fragmented decision making. Jones says three people—me, myself, and I—are always present for the commissioner's meetings. "Sometimes," he says, "me and myself will want to argue with each other."

The disadvantage is that there's only so much one person can do. And Jones understands why counties, including Lumpkin, have since gone to multimember bodies of government. Jones did his best, though, sometimes attending three or four meetings a week, checking roads in the early morning, taking phone calls all day long, working from before sunup to after sundown. And, his supporters say, he wasn't above using a shovel or motor grader himself if he needed to pitch in.

No doubt Jones enjoyed the work, and he laughs heartedly as he recalls humorous incidents from his years with the county. One of his favorite stories involves prison labor. A couple of judges in the court circuit were okay with Jones's using prisoners now and then to work on county property.

"One day," he begins, "L. J. Jarrard came in and said, 'Jones, it ain't none of my business, but you might ought to go up Highway 19. I met them two hands of yours mowing grass, and they were straddling the white line going toward Suches. With two mowers."

Jones went up Highway 19 to see for himself. Sure enough, two prisoners were driving down the middle of the road, attempting to cut grass. "What in the world is wrong with you guys?" he asked. "They were supposed to be mowing the shoulder of the road, but they'd got drunk and were going right down the middle." Turns out, the prisoners had found a case of beer alongside the road. Jones told them, "I want you to sit right here and take a break and get back to mowing the road when you get sober."

Jones retired from the county in 1996, leaving the job to two sole commissioners before the county went to a five-person commission. He may be retired, but he's still active on several boards, including the Georgia Mountains Regional Commission; the Lumpkin County Development Authority; and the Georgia Council on Native American Concerns (Jones is about one-sixteenth Cherokee). He's also a Rotarian.

He still gets up at five o'clock every morning, but now he goes to the chicken house, rather than out to the roads to make sure they're passable

PLATE 68   J.B. and Leslie Jones
at home in Frogtown Community

for school buses. He and his wife, Leslie, tend a garden every summer and harvest twenty-something varieties of muscadine grapes on the farm. They also raise beef cattle.

Jones's visitor asks to see his awards room at home, but Leslie says no, it's too messy. If you ask Jones about his greatest award or honor, he doesn't answer. But he does name one thing he's proud of. "Somewhere in that room," he says, "is a list of a ship's passengers, and the first Sitton, one of my relatives, came over in 1638. That wasn't the first one, but that's pretty early."

One wonders if Jones's ancestors were natural-born politicians like him. Surely there's something genetic about his charm and ability to be elected time after time. But, then again, the secret might just be as Jones says: be a good listener, be a hard worker, and be concerned about people.

Zell Miller, then governor of Georgia, discovered those virtues firsthand. On his way home to Young Harris one Friday, he dropped by the Lumpkin County Courthouse to visit with Jones. While the two were talking, one of Jones's constituents barged in and sat down right between the governor and the commissioner. He wanted to tell Jones about a tree across a road.

"He had a right to do that," Jones told Miller later. "I'm his commissioner." And Miller said, "No wonder you keep getting elected."

THE GREAT OUTDOORS

Catching Violators of Game and Fish Laws

Stories from Calvin Stewart

CALVIN STEWART remembers well the worst day of his life. It was the last day of November 2005. He turned in his equipment and his vehicle, and another officer with the Georgia Department of Natural Resources drove him home to wait for midnight. Technically, he was still a wildlife ranger, or a game warden, to use the vernacular.

"My wife was at work," he said, "and I stayed up, as so often I do, way too late. It got closer to midnight, and I remember that at one minute after midnight, I was no longer a DNR ranger. It just sucked something out of me."

You might think that a fiftysomething-year-old game warden would be a tad tired after thirty-one years of chasing down lawbreakers in the woods, lakes, and streams of Georgia. But Stewart was no ordinary game warden. In fact, you could say he was cowboy Roy Rogers and Superman all rolled into one imposing figure wearing a badge and a pistol, a man who did whatever it took to accomplish his mission.

These days, Stewart patrols northern Hall County, Georgia, as a part-time deputy sheriff. He practices a lot of Andy Griffith law, taking cues from the mild-mannered sheriff that Griffith played on television in the 1960s. He doesn't write a lot of tickets. If he can fix something by talking about it, then that's good. People go out of town, and he checks on their homes. He checks on the elderly when he can. If there's an emergency, he'll spring into action. But mostly he's out there to assist other deputies.

PLATE 69   Calvin isn't chasing game and fish violators now;
instead, he patrols for the sheriff's department.

It's a different life, this deputy sheriff business. As a game warden, Stewart was expected to be away from the radio, usually one ranger to a county, all alone with nothing but his pistol and his wits. He was the sole negotiator for the law when bad things happened. As a deputy, however, he's married to the radio. "They call you once an hour to make sure you're still breathing," he said.

While he was being interviewed for this story, Stewart was the one to call in to the sheriff's department. "I'll be away from the radio for a while," he said. And then, a minute later, he added, "Thank you, sweetie."

Stewart is the epitome of a Southern gentleman, and the women love him for that, one of his former colleagues said. He speaks Southern charm fluently. But don't try to convince the rogue hunters and fishers he's arrested that he's a man of charm. They would laugh. Assuming Stewart is not listening, of course.

Calvin Edward Stewart, Jr., grew up in a rural town called Mountain View, near Atlanta. It was a place with hogs, chickens, cows, and, unfortunately for the residents, later on, airplanes. The Atlanta airport, now called the

Hartsfield-Jackson Atlanta International Airport, with its airplanes flying low and loud twenty-four hours a day, killed off the little town.

Stewart flew the coop as an adult and went to Baldwin County. He had graduated from high school, where he majored in study hall, married his high school sweetheart, Linda Keeble, and was ready for a career. He landed a job with the line department of Georgia Power Company. One day, he was on his way to work when a wildlife ranger driving a pickup pulled up beside his car. "I saw that logo on the door—that deer, turkey, bass, and quail—and I said, 'Boy, that's what I want to do.'" He applied with the Department of Natural Resources and was hired on March 1, 1974. He was a wildlife ranger at twenty-one years old, and later, thanks to night school, a graduate of Georgia Military College with an associate's degree.

Stewart always wanted to live in the mountains of Northeast Georgia, preferably up around Union, Towns, or Rabun County, but first he had to do his time in the middle of the state. He ended up in Jones County, where he was responsible for 402 square miles of land. And that's where he got his reputation as a game warden's game warden, someone with stories to tell.

His best story is one he doesn't need to embellish. The facts themselves are dramatic enough. In November 1982, Stewart was an innocent-looking thirty-year-old sergeant who had been with the enforcement section, then called the Game and Fish Division, for nine years.

Stewart received a phone call about a hunting club operating on the western side of Jones County. The caller said, "I'm a member of this hunting club, and I just don't like what goes on. You've got a lot of them scared because you're working over there, but they're still doing wrong stuff." The rogue hunters had developed a technique to avoid capture, or so they thought.

They would hunt on non-doe days, which is illegal, but they believed the saying "If it's brown, it's down. If it's moving and it's a deer, it gets shot." The men would kill does during cool days, gut and field-dress them, and leave them in the woods, then go back at night and retrieve them. Late the following Saturday night after the phone call, Stewart drove to an area near the hunting club's property and hid his car. He tells the story from here:

"I hadn't been there long when I heard a vehicle coming down through the woods. It was an old logging road. I stepped off in the bushes, and this pickup truck comes riding by. It was a big, jacked-up pickup with big tires and wheels. It passed me. The road went on down another quarter of a mile and dead-ended.

"I waited. Four or five minutes go by, the noise dissipates, and it was real quiet. Then I heard what sounded like a tailgate slamming down. *BAM!* Another minute or two later, the truck was coming back toward me. If I jump out in the road and throw my hand up, *Stop!*, I know what's going to happen. The guy driving will stomp the gas, and I'm going to have to jump out of the way or get mowed down.

"I wait and it comes by me. I ran down the road, it wasn't going that fast, and I caught up with the truck. I stepped up on the back bumper. I could see the silhouette of two people in the truck. The truck was high off the ground. Lo and behold, there lays a doe. So the information I was given was dead-on. So I'm thinking, well, what now? I'm just going to crawl over in the back of the truck, and wherever they go, I'm going to go. So I lay down beside the deer.

"They pull up to a cable across the road, and the passenger has to get out and let the cable down. Me and the driver and dead deer ride through past the cable, and the passenger locks the cable up again. He walked right by the truck bed, and I'm sort of looking up, had my head cocked up, and I could see the top of his head go by the bed. Of course, he don't look over in the truck.

"So here we go. We go on down the road, and I'm going wherever they go. I didn't have a walkie-talkie or anything. But I wasn't sweating it, because I had the element of surprise on my side. We get on down the road a mile or so, and the truck slows down. We're before you get to the turn to go to Macon. It's rural fields and woods. What are we slowing down for? The truck backs up and does a three- or four-point turn in the middle of the road and is going back the same way we just came from.

"Then I feel the truck slow down again; we hadn't gone but a few hundred yards, and the truck slowed again. I could feel the truck swerve at about a forty-five-degree angle and stop. And then it hit me: These guys have seen a deer in the woods or a field, and they're going to collect another one. I'm expecting one of them to get out and to hear *BOOM!* any second.

"Well, the passenger gets out. But instead of hearing *BOOM!*, the passenger reaches over in the back of the truck, unbeknownst to me, looking for a handheld, six-volt light. When he reached over looking for the light, I wished I could've handed it to him. But his hand touches the top of my head. I knew the jig was up then, because my head don't feel like that deer.

"We carried .357 Magnums at the time, and I wasn't taking any chances. There are times you're justified in keeping the gun in the holster, and there are times not to. This was one of the times not to.

"So, I jumped up, and I throwed that .357 on him and said, 'HOLD IT!' Well, that boy jumped backward. I mean if the devil had jumped out of hell, he wouldn't have been any scareder. I said, 'Don't make a move. Game warden.' The last thing they expected was a game warden in the back of their truck.

"The driver, he was sort of stunned. I said, 'Get out of the truck,' and he got out. And I said, 'Get around to the back.' I frisked them down. That's a hazardous situation: one man frisking two guys. 'You're under arrest.' I didn't want them to know where I had my car hid. So, I said, 'We're going to town and we're going in your truck to the sheriff's department.' We got in the truck and headed to the sheriff's office. And these guys were still in a state of disbelief."

But that wasn't the end of the night. On the way to jail, Stewart, who was riding shotgun, spotted another deer camp. He saw eight or ten guys down in the woods with several deer hanging up. After booking the first two violators, he got a deputy to take him to his car, still well hidden, and then went back and arrested three or four men who had shot deer but had no tags to legalize their kills. "That," Stewart said with a smile, "was a good night's work."

Stewart, his former colleagues say, knows how to handle himself when he's making an arrest. "If you walk into camp and you appear to be wobbly-kneed," Stewart said, "they're going to sense it." So, a ranger must set the tone, not belligerent, not haughty, not in an I'm-the-law way. But violators need to understand who's in charge.

Another one of his more memorable escapades occurred one night in 1978. Stewart and his wife, Linda, were returning home from nearby Forsyth, Georgia, where they had enjoyed the first *Superman* movie. They were driving down four miles of desolate dirt road leading to their home when eagle-eyed Stewart spied a spotlight down in the woods beside the road. A game warden is always a game warden, even if he's in civilian clothes, dressed for a night at the movie theater. Stewart got out of his car, told his wife to go home and to call a deputy and tell him what was going on. In the meantime, Stewart would do what he could.

Before too long, a car came out of the woods, nearing the dirt road. As it got closer, Stewart could see that it was a convertible. He also could see four men, two in the front and two in the back. "So, I could either jump out in front or get in amongst them," he said. He chose to get in amongst them, because if you get in amongst them, they can't get away. Wherever they go, he goes.

Stewart didn't say, but one must wonder if the heroics of *Superman* were still flying around in his subconscious. Whatever the case, with his .38 Smith & Wesson drawn, Stewart took a flying leap into the back seat of the convertible, full body, landing in the laps of two occupants. "Halt, game warden," he bellowed. Stewart has a loud voice.

He was sort of lying down across them at first, so he maneuvered himself to be kneeling instead.

"Calvin," the driver yelled. "You scared the —— out of me." People knew each other in Jones County, and the driver knew Stewart.

Turned out, the men didn't have guns, and they were apparently out looking for places to hunt. Technically, it's a violation to harass or blind wildlife at night, but Stewart didn't pursue charges. "It was just some good ol' boys looking for deer," he said. So four men in a convertible, no doubt still shaking, went on their way. "They had something to talk about," Stewart said, "and I did, too."

But some cases required desperate action. Stewart shot a man in the knee one time after the violator raised a deer rifle in his direction. The man later sued, but the jury found in favor of Stewart. After the trial ended, one of the women on the jury came up to Stewart and said, "Next time, Mr. Game Warden, aim a little higher." The violator, incidentally, is serving a twenty-five-year sentence for child molestation, Stewart said. "Bad people hunt and fish, too."

Calvin Stewart is sort of a walking paradox. He is friendly, always a gentleman, always willing to help if he can. He believes law officers should spend more time being friendly to the people they serve. But as a young, gung-ho game warden, Stewart could scare the dickens out of a violator.

"If you look at Hollywood movies and you hear how they portray Southern gentlemen with the big, booming accent. That's how Calvin communicates. He has that typical Hollywood Southern drawl. . . . And Calvin was a

PLATE 70   David Cochran

great officer," said David "Foots" Cochran of Forsyth County, Georgia, who was Stewart's supervisor for about five years.

Actually, Stewart wrote more warning tickets than citations, but he also arrested many lawbreakers, especially people boating under the influence.

"No one ever complained of rough handling, but they felt intimidated." One complaint, Cochran said, came from a man Stewart sent to jail. "Did you see his hands?" the man asked. "His fists are so big." "Did he make a fist at you?" Cochran asked. "No, but he has these clubs sitting on the end of those arms. His arms are huge." Stewart lifted weights back then, building muscles to match his booming voice, which was enough to intimidate most violators when things got tough.

Marion Nelson of Milledgeville, Georgia, worked side by side with Stewart for several years. "Calvin was an unusual sort," he said. "He was not one of these eight-to-fivers who work for a paycheck. He was all-in."

One time, down in the bowels of the Oconee River swamp, Stewart and Nelson were determined to arrest a group of notorious game violators. They couldn't reach the hunters' camp by vehicle, so they walked several miles to reach the darkest part of the swamp. "When we encountered some folks down there," Nelson said, "their immediate response was, 'How did you get here?' 'Where did you come from?' As was quite typical with Calvin, he responded, 'I'll do whatever it takes.'"

In another case, Stewart was desperate to gather information on some illegal hunting taking place in a deer camp. "The story goes that Calvin had eased into this deer camp earlier in the day when no one was around," Nelson said, "and had secreted himself below the floorboards of a cabin. He was alleged to have stayed there all day and part of the evening, gathering intelligence on illegal hunting activity, just taking in conversation inside the cabin." Game violators, Stewart said, "love to brag about their exploits."

Stewart has also been known to spread a sheet inside the dirty trunk of a suspected violator's car, close the trunk, and take a ride, hoping to catch him in the act.

"I should have kept a diary, because I could have sold these stories," Nelson said. "He was legendary for these off-the-wall methods of interdiction back in the day. He was about as dedicated a soul as I ever worked with in my life. If Calvin Stewart made it a priority to go after somebody violating game and fish laws, their number was up."

But too much dedication at work, Stewart said, can cause problems at home. His wife, Linda, a registered nurse, has followed him wherever his career took him. Sometimes, though, a ranger becomes obsessed with his work. "I would go home to eat something and hit the road again," he said. One night, he and a deputy sheriff were working together on a case. The deputy was there to catch cattle rustlers, Stewart was there to catch game law

PLATE 71 Calvin Stewart receives the Medal of Valor at his retirement party. Presenter is Richard Wiley, who was president of Lodge 41.

violators. They were working from the deputy's car when a call came in over the radio. "The game warden's wife called," the caller said. "He needs to get home." The two rushed back to the sheriff's office; Stewart got in his truck and headed home. His wife was in labor with their first child.

"And that was stupid," Stewart said. "Here she was, due to have a young'un any minute, and there I was, out in the woods trying to catch somebody trying to kill a deer." He rushed her to the hospital, and everything went well. But he knows of several rangers who either got divorced or almost divorced "because they didn't have enough sense to go home."

You can't catch them all, Stewart said. Old rangers told him that when he first joined the DNR, but he didn't believe them. He would come home and lie in bed worrying about what was going on down the road. "I got over that," he said. "It took eight or ten years, but I got over it."

When he was transferred to Hall County in December 1986, Stewart told his superiors he needed to live in the northern end of the county. "I wanted to get as far away from Atlanta as possible," he said. "I've got too much Daniel Boone in me to go back living close to Atlanta."

So the Stewarts—Calvin, Linda, and their son and daughter—settled on a mini-farm at the foot of Wauka Mountain, near Clermont, Georgia. They own eleven acres, where they do a little gardening and keep eight acres in hay.

After years of service, Stewart realizes that the chronic offenders, the violent, break-a-law-if-you-can violators, are very rare. "I remember looking upon the average hunter as being probably a violator," he said, "but then it hit me that nobody walks on water. And if these people I'm dealing with only occasionally fudge a little bit, that don't mean they're bad people. I've preached it over the years. I've said we law officers are our own worst enemy, and we need to lighten up a little bit and be friendly with folks."

Stewart is a more relaxed, mellowed officer these days. But he misses fellowship around a campfire, and he misses sitting out in nature and listening to the woods wake up or go to sleep. "I'm going to have to partake of some of that," he said. If he follows through, hunters and fishers might see Calvin Stewart, the retired game warden of fearsome reputation, out in the woods again, just enjoying nature. But this time, they won't have anything to be afraid of.

Turkey Hunting

The turkey-hunting tales of three Georgians

HERB MCCLURE is a student of wild turkeys. Says so on his calling card. Even when he was a student of math, English, and geography, he preferred to take classes on a remote mountain ridge in Northeast Georgia, up where the turkeys gather to talk to one another and, occasionally, to answer an impersonator in the distance.

One March day in 1958, McClure skipped his regular, indoor classes, taking zeroes in each one, to venture into the wilds for outdoor instruction. That was the year he got his diploma from high school, and that year—in fact, the very day he played hooky—he killed his first wild gobbler. But not before he learned an important lesson: Never lie down under a holly tree, with its prickly leaves digging into your skin, thinking a turkey will answer your call, walk up in front of you and stand there politely while you shoot him. No, this turkey circled behind the holly tree, spooked the hunter, and then flew off, leaving McClure with nothing but a few scratches. Later that day, he called up another gobbler during a steady rain and bagged him as he took flight. "That was a lesson," he said. "I never laid on the ground to call a turkey anymore, and I certainly didn't under a holly tree."

Today, about sixty turkey seasons later, Herbert Leon McClure of White County, Georgia, knows enough about turkeys to be a professor on the subject, but he still calls himself a student. Even when he led a wild-turkey seminar at Georgia's Unicoi Park in early 2016, McClure said he wasn't there to tell anyone how to hunt. He was there to talk about his experiences, about how he studied and documented wild turkeys wherever he found them. His stories are worth the telling.

"Herb and I have exchanged stories," said Doug L. Grindle of Dahlonega, Georgia, who has hunted with McClure several times and wrote the foreword to a book McClure authored in 2012 titled *Native Turkeys and a Georgia Mountain Turkey Hunter*.

"You don't turkey-hunt with Herb. You have an adventure. It would be mischaracterizing it if you called it a hunt, because in a traditional sense of the word, it's a ritual. He's the most prepared person I've ever hunted with. Also, he's the stealthiest. He is quiet."

What McClure is trying to do, Grindle said, is to become one with nature. He's trying to make himself part of his surroundings. "If you hunt that way, you'll be more successful. It's just that most of us don't have the discipline to do that."

McClure doesn't talk much about his hunting success, or anything else, for that matter. He enjoys being quiet. You learn, Grindle said, by watching him and asking questions, assuming you know what questions to ask.

Herb McClure grew up in Forsyth County, Georgia, wanting to be outdoors, wanting to learn how to hunt. But, at seven or eight years old, he was too young to carry a rifle or shotgun. So, he just went along with a beagle and his daddy. His daddy made him stay home when he hunted squirrels, because squirrel hunting required stillness and quiet, so young McClure became mainly a carrier of dead rabbits. One day, his daddy killed a couple of cane cutters, rabbits bigger than cottontails, and then told his son to take them home while he continued to hunt.

"I didn't want to go," Herb said, "but he scolded me a little bit and I went on. That was about as big a load as I ever want to take. I took two big old buck rabbits a mile to the house. I was loaded down with rabbit feet." A year or so later, McClure was still too young to hunt, but he wasn't too young to trap.

He set out traps for muskrats, mink, and raccoons, and every so often a man called Trapper would come by and purchase the boy's furs. He also caught his own rabbits, gutted them, and hauled them in a tow sack to the Jot 'Em Down Store on his way to Chestatee School.

"I'd get off at the store—the bus driver knew what I was doing—and

Mark Porter, the store owner, gave me a quarter for every rabbit I brought. Then I'd walk to school about a quarter mile away."

Back in those days, he said, people from Atlanta and elsewhere who wanted a fresh-killed rabbit to eat could buy one at the Jot 'Em Down Store. But the state, no doubt concerned about health and sanitation, put a stop to McClure's fresh-rabbit business.

When he reached the age of thirteen, McClure's parents, Leon and Arrie McClure, finally trusted him to take a gun out into the woods. There was no place he'd rather be.

But he had a lot to learn, he'll tell you. So, he listened. Good turkey hunters always listen to those who know. He listened to the old gentleman walking with a cane on the day of McClure's first turkey kill. "You got to hide your back from them turkeys," the old man from Ellijay, Georgia, told him. But not under a holly tree. Hide your back against a tree that's wider than you are.

McClure listened to Arthur "Fat" Truelove after he and his family had to relocate from the Chestatee River in Forsyth County because the impoundment of Lake Lanier took their land. They moved to Hall County, within a mile of Truelove's home.

McClure went through his new community, called Tadmore, asking

PLATE 72   Herb McClure (*left*) with Fat Truelove

about hunters. "Who hunts around here?" he would say. "Do y'all hunt?" The answer was always the same. Talk to Fat Truelove. He hunts. His daddy, too. Fat Truelove, not really fat, just big and strong, was a block mason part of the year. But along about September, he would stop working. It was time to hunt. "I learned everything from Fat, just about it," McClure said reverently. "There was no better hunter in this area." Truelove died on September 9, 2012, at age eighty-nine. He is memorialized in Herb McClure's book, *Native Turkeys*.

"Arthur lived his life hunting like no other hunter I ever knew," McClure wrote. "He led me into the high mountains as a young lad, and he set the standards very high. Arthur was my mentor, and I idolized his hunting skills."

Every turkey hunter, it seems, has a mentor, sometimes several. Randolph Jones of Union County, Georgia, said he would listen to anybody who knew anything worthwhile about hunting.

"I been hunting turkeys for forty-something years," Jones said, sitting at a picnic table outside the Citgo convenience store, sometimes called the Mulkey Gap Store, just outside of Blairsville. Leonard Frank "Buck" Dills was sitting with him. Both are natives of Blairsville. Dills has bought, sold, and swapped land, and most anything else, in the county for many years. Jones builds houses and preaches every Sunday at the Jones Creek Church of God. He lives on Jones Creek. Buck Dills agrees with the saying that heaven has to be on Jones Creek, because the people there are happier than anybody else. "If they don't want to work, they don't work. If they want to work, they do. If they want to go hunting or fishing, they go."

Jones hunts regularly and has been known to walk ten to twenty miles a day during turkey season. "He is a great hunter and outdoorsman," said Dr. James Jackson of Gainesville, Georgia, who turkey hunts with Jones every year. "I have hunted for fifty years and have seen a lot of great hunters. I have never seen anyone who moves through the woods so quietly and quickly. You cannot hear him. I don't know how he does it. The last time I went hunting with him, we were walking three to four miles per hour in mountain terrain."

Like Herb McClure, Jones knows a lot about how to hunt turkeys, but he's not bragging. He holds back, lest his listener thinks he's full of himself.

So Jackson says it for him: "He is a good teacher and has a wealth of information, not only about the game, but also about the flora. He has always been good about explaining things to us and has insights that I think are unique and I seriously doubt others have thought of."

Jones will share some of his knowledge, but he often credits others. The late Hub McClure of Hayesville, North Carolina, for example, taught him that just lightly scratching dry leaves, not too much, can attract a gobbler. The late Ralph Tritt told him to make sure he's well hidden in the woods, and if a gobbler answers your call, just wait.

"I believe if you were a hundred yards away," Jones said, quoting Tritt, "and you were down in a hole, that turkey can walk up and look in that hole and see you. That's how good they are. It's just like radar. They can pinpoint you. The first turkey I ever killed, Ralph Tritt told me how."

Gobblers have tremendous hearing and vision, and "if they could smell as good as a deer can," Jones said, "they'd be virtually impossible to kill." Which explains why a hunter always celebrates when he kills a native turkey in the mountains. It's not that easy.

Nowadays, most folks hunt for sport and to enhance their store-bought food with wild game. But back during the Great Depression, Buck Dills said, they hunted to eat. "You go to one of the stores and there'd be ten or fifteen men sitting around," he said. "There was no work to do. But if they had a muzzle loader and they heard a turkey gobble, that was going to go on their table."

Wild hogs roamed the mountains back then, before blight killed the great American chestnut trees that provided tons of grain for them to eat. People hunted them. Even groundhogs were not safe. "My grandpa and his brothers—he had seven brothers—they would dig that groundhog out," Dills said. "They'd dig all day to get that groundhog. That was meat on the table."

Raccoons were good to eat if they were cooked right, but they were scarce because they'd been hunted out during hard times. When Dills was a child, his mentor, Kenneth Wright, would take his coonhound into the mountains every Friday night during coon season.

They would kill a raccoon and bring it home. Wright would skin it and save the fur to sell to the fur buyer in town. The next day, Pearl, Wright's wife, would walk into the woods and bring back a bunch of "spice wood." Spice wood made good tea, but it also enhanced the flavor of wild game.

"She would boil that raccoon all day with spice wood sticks," Dills said, "take it out, salt and pepper it, and bake it in her oven, an old wood cookstove oven. She would invite me up for supper. She'd have fried potatoes, cornbread, and raccoon. It was the best darn supper I ever had in my life."

Things have changed considerably since the Depression. Now the state enforces game and fish regulations designed to control the population.

Regulated turkey seasons started in Georgia in 1955. Herb McClure said his mentor, Fat Truelove, shot the first legal turkey that year. But the season was short, one week, and the limit was one gobbler. Then the season was expanded to two weeks and the limit to two gobblers, never a hen. Today, the season is about two months long, and the limit is three gobblers. In 2013, McClure accomplished a rare feat. He got his limit of three gobblers, all taken on the Blue Ridge Wildlife Management Area near the Appalachian Trail. In an article he wrote for *Georgia Outdoor News* magazine, he called that year "a season for the book."

Both Jones and McClure hunt other game. And they fish the streams. Jones hunts deer, bear, squirrels, rabbits, and he's been going to Colorado for twenty years to hunt elk. He eats what he kills or gives it away.

McClure's second-favorite sport is hunting deer. And it was turkey hunting, in fact, that helped make him an avid deer hunter. He couldn't help but notice all the buck sign such as droppings, antler rubs on small trees, or hoof scraping at the base of trees in the winter and spring, while he was scouting for turkey sign or turkey hunting. His prowess as a deer hunter was legendary in Northeast Georgia. For many years, a collection of his best deer trophies hung in the sporting goods section of Big G, one of two large Gainesville stores where he worked for twenty-one years.

But while hunting other game has always excited these two men, nothing compares to hunting gobblers, which inhabit the highest and most remote areas of the Northeast Georgia Mountains. McClure said he was shaking with excitement so much one time, knowing a gobbler was coming toward him, he couldn't even move his shotgun from his lap. Said Jones, "I was shaking so bad one morning, I said, 'I've scared that turkey.' I thought he'd seen me shaking." But he hadn't, and Jones made the kill.

The native turkey is the hardest game to kill, McClure and Jones agree. A deer has good eyesight, hearing, and sense of smell, but hunters can bring him down with a rifle, instead of a shotgun, and at a longer shooting range. But with turkeys, you'd better be closer. These mountain gobblers are a pure strain of the eastern wild turkey, and they have the keenest eyesight and the best hearing of any breed.

McClure and Jones are obviously both successful turkey hunters, but the ways they hunt are completely different. Jones calls and listens for the gobble. Some mornings, he might hear four or five turkeys. Next morning, it'll be quiet as a Monday-morning church. "When they don't gobble, you can't make them gobble," he said. But, eventually, he gets his gobbler, sometimes by moving in closer, if the turkey is far-off, sometimes staying where he is if it is moving toward him.

McClure, however, usually can't hear a gobble. If he takes out his two hearing aids, he can't hear himself talk. Doctors believe a high fever from measles took much of his hearing when he was fourteen. So, like the gobbler himself, McClure is patient. He goes to a preselected "calling place,"

PLATE 73   Herb McClure waits for a turkey to come near.

and, using an old caller invented by Leon Johenning of Lexington, Virginia, he calls and waits. And waits. And waits. He waits until the gobbler comes to him, expecting to find a hen.

"Over the years," McClure told the seminar at Unicoi State Park, "turkey hunters have been a lot like automobile drivers. That is, when a vehicle comes to a traffic light and the light turns green, or when a hunter hears a gobble, they both take off as fast as they can. Whatever happened to having patience and taking your time?" His hearing problem, he said, taught him patience.

Speaking to a group of turkey hunters, or to anybody else, for that matter, is not Herb McClure's favorite activity. He is a private

PLATE 74   Buck Dills (*left*) and Randolph Jones
talk turkey outside a Citgo station in Union County, Georgia.

person, a quiet, humble man who prefers the solitude of a high mountain ridge. And he was not comfortable about some of the things he wanted to say. Some people in the audience might be offended.

First, he wanted to say in as nice a way as possible that he wasn't excited when the government brought in pen-raised turkeys to stock certain areas. Many of those birds couldn't even fly. They roosted on the ground in holding pens. If you want to be a true turkey hunter, you go for the native, the skittish, wary, blackish bird of yore that'll elude you like a moonshine tripper fleeing the law. Second—and he sounded almost apologetic here—he does not kill turkeys anymore.

In 1980, McClure and his wife, Mary, started building a log house next to Horse Range Mountain in White County. It took them about ten years to complete it. They cut trees and hewed them into logs; they did everything themselves. McClure virtually stopped hunting deer in 1980 because he had work to do at his future home. He killed his last deer near Horse Range in 1995. Shot him with a bow, as he did his first. He continued to hunt turkeys. He continued to learn from them. But he killed his last one in 2013, the year he got his limit of three on the Blue Ridge WMA.

"The turkeys off of the Horse Range Mountain and their young," he said in his prepared Unicoi talk, "became like a brotherhood society, with me having strong feelings of goodwill towards helping all of them. When one has lived for over twenty years in a brotherhood's society, with friendship feelings of goodwill for those homeplace gobblers, and now I consider all other gobblers, everywhere else, my friends. How can I keep on killing these other friends just to prove I can kill them?"

He ended his confession this way: "Hopefully some of you will remember an old turkey man as becoming a friend of the mountain gobblers, and not having just been a killer of them."

Come next March, turkey hunters from all over will slip into the mountains of Northeast Georgia to try their luck once again. Many of them will crawl out of bed four or five hours before first light, as McClure did in 1958, and make their way to a high mountain ridge. Few of them will know more about these natives than Randolph Jones, Buck Dills, and Herbert McClure. These three men know when a gobbler has been in an area just by looking at fresh scratching in the leaves. They can tell the difference between droppings from a gobbler and droppings from a hen. They are more than hunters. They are woodsmen.

Lord willing, Jones will be there when the season starts, armed with a Stoeger three-inch magnum camouflage shotgun. Dills will be there with his Mossberg pump-action 12-gauge, and McClure will be there, too. He'll be armed with a forty-year-old Panasonic camcorder with homemade camouflage. All of them will use their callers. They will wait and see—and hope to get their shot.

Legendary Bear Hunters from the Old School

Tales of bear hunting in Rabun County

by Jessica Phillips

TURNING ONTO CONNER LANE, my brother, Ethan, and I discussed how we thought the interview would go. As we drove up, we heard someone greeting us with a hello. As we got closer to the house, we realized it was Steve Conner. Martha, Steve's sister, and Bill Speed were on the porch to greet us, as well. We walked in, and made our way to the dinner table where we conducted the interview.

Steve Conner and Bill Speed have been hunting together for more than fifty years. Steve and Martha are two of the children of Minyard Conner, who was featured in many previous Foxfire books. During the interview, Steve and Bill recalled stories from hunting together, as well as how hunting has changed throughout the years. Bill, along with Ray Conner, Steve and Martha's brother, was the first person to ever hunt bears in Coweeta, an experimental forest located in Otto, North Carolina.

As the stories began to unfold, my brother and I could not stop laughing. We could tell through the looks on their faces and the tone of their voices that Steve and Bill really enjoyed their hunts. They even had special nicknames: While hunting, Steve was referred to as "Hog Jaw" and Bill was "Gray Fox." Bill had a scrapbook with tons of pictures of bear hunting dating back to his first hunt in 1966.

When asked what this article should be called, he grinned with excitement and said, "Legendary Bear Hunters from the Old School." We all laughed, and from that point on, this article had a name.

On their early days as bear hunters:

Steve: Me and Bill have hunted together about all our lives.

Bill: We've got about a hundred years of huntin' between us both. We've both been huntin' about fifty years apiece.

Steve: I guess the reason we always bear hunted was because it ran in our family. My twin brothers, Ray and Roy, always hunted, until they went to preaching. Ray's in one of the Foxfire books. They put Roy's name on [the picture in the book], but it was Ray. He was standin' up there at that barn with a bear hide on it; but, they both quit bear huntin', so me and Bill had to carry it on.

Bill: Steve uses a thirty-five when he hunts. I always liked to use my thirty aught six; but, back yonder when we first started, we just got whatever we could to hunt with. We mostly hunted with buckshot, and that was legal.

Steve: See, the season didn't start in North Carolina until 1966. That's when Bill and [his friend] Ray went to bear huntin'.

Bill: That's when me and Ray Conner got dogs. We started getting us a pack of dogs to bear hunt with. We were the first bear hunters that ever hunted Coweeta the first year bear season opened.

Steve: Coweeta is in Otto, North Carolina. It is all that country around Pickens Nose.

And later:

Bill: I am a year older [than Steve]. I am seventy-two. In 1966, me and Ray Conner were the first two bear hunters that ever hunted Coweeta. Period.

PLATE 75   Bill Speed and Steve Conner

One day, we went after a bear. The dogs treed it. Well, we got to the tree. Ray looked at me and said, "You shoot that thing out of there." I said, "That thing is far up in that tree. All I will do is burn him out." But I said, "I'll burn him out of there." I had a double-barrel shotgun then. So, I pulled up, and I fired both barrels at that rascal. He was in the tip-top of that tree. I call these trees a lynn tree. I don't know what kind they really are. They are a big ol' tree and have big ol' leaves on 'em. They are kind of like a poplar. That was the tallest tree I had ever seen. To make a long story short, I shot that bear with both barrels. He went right up in the air just like that [raising his finger in the air].

Instead of comin' back down the tree, he fell just plumb out of it. I thought that I had killed him. Well, when he hit the ground—kids, this is no lie—he bounced twenty feet up in the air. I had never seen a bear bounce that high in my life. He bounced up about twenty feet. Well, when he came back down to the ground, the dogs covered him up. The dogs thought the bear was dead. Well, that thing came up from there. He whooped every dog we had. He ran about twenty yards down the hill, and every one of our dogs was right behind him. Boy, they was biting him. Well, he started up another tree. My gun was empty now, because I had just unloaded it on him. Ray's gun was loaded. So, he just pulled up and *pow!* The dust just boiled out of that bear. I said, "Well, you got him." I was gettin' two more shells to go in my gun. I was puttin' 'em in, and it didn't faze that bear when we had shot him. That bear turned around, and he whopped every dog again. He saw me, and his eyes were just as focused on me as me and you lookin' at each other. I said, "Oh no." About that time, he laid his ear back like a mule. Ray said, "Bill, he's gonna charge you!" I was just puttin' the last shell in, and I was watchin' him, too. He came wide open towards me. I said, "Oh no." Boys, I reached for my shotgun, pushed the safety off, and he was then about five feet from me. I shot him from the hip right in the face. I pulled both barrels just like that. That tests your grit as bear hunter!

Steve: One day, I was up yonder, and we had one bayed in a rock cliff. There wasn't but one way around there, and it was kind of an old trail that went through there. I was crawling around through there on my hands and knees. You could hear the dogs over there. Son, about that time, I heard a racket comin'. I looked up, and there came that bear right towards me. There was nowhere for me to go. I just dove to the left, and that thing ran right up to me and threw his brakes on just like that [pushing his hands on the table]. He looked at me and blew real big. He blew snot all over me. I came down as soon as he left, and I got out of there. That bear had just ran right up to me, threw his brakes on, and blew just like that. They'll blow at cha', you know. He blew snot all over me, turned around, and went right back in the rock cliff. I didn't go that way anymore. The dogs went after that bear.

On their dogs:

Steve: The best thing you can do is take one dog at a time up a little ways and tie him up. Then, go back and get you another one. By the time you get the last dog up, the bear will hit the ground runnin'. He knows when you get that last dog, because he is watchin' the dogs. I was gettin' [my dogs] back away from a bear one day. I told Marshall that I got my last dog. I told him, "Get your dog out of there." As soon as he got to the tree to get it, that bear started down. You 'ort of seen him, boy. He didn't want to go get that dog! He was afraid that bear was gonna come down. They'll hit the ground. Buddy, as quick as you get those dogs back, they're gone. Sometimes, the bear will not come down.

My favorite part about bear huntin' would be listening to the race, the sound of the dogs. You can tell when they are runnin' by the sound. Then, when they all lock down on the tree, oh boy! That is beautiful! You can hear that from a long way.

Bill: That's the best part about it.

Steve: Bear hunting has changed a lot. When we first started, you didn't have any of this tracking stuff. My brother Ray Conner would take off behind the dogs when I turned them loose.

Roy was a lot like me. He would kind of hang behind. See, Bill and Ray would take after the dogs. You would pull over one top, hear 'em, and you'd go again. If you couldn't hear 'em, you couldn't find 'em. It could be three or four days before you would find your dogs. But now, we've got a tracking system. It used to be just trackin' devices that went around their neck. You would hold it and follow it. It would beep, and you would know where the dogs were at. Now, everything is GPS. Oh, son! You can just watch 'em on TV! I love it!

Bill: That's not bear huntin' the old way. They like the GPS, though. It will tell you right where the bear is, and how to get there. It tells you how far away it is and everything. It saves you a lot of extra steps and lost dogs.

Steve: You know how a mountain is marked at the top, like Jones Mountain? There will be a big survey thing there that says Jones Mountain when you put your arrow from the GPS on it. It will tell you the name and everything about that mountain. You can see right where your dogs are. Then, you can go right straight to 'em. It ain't nothin' to keep up with your dogs now. But, back there years ago, we've had dogs stay gone for a while. There was one who stayed gone for over a week.

Bill: Ole Bullet stayed gone for about a month.

Steve: Nobody could catch Bullet. Bill was the only one who could catch him. Somebody finally told him that they seen him up there in the Flats sitting under a tree. There is a big white fence up there above the Flats on the right. They said they seen him, and Bill went up there.

Bill: I talked to him, and here he came just like that.

Steve: But, son, he was a bear and hog dog. The little ol' dog was a real dog. He'd catch a bear or hog.

Martha: That dog wasn't registered either.

Steve: The last time we'd seen him was when he left here on a bear. We haven't seen him since. That was back before we had all of that trackin' stuff.

Bill: I believe the bear got him. We couldn't find him. I bet I burnt ten tanks of gas huntin' for him.

Martha: Bill generally kept three dogs. Ray would keep two or three. They'd all keep about three. So, that was about nine altogether. Then, when Steve came home, he added some more to the pack.

On controlling the bear population:

Steve: I do think huntin' is valuable to our culture here in Rabun County. You need to keep it a-goin'. There ain't nobody else goin' to keep it a-goin'. We used to have to look for a week to find a bear track. Sometimes we would even go a week without finding one. But now, you don't have to. Son, they are comin' to your house!

Bill: I was sitting out there on the porch last spring, and I look down the road, and there went one across the road just walkin'. We came in from a ball game, and one was walkin' right by the smokehouse out there.

Martha: If you live out like this, they'll get in your garden and eat up all your corn, tear up bee gums and bird feeders, and make a mess out of trash.

On other bear hunters:

Bill: Taylor lived out on Highway 64 out of Franklin. I'd say he was one of the first bear hunters in Macon County. We've hunted with all the Legion bear hunters. We hunted with the old ones like Jess Mason. He lived over yonder on Tellico. We'd go over there and hunt.

Steve: Jerry Ayers come out of the Smokies like my mother. He was my uncle. He was my mother's brother. He hunted with us. He was an old man.

Bill: Jerry went with us huntin'. Me, him, and Ray was huntin' up on Coweeta. We was about the only four up there. We sat down to eat dinner one day, and we was just sittin' there. The dogs were off in there runnin'. We didn't know if they were on a bear or what. But, we would listen to the race and eat dinner, too. He was blind in one eye, and he wore a patch over it. A big, black butterfly came right at him, and went by him right there at his face. Jerry said, "That blame raven like to hit me right in the face!"

On things they've seen while hunting:

Bill: Dillard Green and Chris, his brother, lived up on Betty's Creek. We used to hunt with them a lot. They'd see a bear, and they'd call us until we went up there. They liked bear huntin'. Do you like snakes? Well, we went on a hog-huntin' trip. Me, Steve, Roy, Ray, and David went down on the river. Well, me and Ray went one way, and the other boys stayed there. They sat down on this old log. They was restin'. Well, one of them said, "I'd be dad-burn if I don't believe I seen a snake go up in that log." Steve said, "I know it was." The log was hollow and rotten. Roy said, "Well, we'll just get him out of there, and see what kind he was." Well, ri' here is what they got out of that log. There were rattlesnakes and copperheads. So, they killed 'em all and put 'em in a sack. They thought they had killed all of 'em. When they opened up the sack, they had a bunch of little'ns in the sack.

Steve: The big snakes would open their mouths, and the little ones would run in there.

Bill: The little snakes run down the big snakes' throats. See, we've done about everything there is to do out there. We've killed snakes, and just about every varmint there is. Steve and me are close, and we know each other. We know what each other will do and how we'll do it. We learned that from each other throughout the years.

PLATE 76   Bears that have been left in trees

Steve: I've been huntin' all of these years. The other day was the first time I have ever seen five bears together. There were two that was a little bigger. They had four cubs up there and one sow.

Two of the cubs were a little bigger than the other two. But, that tree was slap full of bears.

Bill: Like he was sayin' a minute ago, back then, bears were hard to come by. Tom finally got to kill one. Steve's and my dogs treed the bear. He didn't even have a dog that would tree, and he had about eight or ten plots. We let him shoot it. He'd been huntin' with us for twenty-five years every day the season was open. But, that's the way it goes.

Steve: Now, we won't hardly kill one unless we've got somebody young with us, or somebody that has never killed one before. If we are just by ourselves, we'll leave it up there.

On eating bear:

Martha: My daddy loved eating bear. He would even render the fat out of it just like the old people used to do. That is what they lived on.

Steve: Mom would make biscuits out of that fat. They would come out just as fluffy.

Martha: When he passed away, he had two big lard cans of fat for Mama to make biscuits out of. It was good.

Bill: You could taste the bear in it, though, but it was a biscuit! . . .

Martha: See, the Indians ate bear. Dad and Mom were raised in the Smoky Mountains. They ate anything Dad brought in. Mom was a good cook. We all ate what she cooked and liked it. We don't eat wild meat much anymore.

Steve: We just divide all the meat up when we kill a bear. We'll take it up there and skin it. We'll take all the good parts and cut 'em up. That way, you'll get some of all of it.

Martha: Steve can cook some good bear barbecue.

And later:

Steve: We skin the bear from the back feetfirst, just like you do a deer. You cut it just down the straddle and pull the skin on down. Then, you start cuttin' it up. If a big ol' bear ham is layin' here like this, we'll just cut it in about three or four different sections where everybody can get some. You'll get some of the good with the bad. You just take a sack with you. When you're cuttin' it up, you make different piles, and everybody gets 'em a pile to take with 'em. We have skinned a lot of bears ri' here on that old tree in Bill's backyard. We had a table to lay the meat down on to cut it up.

Martha: We like to cook bear in the Crock-Pot, the slow cooker, about ten to twelve hours.

Steve: I like bear in Dale's seasoning. Now, son, that's good!

Martha: My daddy, Minyard Conner, loved bear.

Steve: Daddy just liked his boiled. He didn't like anything on it except salt and pepper. That's how he ate it. My uncle Jerry, the man we was talkin' about, had a bad stomach. I mean, a real bad stomach. I've seen him take a biscuit, tear it open, and put plain bear fat in it and eat it. He said that that wouldn't hurt your stomach. I believe it because of the way he ate it.

We was bear huntin' one day, and we accidentally got up on a hog. We killed it, and he was a boar. He had teeth that long [holding his finger so far apart], and he stunk. Man, he was rotten!

We got out of there, and we skinned that hog. None of us wanted any of the meat, so we gave it all to Uncle Jerry. He'd eat anything. He took it home with him. The next mornin', Jerry came back with a sandwich made out of that hog. Shoo! I smelt that just as quick as he got it out.

When you make old boars mad, it makes the meat stink. You have to throw the pot and everything away when you cook that meat! But, he brought me a sandwich made out of that meat. He brought Mike, my brother-'n-law, one, too. Mike looked at me funny after he had taken a couple of bites and smelt that stuff. Boy, in just a minute, I caught his back turned, and I sailed mine down through the woods. Mike's seen me do that, and he threw his down there, too. Boy, we really bragged on that meat, but we didn't want any more.

On their best bear hunt:

Bill: I couldn't name a best time that we've had. I really don't know what the best time we've really ever had. I guess just sittin' down laughing about somethin' that happened on the hunt was pretty good.

Steve: We had to pull a bear through a yellow jackets' nest one time, and everybody got stung. That was pretty good.

Bill: Oh, I won't tell that now. That's bad! That was the most laughin' that has ever been done on a bear hunt. We were bear huntin' with Uncle Jerry, and we killed a bear. It took 'em to almost dark to bring the bear out. There was an old roadbed there, and I was holdin' two or three dogs. Ray and Roy was pullin' the bear, and Steve was leading the dogs. Their uncle Jerry sat down on the bank where the old roadbed was. He wore overalls. Back then, old men didn't wear no draw's. Well, we were sittin' there, and I was sittin' right beside him. All at once, he just jumped up from there. He had sat right in a yeller jackets' nest. He didn't know it was there. He shook them overalls down to his ankles and bowed over and said, "Roy! Get these things off of me! They're eatin' me up!"

Well, Ray and Roy are twins. Any little thing like that will tickle 'em to death. One will get tickled, and then, the other one will get tickled. They'll just get down and roll. They've always been that way. Well, Roy was laughin' so hard at Ray over there, and I just walked off to keep from gettin' stung. I was laughin', too, to tell you the truth. They ate him up. Roy was tryin' to get 'em off of him, and he finally got started.

Steve: Ray hollered at somebody, and they jumped in the truck. We wrapped a rope around the bumper, and we pulled the bear out of the way of the yellow jackets.

On hog hunting:

Martha: A couple of years ago, they killed a bear the first day the season opened in North Carolina. About four hundred yards away, the dogs struck a hog. They ended up killing a hog and a bear the same day. They ran the hog so long that he ran through the cold creek, and it killed him.

Steve: He got in the cold water, fell down, and died. All of his muscles locked down. He was as stiff as a board.

Bill: A bear got into Bruce Kenner and Pledger Thurmond's bee gums one time. They ended up wounding it, and they called me. I took my dogs up there. They bayed it. The bear was down. This picture is Pledger up on top of it. Now, that was a big bear, too.

Steve: Both of them fellers are dead now.

Bill: Mal James owned Osage Mountain up yonder on Hell Ridge. There had been a big hog comin' in and eatin' their corn. He had been rootin' up their fields. I seen Mal one day, and he looked at me and said, "Bill, do you have any hog dogs?" I said, "Well, I've got some hog dogs." He said, "Do you think you can catch a big boar?" I said, "Yeah." Well, he said, "I've had about fifteen different people up here, and it's whooped every dog they've got and ran 'em off." He said, "I want you to come and try your luck." I said, "Okay. I'll be up there in the mornin'." He said, "Well, I'll be waitin' on you." So Steve, Ray, Roy, and me went up there. We found some fresh sign. [One of our dogs] had that hog bayed within fifteen minutes. So, we turned our catch dogs loose.

They caught the Osage boar. Mal and 'em were comin' up from the other side. We could hear 'em talkin'. I told Ray, "I want Mal to see what kind of dogs I've got." They got to see the hog caught, and we brought him out of there.

Steve: Ray had several bulldogs get killed by hogs. Me and Bill have had several good bear dogs killed by bear. They bite them through the back, and they tear the skin open with their claws, knocking out their hip joints.

Bill: Those hogs would stab the dogs. They've got 'em big ol' knives for tusks that are as long as my finger. If they stab 'em in the chest, they'll go right into their hearts and kill 'em dead. We went huntin' up on Messer Creek one time with their uncle Jerry. There was a bunch of hogs up there. Well, we all went a different way. I was comin' in with my catch dog one way. Ray was goin' in another way with a catch dog, and Roy was comin' up with a bay and catch dog. If a dog bayed at the top, then somebody would be there to turn their catch dogs loose. If we could hear 'em, we were going to turn our catch dogs loose, too. They'd go straight to where they heard the racket comin' from. Well, I heard the little bay dog bay, and, boys, I took off a-runnin'. I was tryin' to get there just as hard as I could go, because I knew Jerry was right there where they were. Well, about that time, I heard the gunfire. I said, "Well, Jerry's already shot one of 'em hogs." Well, when I got there, he had shot one. He had a big ol' sow shot. She was as long and high as this table. Well, she had got up on her feet. Jerry had it by the tail, and it was tryin' to get away. He was in a laurel thicket with that big ol' hog holdin' it by the tail. He had it stretched as long as a cow's tail. Well, he'd seen me, and he hollered, "Shoot this thing!" He said, "It's gonna get away, and I'm give out!" I just got down and started rollin'. I was so tickled. That was the funniest sight I had ever seen. There is a man with a wild hog by the tail, and it's tryin' to get away.

Steve: The hog was pullin' him down the laurel thickets. Jerry was puttin' his feet against everything. We now called that place Cal Laurel.

Bill: I finally quit laughin' enough so I could get my gun out, and I was still tickled. I aimed at its head, and I shot and killed it. He said, "I couldn't've held it another second!" That was all he said. He was just plain give out.

Steve: He was mad because Bill didn't shoot it fast enough.

Bill: One time, we was up at Coyle Justice's house. Coyle had a garden up there on Betty's Creek. Steve, Ray, Roy, Jerry, George, and me went up there. They were rootin' up his 'taters like a plow. Well, Coyle said, "You boys are gonna have to come up here and do somethin' with these hogs. I'm not gonna have a 'tater for this fall."

We went up there at night, 'cause we had to work during the day, and the hogs would come out at night. So when we got out, the hogs ran up the hill there above Coyle's. There was a big ol' rock cliff up there. It was about as high as this house. We turned the dogs loose, and then, that hog came right straight over the top of my head. He landed in the brush pile. Roy was standin' to the side of me, and we had just unlatched our two catch dogs. They took off, and Roy went about six feet. That was right where the hog had hit. My dog was black, and he passed [Roy's dog, which] thought that was the hog that went by him. There was a dogwood there. It was about this four inches around and eight feet high. That crazy bulldog locked on that dogwood bush, and he thought that he had the hog caught. He wouldn't turn loose. We left him locked on that bush until everybody saw what he had locked on.

Steve: We had to choke him off of it! A lot of times, you would have to carry a choking stick with you. You would put it in the dog's mouth behind their teeth and twist it. It would make them open their mouths. You could break 'em loose. Pitbulls will lock down like that. You can't get 'em loose. That's the way that dog was.

Roy's ol' Rock was cut all to pieces here. We brought the hog in and put it downstairs. We carried that dog in, because he was cut all to pieces. We laid him down over there on a coat. He saw that hog, and he went to wobbling towards it. He was gonna catch it again!

On other hunting adventures:

Bill: We would go anywhere that people called us about a bear or hog. We've had some times, and some good times at that!

Steve: We've been at it fifty years, buddy. That's a long time to be huntin'.

Bill: We ran a bear through the Owl's Den over a rock cliff. In our party this time was Steve, Eddie, Clayton, Conner Speed, my fourteen-year-old grandson, and Marshall. Eddie and Clayton went to the barking dogs. Two were hung up on the cliff. The bear had jumped off the cliff and left.

Clayton's dog was about forty feet from the ground on a tree that was leaning up the rock. They watched the dog go as far as he could up the tree. The bear turned around on the dog and came back down. They knew if he fell that he was a dead dog. He made it down. My dog was on about a ten-foot ledge. He had fell over the top and landed on the ledge. Eddie and Clayton looked at him about seventy feet up, and they couldn't see any way to get the dog out. They said, "You'll have to shoot him." They went back to the truck where Conner and I was, and they told me what they thought. Conner and me wanted to see what we thought. I had two dog leashes which I tied together, and I found a ledge to put my toes on to creep around to the dog. I saw I needed some help, so I called Steve on my handheld radio. Steve and Marshall came.

Steve: When I saw Bill up on that cliff, he was tied to his dog leashes and holding on to a little old scrub tree. I said, "I can't believe you are out on the face of this cliff holding on to a scrub tree that is coming out of a crack." Conner was on the top telling his grandpaw to come back because it was too dangerous. When Marshall came, he had a short rope that he tied to a tree on the top. We retied ourselves and sent Marshall to Dillard to get a longer rope about one hundred feet.

Bill: When Marshall came back, we were about twenty-five feet from the dog. I tried to lasso the dog four or five times, but I couldn't get him. Steve

PLATE 77 Bill Speed, Martha Speed, Jessica Phillips, and Steve Conner

PLATE 78 Steve Conner and Bill Speed with Steve's hunting dog

said, "Let me try." He threw three times and caught the dog on the last throw. We pulled the noose tight, and together, we pulled the dog up over the ledge and on up to the top on his side.

Conner and Marshall said that they were glad they saw the dog make it out, because it looked impossible. Eddie and Clayton's eyes popped, because they didn't believe this rescue. That was one of the most dangerous hunts we have ever had. That is what a hunter will do for his best dog!

Steve: My dad, Minyard Conner, hunted in the Smoky Mountains before the park came in. He said he had heard the old men saying a bear would pack his wounds and get well. I killed a bear that had a funny-lookin' place on his back leg. I showed this to Dad. He said, "He has packed his wound." As I examined his leg, the hair stuck straight out and it had crushed acorns in it that had been half digested and threw up. Both sides of his leg had this packed into his hair about a half-inch thick. The bullet didn't hit the bone, just the flesh wound. The old people always said that the animals knew how to doctor themselves. I have never seen this before or even after that.

One training season on Commissioner, the dogs were after a walking bear [a bear that is too big to tree]. They were going up the small creek because the hill was steep. I went up on a rock cliff where I could see where the dogs and bear had come below me. I watched them go behind the rock, and in just a minute, the bear came up on the top of the rock where I was. I couldn't run or jump. I went to yellin' and wavin' my arms. The bear kept coming towards me. I thought maybe that I could hit the top of a tree when I jump. The dogs were after him real close. They must have nipped him. He made a sharp turn and went by the dogs. Now, that was when I was between a rock and a hard place.

We were huntin', and I had killed a hog with about an eight-inch-by-two-and-one-half-inch stick. It was comin' out of his chest. As he was runnin' through the brush, a limb off a dead tree had went between his rib cage and his shoulder. The wound had healed with scar tissue all around the stick. This had tapered and sharpened on one end. This is probably a once-in-a-lifetime sight.

Two hours had passed by, but I felt like we had just gotten there. As we left, you could hear Bill's hunting dogs barking in the distance.

WHERE MUSIC DWELLS

Music in Southern Appalachia

Bluegrass, country, and shape note singing

PLATE 79   Pickers and singers at Clay's Corner on a typical Friday night

PICKERS OF MUSICAL INSTRUMENTS are everywhere in Southern Appalachia. They're playing in senior centers, in auditoriums, in town squares, in state parks, in gas stations, at family reunions, at campsites, in living rooms—even in a McDonald's restaurant—wherever people gather, all over the region. The hills and hollers are alive with the sound of music that some people may have thought dead.

"There's a whole generation of people in their twenties and thirties for whom there's a pique of interest in the old-time Southern string band music," says David A. Brose, folklorist at John C. Campbell Folk School. "Young people are taking it up with a vengeance." Other styles of old-time music, folk songs, ballads, early country, and even shape note singing, which dates back to the early nineteenth century, are thriving in the South.

You can't really call it a revival of Southern string band music because it never left, Brose says. It's just that young people are catching on to what their elders have known all along: that there's beauty, emotion, and grace in the old-time music. And it's downright fun to play. That's why pickers in places like Brasstown, North Carolina, and Auraria, Georgia, don't give up their jam sessions without a good reason.

Clay Logan, proprietor of Clay's Corner in Brasstown, says he's closed his store to musicians only about ten times in twenty-eight years. Admission is free, but Logan would appreciate your buying a pack of Nabs and a Coke, or something.

"Sometimes we'll have just three, and other times we'll have more pickers than we do listeners," Logan says. You'd be surprised, he adds, how many people can crowd into a back room that measures twelve by thirty feet. "Some are sitting, others are standing, folks just eating ice cream and having a good time."

(Logan, by the way, became regionally famous, or infamous, several years ago when he started competing with the Peach Drop in Atlanta and the Times Square Ball Drop in New York City to count down the last minute to the New Year. He decided to lower a live, caged possum, safely and slowly, outside his store in unincorporated Brasstown, as the year's final seconds ticked away. However, in 2003, threatened by a lawsuit from PETA, People for the Ethical Treatment of Animals, Logan opted instead to use a dead possum, roadkill that had been washed and blow-dried, he says, tongue in cheek.)

In Auraria, the only thing that'll keep the pickers away is voting day, says Ray "Cowboy" Harris, a former rodeo rider who's keeper of the key to the community house, which is also used as a voting precinct. "On voting days, we go

PLATE 80   Rebecca Carter watches her fellow musicians.

somewhere else," he says. Even a small flood that sent water under the door
in the spring of 2015 didn't stop the show, which costs you a dollar admission to help pay the night's rent of twenty-five dollars.

Auraria attracted a passel of prospectors in 1832, when gold was discovered, and then a hotel and a bank, everything now long gone. But on a sultry
Monday evening, relative newcomers to the jam session are trying to discover, not gold, but the right chord. Rebecca Carter is there with her guitar,
but she uses prompts on major and minor chords because she's still learning.
Doris Burzynski uses a tablature to find the right notes on her Q-chord.

Everybody who shows up with a stringed instrument is encouraged to
join in, and sing, too, even if he or she is not ready for prime time. "Some are
good, some are not so good," Cowboy Harris says. But having fun is the goal,
not proving perfection.

Madge Whelchel has been an Auraria regular for years and used to run
the show. "I grew up with music," she says after refusing to tell her age,
although she admits she's older than Judge Judy on TV. "All we had was a
radio. People would come to our house to listen to the radio, to listen to the
Grand Ole Opry. We'd have a house full, and I lived way out in the country."

It was the advent of radio that changed music everywhere, including,
eventually, the mountains of the Southern Appalachia.

PLATE 81   Waiting for their time to sing . . . Jamie Shook and Wayde Powell, Jr.

"It opened up music," says Wayde Powell, Jr., "but it diluted it at the same time, because it was more composite, and the various strains of mountain music began to disappear. There were certain people who tried to preserve them." In the remote, isolated mountains, however, change came slowly, and the sound "maintained its novelty as Southern Appalachian music."

Powell grew up in those mountains, in Towns County, Georgia, and he's been a follower, an aficionado, really, of old-time Southern music all his life. At one time, he published a magazine, *Precious Memories*, which covered it all: gospel music, bluegrass, old-time, and country gospel. He and longtime friend Jamie Shook play in a group called the Ellis Walden Band, and they're joined occasionally by versatile Wayde III, whom Brian Littrell of the Backstreet Boys referred to as "one of the best and most professional musicians I have had the pleasure of working with," sometimes performing in state parks.

In the early 1900s, mountain people told their story in song, Powell says. Singing was part of life; it wasn't separated from everyday events. "If you were hoeing corn, you sang. The family got together at night, you sang. You sang about events that took place in your life."

Young people, however, even those who grew up around old-time music, sometimes miss the stories altogether. Powell's sons, Wayde III and Nicky, "were pretty good size before they realized what songs were saying," their father says. "They sang songs, they played songs, but they didn't listen to the words."

But music, like food, depends on a person's taste. Powell's young daughter wants to listen to Taylor Swift, while Wayde III would stay up all night trying to master the banjo if he could. "It used to be I couldn't sleep if I didn't hear a banjo playing," Powell says.

Today, the emphasis is more on the beat and the voice, which may have been doctored in a studio. "But can they go out onstage and duplicate what comes out of the studio?" Powell wonders. "Nowadays, people dismiss what they consider not quality voice. They're used to having these professional voices and commercial songs. Like growing tomatoes, who wants to hear a song about that? But people used to sing about things like that."

The roots of the old-time Appalachian music grow deep and far, and not just to Ireland, Scotland, and England. Almost as important, David Brose says, is the influence Africans and African Americans had on Appalachian mountain music. The fiddle is a Western European instrument, but the banjo came from Africa.

In Ireland, he says, a fiddle tune must be played a certain way. If a fiddler slips in a note that doesn't belong, one that's not *right*, he might be asked to leave the session. "But Africans, when they took up the fiddle, brought a whole syncopation to the music," says Brose, who plays guitar, banjo, mandolin, and several West African instruments. "Fiddle music changed in the Appalachian Mountains because of blacks bringing syncopation into the fiddle music."

Brose teaches the history of Southern Appalachian music and its instruments, but during Morning Song, when students at the folk school gather to greet the new day with music, they like to mix it up. He's likely to open with something like "Waterbound and I Can't Get Home," an old folk song with repeated lyrics, and then follow with "King of the Road," a Roger Miller favorite that dates back more than fifty years. "People love it," he says, and they sing along. "Some songs are literally a hundred years old."

Shape note singing goes back even further, more than two hundred years. And it's still being taught, thanks to groups like the North Georgia School of Gospel Music. Lilly Vee Adams of Blairsville, Georgia, was partly responsible for the school's development. She grew up with shape note music. "My daddy, the late Paul Gibson, taught singing school," she says. "There were four of us girls; one of them was older, so she could sit where she wanted to."

But the other three were told to sit on the front bench while Adams's father taught shape note and lines and spaces, two ways to sight-read songs without learning by rote the scales of all twelve keys of music.

"We'd get a new singing convention book," she says, "and Daddy would sit there and hum and sing those songs. I was raised on it. I'm still not absolutely perfect in it."

The gospel music school meets annually for two weeks at various colleges in North Georgia. It's open to everyone, but most of the students range in age from seven to eighteen, with a few older people there, some to chaperone the children.

"The reason it's so easy to sing shape notes is because the shapes are right there in front of your eyes," Adams says. Shapes were added to the note heads in written music to help singers find pitches within major and minor scales. "You don't have to worry about a C or a D or anything like that. You know C is a do," as in do-re-mi-fa-so-la-ti-do. Here's what Adams teaches her grandchildren, who have attended the school: Do is like a triangle; re is a half-moon; mi is a diamond; fa is a flag; so is like a zero; la is rectangular; ti is shaped like an ice-cream cone, then you're back to the high do. The children love shape note singing, she says. "They think it's something else."

Not everybody, however, is only enamored with bluegrass, string bands, and old-time mountain music. One of them is Sharon Thomason of Dahlonega, Georgia, author of *Sing Them Over to Me Again: Loving Memories of Classic Country Music*, published in 2013. As the book title implies, Thomason loves the singing of such country singers as Eddy Arnold, Bill Anderson, Johnny Cash, Merle Haggard, Ernest Tubb, Dolly Parton, and Loretta Lynn. She was turning the radio dial to find good country music when she was just a small child.

But, she says, "if you go back and try to listen to the Bristol Sessions of the 1920s, to Jimmie Rodgers and the Carter Family, it's kind of hard to listen to, almost." Ralph Peer, producer for the Victor Talking Machine Company, held the Bristol Sessions in 1927 in Bristol, Tennessee, and turned out recordings of blues, ragtime, gospel, ballads, topical songs, and string bands. The sessions marked the commercial debuts of Jimmie Rodgers and the Carter Family.

And she's not crazy about many of the singers, country and otherwise, who are popular today. Listening to Willie's Roadhouse on satellite radio one day, she heard two performers, Canadian singer and songwriter Michael Bublé and Eddy Arnold, sing the same old Arnold song back to back. "Michael sang, and I thought, 'Oh, he did good.' Then Eddy comes on and sings, and I think, 'Oh my god, there's no comparison.' The emotion that Eddy Arnold could put in a song. These people today just don't have any emotion. But twenty years from now, will we look back and still feel that way about it?"

That's because tastes in music change a little with every generation, she says. And people of each generation think their music is the best, and that any music that comes later has lost some of the real stuff. When the Nashville Sound came along in the 1960s, singers like Jim Reeves, Patsy Cline, and Ray Price offered a smoother kind of country, and some folks complained it wasn't country anymore. "Now we see that the Nashville Sound saved commercial country music," Thomason says.

But old-time music did have a positive effect on the country stars of a couple of decades ago. Back when the Jordanaires were backup singers for Elvis Presley, Patsy Cline, and Eddy Arnold, Thomason says, the "cheat sheet they used when they were recording, they wrote that out in shape notes. They had all learned that in church."

Regardless of the style a person enjoys, the fact is music is soothing to the soul. Psychologists recommend that their anxious patients listen to good music, the kind that represents how they want to feel, and hospice staff and volunteers know that songs often are the last thing a person dying with dementia will forget. Hugh P. Minor III of Danielsville, Georgia, a spiritual care coordinator with Gentiva Hospice in North Georgia, tells this story about a patient:

Minor was called out to an assisted-living facility to help a family through their grief. A loved one was dying (hospice calls it transitioning). He sat and talked to the patient's family members for a while, and then, "I don't know what it was, but something struck me and I offered to the family to sing," he recalls. "I knew the words of 'Blessed Assurance,' so I asked the family if it was okay to sing. They said sure. So, we were holding hands. We prayed and then I sang the first verse.

"The patient hadn't said a word, hadn't said anything for many, many hours to her family. When she heard that song, she opened her eyes and sang parts of the chorus. When we finished, she looked over at her family and closed her eyes. She died several hours later."

The part of the brain where music resides is the last part to deteriorate with dementia diseases, Minor says. The patient may not have known him, and she may not even have remembered the song after he walked away thirty seconds later. But she knows she had a nice, warm feeling hearing the music and maybe singing the song. "That's why," he says, "I sing the praises of the group of people who come together to do this thing called hospice."

Music can be used in teaching many things. Writing good storytelling ballads, for example, Kate Long will tell you, is like writing a good newspaper story. It's all about communication. Long should know. For thirty-two years, she was writing coach for *The Charleston Gazette* in Charleston, West Virginia. She has led seminars and conferences on newspaper writing and songwriting all over the country, and she's also a storyteller, singer, and songwriter whose songs have been recorded by dozens of artists.

"The same kinds of principles that apply to newspaper writing also apply to lyrics of song, poetry, and what have you," she says. You're trying to communicate with people by using straightforward sentence construction, plain English, vivid details, movement through time and space, inventorying a cast of characters to convey an idea, all those things Long taught in her writing sessions.

She quotes William Zinsser, author of the classic *On Writing Well*, in making her point: "Clutter is the disease of American writing."

"One of the reasons I love Southern string band music," she says, "is that the best Southern songs are excellent examples of straightforward, lyrical storytelling. They usually involve a tightly spun plot and memorable detail, all put together in a short, compact package.

"And more and more young people are attracted to this kind of music," Long says, agreeing with Brose. "They show up in droves, musical instruments in hand, at the Vandalia Gathering in Charleston. They're everywhere at West Virginia State Folk Festival in Glenville, West Virginia. At the Appalachian String Band Festival in Clifftop, West Virginia, about forty percent of the participants are under thirty years old. What young people may not learn in school, they might well learn in writing and performing good storytelling songs, and that is: If you wouldn't say it that way, you shouldn't write it that way. Just use simple, comfortable words that people can identify with."

Long mentions Jean Ritchie and Hazel Dickens, two songwriters and icons in Southern music, as role models. But Long herself, a singer with a dusky, alto voice, has written ballads that have won national awards. Here are the lyrics of one that strikes home with people of Southern Appalachia:

Who'll Watch the Home Place?

Leaves are falling and turning showers of gold
As the postman climbs up our long hill.
And there's sympathy written all over his face
As he hands me a couple more bills.

Who'll watch the home place?
Who'll tend my heart's dear space?
Who'll fill my empty place
When I am gone from here?

There's a lovely green nook by a clear running stream.
It was my place when I was quite small,
And its creatures and sounds could soothe my worst pains
But today they don't ease me at all.

In my grandfather's shed there are hundreds of tools.
I know them by feel and by name.
Like parts of my body, they've patched this old place.
When I move them, they won't be the same.

Now I wander around touching each blessed thing,
The chimney, the table, the trees
And memories swirl 'round me like birds on the wing
When I leave here, oh, who will I be?

Most of what they're singing in Auraria or in Brasstown and elsewhere are not necessarily songs of Southern Appalachia. They're just songs people want to play and hear. Besides, old folk songs and ballads of the Appalachian Mountains and Western Europe often get reworked and reworded, copyrighted and commercialized into a hit, and it's hard to tell sometimes which songs are true Southern Appalachian and which ones are pretenders.

Says David Brose: "Bob Dylan stole many, many classic ballads very early in his career, changed them only slightly and slapped a copyright on it, claiming authorship. Nobody called neither Bob nor Paul Simon out for doing this, because ninety-nine percent of Simon and Garfunkel and Dylan fans were not themselves ballad scholars. Just a few of us knew where Paul Simon got 'Scarborough Fair.'" He obviously got it from "The Elfin Knight," one of the oldest ballads in the English language.

The same thing is true of "Tom Dooley," made famous by the Kingston Trio. It was first collected from a North Carolina tobacco farmer named Frank Profitt, Brose says, and later by folklorist Frank Warner. Alan Lomax put Warner's version in a book, and the Kingston Trio found it there. "The Kingston Trio made it sound 'modern' and made a multimillion-selling hit out of it," Brose says.

And if you've seen the movie *O Brother, Where Art Thou?*, you no doubt remember the hymn with these words: "When I went down to the river to pray," which was adapted from a traditional hymn with the lyrics: "When I went down to the valley to pray." It was changed to fit with the baptism scene in the movie.

"Now I hear it many places," Brose says. "At weddings, funerals, church services, and it has entered popular use with the word 'valley' being replaced by 'river.' Pop culture strikes again."

Meanwhile, back in Auraria, Georgia, Cowboy Harris kicks off the singing with "Crystal Chandeliers," a song made famous by country singer Charley Pride decades ago.

Mark Kersh follows up with "Blessed Jesus, Hold My Hand," and then singing flows clockwise around the room, starting with Kenny B. Bowers with "I Can't Stop Loving You." As couples begin to pair up and dance in the adjoining kitchen, Doug Cook yells out, "Give me a D as in dog," and then sings "When You and I Were Young, Maggie," a song whose origin is in dis-

PLATE 82   Fred and Drucilla Stowers

pute. Springtown, Tennessee, claims that a local, George Johnson, wrote the lyrics for his Maggie in 1864, and the town even erected a small monument in Johnson's memory. Others say the lyrics were part of a poem by George Washington Johnson, a teacher from Hamilton, Ontario, Canada, who lost his Maggie at a young age. Whatever the case, some Maggie was immortalized in Auraria, Georgia, on this Monday night.

Fred Stowers of Dawson County, Georgia, a lawyer turned businessman, steps up to the microphone and announces that he wants to experiment with a song. "Dad told me that life is a gamble," he says, so why not enjoy yourself and try new things while you can? "If you're alive, you're still in the game."

Stowers is proficient on the mandolin; he's a good strummer, not a picker, on the guitar and banjo and even plays fiddle sometimes. He keeps a couple of changes of clothes in the trunk of his car, along with his golf clubs, so he can be ready for whatever occasion.

A few weeks later, Stowers and the Porch Pickers band are performing under a giant white oak tree at the Stowers family reunion, held on his hundred-acre farm, of which the main dwelling house was built in the 1830s. He performs somewhere every week, sometimes three times a week. He's a regular at an assisted-living home nearby.

PLATE 83   Madge claps at Stowers reunion.

Some of the same pickers who show up in Auraria on Monday nights are performing at the reunion. There's Dave McLaughlin on the banjo, who sings "Heartaches by the Number," a hit by Ray Price fifty years ago. "He's got a good, strong voice," Rebecca Carter comments. "His voice has that country edge."

There's Maxx Bevins with his fiddle, a man who once lived in Baltimore, Maryland, and operated nightclubs on the Chesapeake Bay. "He had big-time bands coming through," Stowers says, "and chaired the Appalachian Jam on the square in Dahlonega for a while." (Bevins was seriously ill at the time of the reunion and died about a year later.)

Madge Whelchel is there at the reunion, clapping in time with the music and perhaps wishing she were up there on that stage, too.

In Auraria, Whelchel sings and plays "Goin' Down the Road Feelin' Bad," a song first recorded in 1924 and made famous by Woodie Guthrie. But then she gets to "feelin' bad about singin' it," she says, and quits before the song ends.

But nobody feels bad at the end of the jam session. That's what music does to people. It makes them feel a little better about life and where it's taking them. Sometimes it makes them smile. Sometimes it's a catharsis, something to purge the tensions of everyday living. Most times, it's nice to just sit back and listen.

Every person has his or her preferences. But, thank goodness and thank musicians, good music—old-time and more modern—is still wafting through the hills and valleys of Southern Appalachia. May it always be so.

A SHORT PRIMER ON MUSICAL TERMS

Folk song: A folk song has no known author. It has been handed down from generation to generation. A folk song does not tell a story; it has no narrative quality. An example is "Old Joe Clark," every verse of which may be coherent unto itself, but taken together, the verses do not tell a cohesive story.

Ballad: A ballad does tell a story; it is a narrative folk song. Sometimes, songwriters will use the term "lyric song" to mean a folk song that does not tell a story, and the term "ballad" to refer to a traditional song that does. "The House Carpenter" is a ballad. "Barbara Allen" no doubt is the best-known ballad in America. Sometimes, the lines between folk song and ballad can get blurry.

Shape note: Shape note music is a system of efficiently learning the basics of music theory. With an understanding of shape notes, one can sight-read songs without needing to depend upon learning by rote, or by "ear." Young people throughout the Southeast today are being trained in shape note music (particularly the seven-note system) so that they can lead music in their local churches with conviction and confidence. The shapes (do-re-mi-fa-so-la-ti-do) correspond to the relativity of pitches found within any musical key. The beauty and power of the shape note system is that once a singer understands and can hear the relativity of the pitches within the musical scale, he can then transpose that relativity to any chosen key of music, thus eliminating the need to learn the scales of all twelve keys. Learn one scale and transpose it eleven times. Because of shape notes, when the newly published annual songbooks are brought out at today's local, state, and national singing conventions, all singers can sight-read (i.e., sing without previous rehearsal) every song in the book, because they understand the relativity of the pitches displayed by the various shapes on each page of music. They quickly master the tune of each song and can focus more intently on the words they sing.

Grounded in Folk Tradition

The story of Hedy West

HEDY WEST had a knack for getting her way, even as a child. If she didn't want to help her older sister wash dishes, suddenly it was time for piano practice. And no one could disturb Hedy when she was at the piano.

Hedy was brilliant—she began first grade at four years old and graduated high school at fifteen—and she had little patience for stupid people doing and saying stupid things. Nothing changed when she became an adult.

She was a magnificent musician, songwriter, and folk singer who made a name for herself wherever she went, even in England and Germany. She was performing in the Jacksonville (Florida) Symphony Orchestra when she was thirteen and could play practically any musical instrument she picked up. She wrote many folk songs, the most famous being "500 Miles," made popular by Peter, Paul and Mary. The great English folk musician A. L. Lloyd reportedly called Hedy "far and away the best of American girl singers in the [folk] revival," the era of Joan Baez, Jean Ritchie, and Judy Collins. Today, more than ten years after her death, Hedy's original compositions, along with traditional songs she collected in Appalachia, are still popular with folk music fans.

Hedy grew up in a working-class family in the mountains of North Georgia and received the bulk of her repertoire directly from her family's musical heritage. Because of that, music historians have said, she was more grounded in the folk tradition than other prominent folk musicians, such as Baez and Collins. Her father, Don West, introduced her to songs of Southern textile mill workers and miners, and Hedy herself described her work as chronicling the "lower classes" with songs like "Cotton Mill Girls," "Whore's Lament," and "Come All Ye Lewiston Factory Girls." Her music often reflected social and political problems of the twentieth century. Her songs gave voice to children and parents forced to work twelve-hour days in textile mills to support their families.

Hedy despised President Lyndon Johnson's administration and delighted in singing songs opposing the Vietnam War. She sometimes turned familiar melodies into cutting lyrics of her own. "Jingle Bells," for example, became "Riding Through the Reich," a sarcastic Nazi commentary, and "Go Tell Aunt Rhody" morphed into "The Poverty War Is Dead," a humorous slap at Johnson's attempt to eradicate poverty in America.

Hedwig Grace West was born in Cartersville, Georgia, on April 6, 1938. At the time, her family was living on a farm just outside of Cassville, at one time a sizable Appalachian town that was brought to its knees during the Civil War when General William Tecumseh Sherman and his troops came through on their way to Atlanta, burning practically everything.

Don West had built a house with knotty pine walls for his family, while his mother, Hedy's grandmother, Lillie Mulkey West—"Bamma," one of the grandchildren started calling her—lived in the old homeplace on the property. Don was a well-known Southern poet, an educator, an ordained minister, a labor organizer, and a leftist activist who moved from one activist project to another and from one teaching job to another. His wife, Mable Constance "Connie" West, was also a teacher.

Hedy's sister, Ann West Williams, five years older than Hedy, had already started school before her family moved to Cassville from Bethel, Ohio, where Don West had been preaching. The Wests knew many homes over the years. They lived in several places in Georgia: in Lula in Hall County, where Don West was superintendent of Lula High School and where his wife taught; just outside of Atlanta, while he taught at Oglethorpe University; in Meansville, where he was minister of a church; in Ringgold, where Connie West taught school while her husband was in New York working on his doctorate at Columbia University; and on a farm on the Chattahoochee River near Douglasville. For a while, Connie and the girls lived in Fernandina Beach, Florida, where their mother taught school while her husband stayed on the farm to grow and sell vegetables. At one point, Don West landed a job in Texas, but he didn't like it there, so he left.

If Hedy were alive today, no doubt she would say it was her grandmother, Bamma, who lit the musical fire in her. Bamma [herself profiled in the story beginning on page 235] was a folk singer, songwriter, and storyteller who ran a country store near Blairsville, Georgia. She sang a folk song similar to "500 Miles," could play the banjo, guitar, and Dobro, and like Hedy, she had a quick wit and a sharp tongue. One day, a city slicker walked into Bamma's store and said, "Ma'am, can you tell me where this road's going?" She replied, "Sir, this road's been sitting here for thirty years that I've been living here, and as far as I know, it's not going anywhere."

Hedy also learned songs from her great-uncle Gus Mulkey. In an interview years ago, Hedy said her grandmother "specialized in sober or tragic songs, perhaps conditioned by her hard life, but Gus preferred humorous songs; indeed, he was not likely to sing unless he could extract a bit of fun out of the song." Hedy combined both humor and sadness for her own songs.

Recalling their childhood, Ann Williams remembers, "In the evenings, after supper, we would sit on the floor in front of the fireplace in the bedroom, and Bamma would tell us stories, play her guitar, and we would sing the old songs she knew." Her grandmother also had a Victrola record player on tall legs. She would wind up the arm on the side of the machine and play some of her favorite songs for her grandchildren.

Hedy was a quick learner on practically any musical instrument. She could play flute, piccolo, banjo, guitar, fiddle, and, of course, piano. When she and her sister were living in Florida, she took up the accordion. She would play at women's club meetings, and her sister would do a monologue.

Williams, a retired teacher and mother of five, admits she didn't enjoy piano as much as Hedy. She would rather sing, dance, draw, and act. "I loved being onstage," she says, "and would have welcomed lessons in anything other than piano." She excelled in public speaking and won a national oratorical contest with a speech about the Statue of Liberty.

"Hedy's inspiration to do anything was to beat [me]," she says, recalling growing up with Hedy. "She was very competitive, and I was not. . . . I sang, but I didn't like playing the guitar because it hurt my fingers. She wanted to do better than me. She was four years old when she started piano lessons, and by the time she was five, she *was* better. She took to music at the first opportunity."

The girls lived in what Williams called a "split" family. Ann and her mother were close, while Hedy was Daddy's girl. "Hedy could get anything she wanted from Daddy," Williams says, but she was sometimes confrontational with her mother. "Daddy would get both of us girls in bed and read books to us. Big books. I remember him reading *Cry, the Beloved Country*, a novel about South Africa. "She would snuggle up to Daddy. She wanted to show that she was the favorite. She really was."

"Hedy had a twangy, nasal sound to her voice," Williams says. "She did that on purpose, imitating people in the mountains who sang that way." And she refused to change her style to become more commercial.

But her twangy, lonesome sound didn't hurt her popularity at all. She won a prize for ballad singing when she was only twelve, and as a teenager, sang at folk festivals near her home and in neighboring states.

After graduating from Murphy High School in Murphy, North Carolina, Hedy left home for Western Carolina College—now Western Carolina University—in Cullowee, North Carolina. She was an A student—school was always easy for her—but she was not impressed with her fellow students, or, for that matter, her professors, some of whom she challenged openly in class.

"She was already sort of raising hell as a college student because she disapproved of some of the activities of some of the fraternities and sororities on campus," says Hedy's daughter, Talitha "Tai" West-Katz. "She protested against the panty raids that were going on. That may have won her a few friends, but probably more detractors.... She didn't feel challenged at college.

"I don't know if I would say my mom was confrontational, but she was principled. If something struck her as not being right, she never hesitated to speak out about it, and sometimes pretty bluntly."

After getting her college diploma, Hedy headed immediately to New York City, where she studied music at Mannes College and drama at Columbia University. And she sang whenever and wherever she could. She was a fixture of the Greenwich Village folk scene, where people were singing the kinds of songs she grew up with. Pete Seeger, who became a good friend, invited her to sing with him at a Carnegie Hall concert. Soon she was making albums; the first one of which, *New Folks*, was released on the Vanguard label.

Ann Williams says Hedy went to New York and then overseas "to get away from her daddy. He wanted to tell her how to play, what to play, where to play, what to wear. He was very controlling—and to everybody. And Hedy was not going to be controlled." Hedy also wanted to see the world beyond America, Tai says.

In the early 1960s, Hedy married a man in New York City. The couple later divorced, but remained good friends and kept in touch. Spreading her musical wings, Hedy moved to Los Angeles, where she established a new home base and continued to sing at events across the country. But she was also taking frequent trips to England. Before long, she moved to London full-time and lived there for seven years. She sang at folk clubs and appeared at the Cambridge Folk Festival and the Keele Folk Festival. She recorded three albums for Topic Records—*Old Times and Hard Times*, *Pretty Saro*, and *Ballads*—and one album for Fontana Records called *Serves 'em Fine*. In the early 1970s, she made her home in Germany, where she turned out more albums, including *Getting Folk Out of the Country* and *Love, Hell and Biscuits*.

"She told me she wanted to go to Germany [because] after the Second World War everyone had told her that Germans were the worst thing ever, and she wanted to find out for herself," her daughter says. "I don't know what she concluded about that, but I know she learned German, and she ended up singing a lot of songs in German and translating English songs into German."

German audiences loved hearing American folk songs in their native language while American fans wanted the traditional folk music they were used to. But Hedy West was her own person, and she didn't always abide by what others wanted.

Actually, she was a musical paradox. She had a voice from the hill country of Georgia, and yet she sang fluently in German. She wrote folksy ballads about love, marriage, and loneliness, yet she was trained as a classical pianist and was a devotee of Karlheinz Stockhausen, a controversial German composer. She received high praise from her fans everywhere, and yet she couldn't always get along with her own family. "I loved my sister," Ann Williams says, "but I will never understand her."

Sometimes Hedy made choices simply out of convenience, as with her second marriage, to a man she met overseas. He was gay and worked for the BBC. She married him, her daughter says, so that she could work legally in the United Kingdom. That marriage also ended in divorce.

One of Hedy West's best friends, Judith N. Drabkin of High Falls, New York, first saw Hedy perform at a concert in Manhattan and "was simply captured by her playing," she says. Later, she telephoned Hedy and asked if she would be willing to give her banjo lessons. "And she agreed, which was extremely generous of her, to say the least."

So for the next few months, Drabkin drove three and a half hours from Westchester, New York, to Stony Brook on Long Island, where Hedy lived, to receive lessons from the master banjoist. "She was one of the finest teachers I've ever encountered," she says. "What she was endeavoring to teach me on banjo, she would somehow convert to theory taught from the piano. And it was the most brilliant teaching."

The two enjoyed each other's company, and the teacher-student relationship developed into a friendship that lasted more than forty years. Besides the banjo, Drabkin learned about gardening from Hedy, something the city girl knew nothing about. "In my opinion," Drabkin says, "there was a force within her even more powerful and fundamental than her music. Deepest down at her roots, she was a farmer. That's how I think of her." Unfortunately, the township of Stony Brook was not as impressed and forced Hedy to remove a thriving, chest-high hedge of *Rosa rugosa* from all around the margin of her property.

It was on Long Island, at a faculty reception at Stony Brook University, that Hedy West found love that endured. His name was Joseph Katz, a professor at the university and a native of Germany. At the time, Hedy was a graduate student studying composition and teaching folk music. The first time Katz telephoned his future wife, she said, "Oh, you're the man who can't pronounce his 'r's."

Drabkin knew Hedy as well as anybody, but she finds it hard to describe her friend's personality, even though her outward appearance was powerfully impressive. "She would come into a room, and she might be inconspicuous at first, but inconspicuous rarely. She didn't come in with a flourish. It was her very entry, her very movement. She did not have a dancer's grace. . . . She didn't have a beautiful walk, but there was something about her presence that was attracting, very attracting."

Hedy was a person of enormous complexity and dimension, Drabkin says. She loved her new man, Joseph, but she had a difficult relationship with his family. Still, she cultivated that relationship, dutifully attending the family's Passover seders and other Jewish rituals. She did it, Drabkin believes, for her daughter. She wanted her to have a better sense of family than Hedy had herself.

Hedy had a profound sense of humor. At a performance in a little concert hall for Drabkin's music club, she came out with a little sheath of notes—obviously her playlist. Each time she performed a piece, she would rip a note off the deck, crumple it up, and throw it on the floor. She told her listeners, "You should see my living room." The audience burst into laughter.

She also was a visual artist. "If I weren't a musician," she told Drabkin, "I would have been an artist." She gave Drabkin her very first oil painting,

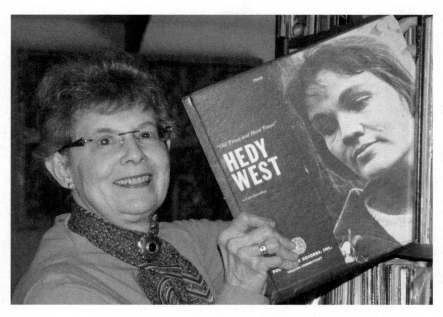

PLATE 84   Judith Drabkin holds one of Hedy's albums.
Mrs. Drabkin died February 7, 2017.

which, interestingly enough, was of her mother, Connie, with whom she was never close, Hedy's sister says. That painting is now part of the Hedy and Don West collection at the University of Georgia.

Hedy could be generous. During the late 1970s, while living in Stony Brook, she donated her talents to many benefit concerts for causes that met her approval. She was all of these wonderful things, but she was still an enigma. In a poem, her father described Hedy as a "strong and tender-hearted [person] whose troubled thoughts coursed deeply beneath a smooth surface."

Hedy encouraged her daughter to learn to play the violin, and she did. Tai performed at her own bat mitzvah when she was thirteen. But near the end of her life, Hedy herself lost interest in performing, Tai says. She was more interested in the history of music.

By that point, she had turned out many great songs, and, much to the delight of her fans, some of her albums have been rereleased on CD. (In 2017, Tai says, a British record company, Fledg'ling, announced plans to produce an album of previously unreleased works, *From Granmaw and Me*, featuring several songs Hedy learned from her grandmother Lillie West.) Hedy also set some of her father's poems to music, "Anger in the Land" among them.

Hedy was an innovator on the five-string banjo, a perfect instrument for her long arms. She developed her own style of playing, combining the claw-hammer technique with three-finger picking. She also had her own style of singing. In fact, she sang a third above the tonal pitch, something she discovered with the help of a prominent researcher of ethnic music, Drabkin says. "So if you were playing in the key of C," she explains, Hedy "wasn't singing exactly in the key of C. . . . She was singing a third sharp of that tone." Nonetheless, Hedy's singing melded beautifully with the music she played.

"I think she deserves a place of recognition," Drabkin says, "not only because she was a girl who played a banjo, certainly a curiosity in those years, but because she was unafraid to bring the discipline, the excellence, the work, the perfection, to what many would think is—and has been—an informal music. And it takes a special brilliance to achieve that."

Hedy became more introspective in her last years, her daughter says. "She believed that the most important thing in life was to develop understanding of the way the world worked, and ethics. She began to believe that having a sense of ethics and a moral compass was the most important thing in life."

Hedy West died of breast cancer on July 3, 2005. She wanted no funeral.

"Lord, I can't go back home this a-way," goes a line from perhaps her most famous song, "500 Miles." Maybe not. But a lot of people believe that Hedy West's music, born in the mountains of North Georgia, has never left.

Lillie Mulkey West

Inspiring a new generation of folk singers

I interviewed Lillie Mulkey West, grandmother of folk singer Hedy West, in June 1972. The resulting story, most of which follows, was part of a series of pieces on Appalachian folklore published in The Times *of Gainesville, Georgia. Lillie West died in 1982, but her songs, her stories, and her impact on the West family are still felt in the hills.*

MRS. LILLIE MULKEY WEST leans back in her chair, smiles when she recalls the song she wants, strums a guitar that has one string missing, and begins to sing. Her voice, though cracked occasionally with age, is brimming with love for music that dates back about eighty years.

The song she's chosen is about a man named Johnny Sands who married Betty Hague, who turned out to be a plague. Finally, Betty told Johnny that she was tired of life and tired of him. So Johnny said he'd drown himself in a river that ran below, and she said she'd wished that long ago.

Johnny asked Betty to tie his hands for fear he would try to save himself. She did. The couple walked to the hill; Johnny asked Betty to push him into the river, and just as Betty reached for his back, Johnny stepped aside and his wife fell in. Mrs. West sang the last stanza:

She's splashing, dashing like a fish,
And cried, "Save me, Johnny Sands."
"I can't, my dear, though much I fear,
"For you have tied my hands."

Mrs. West laughs with me, pleased that I have enjoyed the ballad. She gives another sample of her folk singing. Unafraid of political correctness, she sings several verses about how a woman's tongue will run forevermore and ends the song this way:

There's a lot of fun in sporting,
There's a lot of fun in courting,
Pa says do begin it when you're young.
If you want to marry a wife,
And be happy all your life,
Marry one that's blind, deaf, and dumb.

A car pulls up outside Mrs. West's small country store near Lake Nottely in Union County, Georgia. Sitting on the front porch, she finishes her song, not even noticing the waiting customer, who apparently doesn't want to get out and interrupt her singing.

Finally told that it looks like someone wants to buy something, Mrs. West retorts: "Well, I reckon they can get out and come in if they want something. I don't have a habit of running out to cars."

The customer leaves, and Mrs. West settles back down to more songs and stories. In singing serious ballads, her whole personality seems to change. More of a country twang comes into her voice, and she holds her notes and stretches out her words. She sounds like a female version of recording star Bill Monroe. She'll start singing a line with low volume, hit a peak in the middle, and then let the last word fade off at the end.

Singing has been part of Mrs. West's life ever since she was old enough to learn a few words of song. Eighty-four this month, she was born and reared in Gilmer County, Georgia, and has lived in Union County since 1946. When I ask if she's learned any mountain songs, she says she is about the only one who knows any.

PLATE 85 Mrs. West picks and sings in a 1972 photo.

"People don't sing around here. They do at church, but the songs they have in church now are not like those I was used to singing in my younger days. I think this singing today is more jazz than anything else. Anybody that can dance can dance to the songs they sing in church."

Mrs. West's love for singing has touched many in her family, particularly one granddaughter, Hedy West, daughter of her oldest son, Don. Hedy learned many songs from her grandmother. She later wrote and recorded songs of her own and set several of her father's poems to music as well.

Mrs. West is one of ten children in a family of Scotch-Irish descent. Growing up, the family would gather around the fire most every night and sing a few songs. There were always visitors on Sundays, and there'd be more singing.

Mrs. West rocks back under the snuff signs that decorate the old store front and sings another song her daddy used to like. And if a customer drives up, he won't mind waiting till she's finished.

John Jarrard and Bruce Burch

Writers of country music

SOMETIME BETWEEN FINISHING high school in Gainesville, Georgia, and graduating from the University of Georgia in 1975, John Charles Jarrard and Walter Bruce Burch learned a little something about each other. They learned they each liked—and sometimes wrote—country music.

It happened this way: Burch was working as the night auditor at the Days Inn in Gainesville when Jarrard dropped in for a visit. A guitar was propped up in the office.

"I've got one of them, too," Jarrard said. It wasn't long until they were singing together in a bathroom of the motel. "We'd heard that the acoustics in a bathroom most closely approximated a recording studio," Jarrard said in an interview in 1988. So one morning when Bruce got off work about seven o'clock, they went down to the bathroom of the manager's suite.

The recording was horrible, Jarrard said. A little flushing in the background might have improved the sound. But they weren't discouraged for long.

In March 1977, Burch decided to try his luck in Nashville. Jarrard helped him move.

"I took John to the bus station to go back to Gainesville and then cried like a baby," Burch said. He was in Music City all by himself. About nine months later, Jarrard moved to Nashville as well. They were together again.

Writing songs was going to be easy, Burch thought. After all, he had found a company that liked some of his songs and had published them. Trouble was, published was as far as he got.

"I went to some hole-in-the-wall publishing company," he said, "and they'd say, 'Yeah, that one's pretty good.' I'd call John and tell him, 'Hey, I got another one published today.' I thought that was the greatest thing, to get one published. Of course, they didn't give you any money for it."

At this point, income had become more important for both men than it had been when they were younger: They had married women who weren't willing to wait for number one songs before they ate again. The two men didn't write much together because now they had reasons to stay home. Besides, both were lyricists, and lyricists normally cowrite with people who are more melodic. And then children came along, Matthew and Sarah for Bruce and wife Cindy, and Amanda for John and wife Beth. "We were busy with all that," Burch said. "We were going our separate ways. But we talked every week or so. We kept the friendship up."

Burch knew things were looking up one night in the late 1980s when he stopped at a Waffle House on his way back to Nashville from a friend's wedding in Knoxville. As usual, he checked out the songs on the jukebox. And he smiled.

"I called John the next morning and said, 'Man, we have finally made it big. We are both on the Waffle House jukebox.'" There they were, two country songs written by two city boys from Gainesville, Georgia, guys who

PLATE 86   John Jarrard (*right*) with Whispering Bill Anderson

had been together nearly as long as Homer was with Jethro. And both on the jukebox at the Waffle House.

But getting a hit wasn't easy. "I didn't think I was going to make it for a while," Burch said. In fact, he came close to boarding that midnight train to Georgia, taking a regular job, and forgetting the country music business.

Jarrard's breaks came first. His first hit song, "Nobody but You," sung by Don Williams, was in 1983. Before it was all over, he had written eleven number one hits and scores of other tracks for most of country music's top artists, including Alabama, Don Williams, George Strait, and John Anderson.

The number one hits didn't come as often for Burch, but they came. In about 1984, he got a cut on an Oak Ridge Boys album that went multiplatinum, meaning he received a fifteen-thousand-dollar advance. "I was probably making that in a year," he said, and grinned.

Later in 1988, the hits began in earnest. "The Last Resort" was followed by "Out of Sight and on My Mind," a song performed by Billy Joe Royal. At one time, in early 1988, Burch and Jarrard had five songs, three of Jarrard's and two of Burch's, on the country music top-fifty list.

Burch met singer Reba McEntire when she checked in at the Hall of Fame Motor Inn, there for her first time singing at the Grand Ole Opry, and waited on her at Houston's Restaurant later. Coincidentally, it was Reba who recorded his two number one hits: "Rumor Has It" and "It's Your Call," which were also the titles of two of Reba's most successful albums. He cowrote songs on two other Reba albums, which have sold more than fifteen million copies, and has also had platinum- and gold-certified albums for other top artists. "There was a time when we were doing pretty well," Burch said. "It started slacking off about the mid-nineties. The business was changing."

Undaunted, he started his own publishing companies, first as Burch Brothers Music and then as Bruce Burch Music. He pitched other people's songs as well as his own.

A few years later, Burch became creative director of EMI Music Publishing, a big, successful company. While still writing himself, Burch also worked the classic-song catalogs, arranging new recordings of old songs by such successful songwriters as Kris Kristofferson, his hero; Tony Joe White; Smokey Robinson; Dolly Parton; and Mac Davis.

Burch wrote a number of top-ten, top-twenty, and top-forty songs. But successful though he was, he sometimes seems almost apologetic about not writing more hits. "Jarrard had a lot more success than I did," he said, "so he celebrated more than I did."

"Bruce was very generous with his talent back in those days," said Jeff Stevens, a singer and songwriter in Nashville. "I learned a lot about the cowriting process from him and realized as I was writing with him that I had a lot to learn about the craft. Over the years, I have found Bruce to be not only a super talent as a writer but also as a teacher/mentor. Bruce has a very approachable and down-to-earth personality and is very giving."

PLATE 87   Jeff Stevens

And Stevens wasn't the only one Burch helped. "I have many very successful friends that in some way or another Bruce has contributed to their career," Stevens said.

Like Burch, Jarrard also mentored other musicians, including Wendell Mobley, a singer/songwriter who moved to Nashville in the early 1990s to make it big. "I remember getting with John, as a cowriter, and that's when it hit me that I wasn't as good as I thought I was."

"I don't know why he liked me, but he liked me," Mobley said. "He took me under his wing, man, and showed me how to do this. I am so thankful for that. I promise you I would have been gone a long time ago if it hadn't been for Jarrard's coaching."

About a year after moving to Nashville, Jarrard started losing his eyesight. A diabetic since childhood, he suffered from health problems his entire life, and his vision was one of the victims. When he was twenty-six years old he had to quit his job at the Hall of Fame Motor Inn and concentrate strictly on writing songs.

"He said he could go back to Gainesville and learn how to be a blind man or stay in Nashville and learn how to be a songwriter," said Janet Tyson Jar-

PLATE 88   Jarrard (*right*) picks and sings at
Nashville's Bluebird Café with legendary Waylon Jennings.

rard, whom John married in 1995, after his first marriage failed. "One of the things that I respected the most about him and that fascinated me the most about him was with all of the physical challenges he went through, he was the most positive person I've ever met."

And the word "daring" should fit into that description somewhere. To raise money for the Tennessee School for the Blind, for example, Jarrard rappelled off Nashville's ASCAP building, three stories high, in 1993. "Somebody told John, 'You can't do that. It's too dangerous,'" Janet Jarrard said. "And John said, 'Dadgummit, who says I can't?'"

Some people might have thought that Jarrard would stop going to the office to write, because it's not easy even for a sighted person to negotiate some of Nashville's sidewalks. But he did it. He hired a mobility trainer to teach him how to get around using a cane. "It was superhuman," Burch said. "He walked Music Row every day. He was a legend in Nashville. He'd get to the office and he'd be bloodied up from running into a stop sign or something, especially when he was just learning his mobility training. He used to make himself come downtown just to get practice. It was like learning to drive in Atlanta."

On Fridays after work, Jarrard and Mobley would sometimes find a place to drive go-carts. "He would follow me around and listen to my motor," Mobley said, "and he would hit me in the corners and stuff and burst out laughing. He loved racing, so we had to do that all the time."

John Jarrard loved to have fun, but songwriting always came first. Some writers would wait for inspiration. Jarrard didn't. For eighteen years, he was with Maypop Music Group, the publishing company for the band Alabama, and he wrote there, or somewhere, every day he could move about.

"He literally said in his later years that he came to view his blindness as a blessing," Janet Jarrard said, "because if he had not gone blind, he would not have had to make that decision to pursue music with everything he had."

Burch moved on with his career. He had taught a music-publishing class at Belmont University in Nashville and enjoyed it. So in 2005, he approached officials at the University of Georgia, his alma mater, about starting a music-business program. They agreed, but said they needed financial support. Burch raised the money himself.

Five years later, he started a similar program at Kennesaw State University in Kennesaw, Georgia, and again raised the start-up money. In 2012, he moved back home to Gainesville, where he taught four courses at Brenau University: entertainment management; careers in music, sports and entertainment; event planning; and an adult-education class in songwriting.

In the 1990s, Burch and Jarrard teamed up for a series of benefit concerts in Gainesville, raising money for local charities. The concerts became more popular every year. But Jarrard's health was declining rapidly. Besides losing his eyesight, his kidneys failed, and he underwent kidney-transplant surgery. That kidney failed in 1995, about a month before he and Janet were married. He went back on dialysis for eighteen months and received another kidney in 1997. He lost both legs in below-the-knee amputations and part of a finger on one hand, spending most of 1997 and part of '98 in and out of the hospital.

Bruce Burch had his own health problems. In 1991, he was diagnosed with chronic lymphocytic leukemia (CLL) and underwent chemo treatments. Those treatments are over, he hopes, but he still receives infusions every three months to boost his weakened immune system. He is susceptible to infections and came down with double pneumonia in 2014. CLL is not curable, he said, but is treatable.

Now divorced, Burch is a proud grandfather of four and still writes some but also spends time helping others write. Low-key about his own accomplishments, he likes to brag on former students who are now doing well.

Writing songs is hard to teach because the really good writers, like athletes, are born, not made, Burch explained. He is not a born writer, he said.

PLATE 89   Bruce picks it out.

He works hard at it. If he didn't make it as a songwriter, he figured he could teach and coach football. But writing songs was what he loved to do. As a young man, he loved the storytelling songs of Kris Kristofferson, so one day, he picked up his brother David's guitar, learned three chords, and strummed a few songs by Kristofferson and Hank Williams. "You didn't need but three chords for most of Williams's songs," he said.

The worst thing that can happen to a songwriter is to come up with a great idea and then forget what it was. After he lost his sight, Jarrard always carried a hand Dictaphone with him as he made his way with a cane, and later prosthetic legs, from home to office and back. Burch keeps a pad and his cell phone handy for the same purpose.

The best songs, of course, come with a message that touches people, sometimes in a way the songwriter didn't expect at all. When Jarrard and his cowriters, Lisa Palas and Will Robinson, were writing "There's No Way," an Alabama hit, they thought they were turning out a traditional man/woman love song. But Tony Franklin Moore of Munford, Alabama, thought of his mother.

Tony, you see, was born in 1972 with spina bifida, which develops when the bones of the spine don't form properly around a baby's spinal cord. Burch wrote about Tony in his book, *Songs That Changed Our Lives*.

"My parents were asked by the hospital staff if they would put me in a nursing home," Tony told Bruce in 1995. "They said I wouldn't live anyway, but my parents kept me. The nurse told my parents that if they kept me, I would live longer if I had lots of love." And then one day he heard the song "There's No Way." To most people, it was indeed a traditional love song. But to Tony, it was a song to his mother.

"You see, I'd lay my head on my mother's chest when I was little," Tony said, "and she would tell me how much she loved me. All my life, she has told me over and over how proud she was of me and how much she loves me. I sure do feel her love in the chorus of the song."

Jarrard met Tony in 1985 at an Alabama concert in Northeast Georgia, and they became friends, friends who were there for each other over the coming years. They inspired each other. "When John reached his lowest emotional state," Burch wrote, Tony Moore's inspiration kicked in. Whenever he felt robbed, he would think of Tony. "I knew that no matter what I was going through, Tony had been through worse," Jarrard told Burch.

John Jarrard died on February 1, 2001. He was forty-seven years old. Two memorial services were held, one in Nashville, another in his hometown, Gainesville, Georgia. Some of his fellow songwriters and singers were there in Nashville. "I didn't make it through very well," Wendell Mobley remembered, "but I was there. I was a mess."

About two months later, Jarrard's ashes were scattered near what the family called Jarrard Creek, at the base of Blood Mountain in Northeast Georgia. Jarrard, already blind, had climbed that steep mountain at night with his brother, Tom, and other family members and friends.

Not long after Jarrard's death, the late Mike Banks approached Burch about continuing the benefit concerts that he and his friend had performed in the 1990s. Burch was reluctant at first. But then he reconsidered. Perhaps this would be a good way to remember his buddy and to help worthy charities at the same time. That same year, Burch got together with several Gainesville friends, among them Banks, Philip Wilheit, Charlie Strong, Jim Mathis, and Allen Nivens, and formed the John Jarrard Foundation. Since that time, the foundation, holding one major concert every year, plus several smaller events, has raised nearly two million dollars for charity. The sixteenth annual concert was held in September 2017 on the campus of Brenau University, where Burch taught.

Songwriter Jeff Stevens was one of the performers in 2015. "I came down to Gainesville for two reasons," he said. "Number one, because I knew John Jarrard and admired his talent and fortitude when faced with illness, and I wanted to support the foundation, and number two, Bruce Burch was the first Nashville songwriter that I wrote with, and I wanted to repay him for that."

Wendell Mobley was there, too, and also performed at the first concert after Jarrard's death. "I still write like he wrote, his process," he said. "He taught me to close my eyes and drool and think for four hours. I still think about him when I'm writing. What would John do? How would John do this or look at this?"

Now, every September, successful songwriters travel to John Jarrard's hometown to sing and play, not for money, just for a friend they remember, and for Bruce Burch, his best friend.

"I see the benefit concerts as an extension of his life, the way he lived his life," Janet Jarrard said. "Whatever that spirit of transcendence with John came from, I think it's been passed along to this event. It's been so beautiful to watch it happen."

In late 2016, Bruce Burch resigned his teaching job at Brenau University and moved back to Nashville to be near his four grandchildren and, of course, to write country songs.

Jarrard was inducted into the Georgia Music Hall of Fame in 2010.

It's been more than fifty-seven years, but Burch still remembers their first meeting. It was on the playground of Enota Elementary School in Gainesville. "He said, 'Hey, Johnny.' He thought I was Johnny Yarbrough, another friend. I said, 'No, I'm Bruce.' We had just moved to Gainesville from Hiram [Georgia], and John Jarrard was the very first person I met."

So, in the beginning, it may have been a friendship by accident. But in the end, after all the dreams, the love, the heartaches, the laughter, the failures, the triumphs, it's actually a country song waiting to be written.

Southern Gospel Singing

Still a favorite for many

MARILYN AYERS BERRONG isn't much for what she calls "seven-eleven songs," those repetitive pieces of praise popular in many contemporary church services, where worshippers sing the same seven words eleven times. But give her a good old Southern gospel song, and she's in heaven. "It touches the soul," she says. "It's got a message. It's got a beautiful melody."

With many of the older Southern gospel songs, "Neither Do I Condemn Thee," for instance, the message of salvation is complete, from beginning to end. Songs today just don't do that, she says.

Berrong grew up in Habersham County, Georgia, listening to such gospel groups as Hovie Lister and the Statesmen Quartet, the Blackwood Brothers, and the LeFevre Trio. Starting when she was about eight years old, her parents, Winston and Cleo Ayers, would drive eighty miles to Atlanta to attend all-night gospel singings at the Atlanta City Auditorium. And they kept going back every year, mainly because their daughter insisted.

"It was really great," she says. "It was something you never forgot, especially for a little mountain girl from nowhere. It was wonderful." The family never took vacations, but, to Berrong, all-night singings were close enough to basking in the sunshine on a sandy beach.

Most of those all-night gospel singings are gone now. Most of the singers in the old groups have realized the heavenly reward they sang about for years. Others are spending the winter of their lives surrounded by photographs and memories of concerts long ago.

The biggest gospel events now are the Bill Gaither concerts and the annual National Quartet Convention, moved a few years ago from Louisville, Kentucky, to Pigeon Forge, Tennessee. Gaither, a popular songwriter of Southern gospel and contemporary Christian songs, appears in several major cities every year and draws crowds of several thousands.

"I like them," Berrong, who now lives in Hiawassee, Georgia, says of the Gaither concerts. "They're not as good as the all-night singings. They don't do as much of the old gospel music that I like, but, you know, they're good."

Calvin McGuyrt, a historian of Southern gospel music, remembers the all-night singings vividly, because he was one of the singers. He's been singing with the Georgians Quartet since the 1950s, when the group was first organized. "If you made that venue in Atlanta, then you were considered to be in the elite," he says. Apologizing for getting a bit secular with a spiritual subject, he explains that taking part in the all-night singings of old was akin to a Super Bowl experience. "Your blood was already boiling by the time you got there," he says. "It was a great atmosphere; the crowd was big, and most of the time, it was a sellout," especially when two, three, or four of the top groups were there.

Wally Fowler, sometimes called "Mr. Gospel Music," organized the first all-night singing in 1948 in Thomasville, Georgia, and then started a circuit of performances, says McGuyrt. Before long, all-night singings were being staged in the Waycross Memorial Stadium in Waycross, Georgia, where twelve-to-fifteen thousand people would sit from sundown to sunup as group after group sang the night air full of gospel praise.

Other singings were held in many cities, including Bonifay, Florida; at the Ryman Auditorium in Nashville, Tennessee, home of the Grand Ole Opry; in Greenville, South Carolina; and in Birmingham, Alabama.

McGuyrt started singing gospel in 1949, when he was twelve years old. He sang tenor, but then his voice lowered to baritone. His father, W. L. "Smiling Mac" McGuyrt, had led the Stamps Melody Quartet, a shape note singing group, in the mid-twentieth century, and in 1955, Calvin became the leader. The quartet changed its name to the Georgians Quartet, following a recommendation from Hovie Lister of the Statesmen Quartet.

The Georgians—who were named the Southeastern Southern Gospel Music Conference's Male Quartet of the Year in 2012—recently added another member, meaning that McGuyrt, now in his seventies, no longer sings at most of their concerts. "I don't have to work so hard," he says, "but I'm still the leader and the quarterback." McGuyrt writes most of the group's songs. In fact, the quartet has recorded more than one hundred of his pieces.

Gospel music has changed since its glory days of fifty or sixty years ago. Audience members are grayer; opportunities to sing are fewer; crowds, except those for the big-name groups, are smaller; contemporary Christian music is bigger. But whether the popularity of Southern gospel is waning depends on who's talking.

It's very much waned in the Southeast, says Alan Kendall, who has forsaken singing with a group and gone to a solo ministry. "To me," he says, "there's an oversaturation of artists and groups. And some of them don't have quality music. I think a lot could be done to raise the bar quality-wise, entertainment-wise even."

Some gospel fans and singers think "entertainment" is a dirty word, but not Kendall.

People who say that gospel singing shouldn't be entertaining are pigeonholing God, he says. "I've been learning that the more you keep an audience engaged, the more receptive they are to the gospel. A lot of practice needs to

PLATE 90   Alan Kendall

go toward better music, better entertainment value. But it'll take a long time to change the present mind-set."

Gospel music, he says, is bigger in the North and West, a reverse from the trend decades ago. People in those regions tend to get out more and make concerts part of their weekly ritual. And there's a push for the music overseas, too.

The last group Kendall performed with was a revamp of the Rebels Quartet. He went solo in 2015 and since then is busier than he's been in four years. "I sing in churches, to senior groups, at festivals, concert settings, anybody that'll have me," he says. The father of two young girls, Kendall, who lives in Towns County, Georgia, can do more solo appearances than group singings and still have more time with his family.

Donald A. "Don" Elrod has retired after singing in Southern gospel groups for thirty-five years, eight years with the Singing Deacons of his church, twelve with First Corinthians, and the last fifteen with Georgia, a trio.

"I could see from the time we started until I retired, opportunities to sing were fewer and fewer," he says. "Primarily, we sang in churches, but it's true of these auditoriums, too. Fewer churches are having Southern gospel concerts."

And he agrees that the audience is getting older. Even at the National Quartet Convention, held annually, the listeners are senior adults, or at least fifty and older. "Who's going to support gospel music later on?"

Elrod became interested in gospel music just out of high school when he worked at a radio station in Gainesville, Georgia. But today, radio stations that play only Southern gospel music are almost a thing of the past.

He says the market for Southern gospel is shrinking; CD sales are down; Christian bookstores offer few, if any, selections in the genre. That means Southern gospel groups must sell their music at concerts, sometimes at considerably reduced prices.

"I'm an optimistic kind of person," he says, "and I hope it will continue and do well. My point of view: It's certainly not growing."

"To some degree," Danny Ray Jones says, "Elrod is right. There's plenty of room to argue either side." But it all depends on how you look at the trend, and it's certainly too early to write an obituary for Southern gospel music.

PLATE 91 Danny Jones

Jones, editor in chief of *Singing News*, the chief publication for Southern gospel music, can rattle off several popular gospel events to support his claim, including Silver Dollar City's largest amphitheater, Echo Hollow in Branson, Missouri, filled to capacity twelve nights in a row; sold-out concerts of the Booth Brothers and the Collingsworth Family; and monthlong capacity concerts at Dollywood, a theme park in Pigeon Forge, Tennessee.

Jones believes attendance in the United States has held steady through the years except for the all-night singings that were popular and prolific decades ago. Southern gospel music, he says, has gone more international these days. "Thanks to Bill Gaither, radio, and a whole bunch of things thrown into the pot, Southern gospel is actually reaching more people than ever. We have large pockets of Southern gospel in Ireland and some of the other European nations. There's even a decent-size following in Brazil." Other promoters have succeeded with multiday tours across Canada and along the US West Coast.

But he does see differences in church music. At one time, he says, Southern gospel was the music of choice. Then contemporary Christian music came along as the favorites of seminary graduates. But in certain parts of the country, that trend is changing back. "It's not a sweeping movement," he says, "but it's there."

Jones retired in 2015 as executive director of the Southern Gospel Music

Association. But he's still devoted to Southern gospel. "This is all I've ever known," he says. "I really got into it when I was two weeks old, because that's when my parents took me to my first event."

Marilyn Berrong can relate. She grew up attending singing schools and singing out of Stamps-Baxter books.

"Everything we used back then was shape note singing," she says. And today, as choir director at Woods Grove Baptist Church in Hiawassee, she'll occasionally have choir members pull out one of the old books and sing notes instead of words, causing some listeners to think they are singing in tongues.

Berrong and her family operate the Mountain Home Music Theater in Hiawassee, which features bluegrass, country, and gospel music. She sings backup and solos, and her husband, Larry, who can play ten different instruments, leads the band.

The music theater is all about singing and having fun, rather than making money. Adults pay eight dollars, and children under ten are admitted free, just about enough to cover utilities, she says.

Occasionally, Berrong will book a Southern gospel group to sing at her church. The crowd is big when it's a well-known group like the Chuck Wagon Gang. But when it's a lesser-known group, maybe a hundred people will show up. "And unless your church guarantees them money," she says, "they only come for a love offering. And when you have only a hundred people there, you're not going to get a lot of money."

Berrong is doubtful about the long-term future of Southern gospel music as she knew it, and for one reason that no one else mentioned: lack of live piano music. "One of the things that made Southern gospel music was the piano playing of a person in the quartet. And now, of course, they use tracks. A lot of people just don't want to hear tracks. They want to hear live music when they go."

And people don't want to hear a whole lot of talk from the singers, she says. They come to hear singing, not talking.

Everyone agrees that songwriters Bill Gaither and his wife, Gloria, have done a lot for gospel music. They have written such favorites as "The Longer I Serve Him," "Because He Lives," "The King Is Coming," and "He Touched Me." Their concerts and homecoming videos sometimes feature well-known singers from the past. They have been able to cross over and attract fans who are not die-hard Southern gospel devotees but love other gospel music.

But Gaither concerts, Berrong says, are not like the all-night gospel singings she knew as a little girl. She misses people like pianist Hovie Lister, who always impressed her with his antics onstage. She misses the old songs that told the whole story of salvation through Jesus Christ from beginning to end. She misses the Martha Carson–type music. She misses "Satisfied" and "How Great Thou Art."

She also misses *Gospel Singing Jubilee* on television. "I know at our house," she says, "it came on at nine o'clock, and it was a signal that you better almost be dressed to go to church. Then you'd hear 'Jubilee, Jubilee' and know that you were in for thirty minutes of the best in Southern gospel: the Florida Boys, the Happy Goodman Family, the Palmetto State Quartet, Naomi and the Sego Brothers, just to name a few. Then you would hear 'you're invited to this happy Jubilee' and know it was time to get in the car and go to church." The Jubilee singing, she says, got her heart and mind ready for church and the pastor's message.

Gospel Singing Jubilee, the longest-running television program in the history of gospel music, lasted for three decades and was seen throughout the country. Other lesser-known gospel programs are still televised in parts of the nation.

Marilyn Berrong cherishes her memories: of the all-night singings when she was a girl, of the Jubilee TV program, of enjoying gospel songs with her parents. And, like many fans, she's hoping and praying for a great revival of those old songs that still touch her soul.

Lighter Moments
from Gospel Groups

The Lord's work is serious business, most of the time

YOU MIGHT THINK that the lives of gospel singers are all serious business. After all, they're doing the Lord's work. But they do have their lighter moments. Just ask them.

We asked Don Elrod to ask them for us. Elrod sang with Southern gospel groups for thirty-five years, eight with the Singing Deacons of Central Baptist Church in Gainesville, Georgia; twelve with the First Corinthians; and the last fifteen years with Georgia, a trio from Gainesville. So he knows a lot of gospel singers and is not bashful about asking them about funny incidents.

Here's one that happened to Elrod himself:

Georgia was singing for Apple Savage at Carver's Chapel Baptist Church in Rabun County. Apple oversaw the service, and after he introduced us, we began to sing. Well, everyone seemed to be enjoying themselves, and many were raising their hands and shouting "Amen." After we had sung for about thirty minutes, Apple stood up and announced, "Prayer time. Anyone that wants prayer should come to the altar."

One dear old gentleman came forward and said he had cancer and he requested prayer. We're still standing on the platform, so Apple turns to me and says, "Don, will you come down and anoint 'Brother Jones' with oil and pray for him?"

PLATE 92   Don Elrod

I had noticed a bottle of anointing oil in the pulpit earlier in the service, so at this point I turned to Terry Dale, our tenor singer, and asked him to give me some oil. If you've never been in a service where folks are anointed with oil, let me explain that you can anoint a good-size congregation with just a few drops of oil. Keep in mind there was one man waiting in the altar to be anointed.

Now my microphone is in my left hand, and I hold out my right hand, expecting Terry to give me one or two drops of oil. Apparently, the boy had no previous experience with this procedure, so I got a handful of oil. I mean it was running over. Let me digress and explain that this dear man, who was on his knees in the altar, had undergone chemotherapy and had lost all his hair. I immediately began to pray and spread the oil on this sweet man's head at the same time. When I thought I had disposed of as much of that oil as I could, I closed the prayer and went back to the stage, and we continued to sing.

I thought the worst of this entire experience was behind me, but I quickly realized I couldn't hold the microphone in the hand that had held the oil; it kept sliding down. And apparently, without realizing it, I had gotten enough of the slippery substance on the other hand to cause the same problem there. Luckily, we had mic stands onstage, and so I finished the concert with my mic on the stand.

Unfortunately, "Brother Jones" was having a problem, too. He was sitting on the front pew where we couldn't help but see what was happening. With all that oil on his head, it had to go somewhere, and it began by running down his forehead; he wiped there. Then it began running down his temples and behind his ears; he wiped there. Finally, it must have run down the back of his head and neck, because he was using his handkerchief there, too.

Now, here is the rest of the story. We went back to the same church four or five years later, and "Brother Jones" was there, and he told us how the Lord had healed him of cancer.

True story, you couldn't make this up.

Here's a story from Judy Clapsaddle of Soul Purpose Quartet:

We were singing at a beautiful church with a very long middle aisle. Everything was going along fine. Shortly after the service had started, the church bus carrying many people from a nearby extended-care facility had arrived. A sweet gentleman using a walker entered the main aisle of the sanctuary.

Evidently, he didn't feel he was moving fast enough and decided to pick up his walker and carry it. As he continued up the aisle, we noticed, as did others, his pants started sliding to his knees. He must have felt a draft, because he stopped quickly, pulled up his pants, lifted his walker, and kept right on coming up the aisle.

Now remember, we're still on the platform trying to sing while all this was happening. People would watch him, and then watch our reaction. We smiled a lot, but we kept our composure. The gentleman finally made it all the way to the second row to sit down. Bless his heart.

We had my husband's eighty-year-old mother with us that day. After the service, she said to us: "I think that's the first time I've ever come to church and was mooned."

Robbie Maxwell of New Ground offers this story:

On a hot Sunday night in July, we were singing in a church in Alabama. We were singing a song entitled "He'll Hold My Hand." The main line in the songs says, "He'll hold my hand no matter what comes my way." We were getting ready to go into the second verse, and we hear a lady scream.

Now, having been raised in a Holiness church, that was nothing unusual for us, so we just kept singing. In a split second, another one screams, and about that time two grown ladies in the church are duking it out. They are pulling hair, they are hitting each other in the face; it was an all-out brawl.

We never let up singing. Just kept bellowing out those lyrics like nothing was going on. The pastor, his wife, and mother-in-law jumped up between the two ladies and separated them, leading them outside to try to defuse the situation. We could see them through the windows on the front door as we were facing the doors. The pastor would talk, then the wife and mother-in-law would talk, and finally the two ladies had a few more words to say and went on their way.

The pastor, his wife, and mother-in-law came back into the building, and we acted as if nothing had happened. We never let up singing. We continued with our program, and I'll have to commend the other church members: I think they were caught a little off guard, but they continued to encourage us to "just keep singing."

We learned later that the two ladies had a little bad blood between them. And when one of them laid her arm on the back of the seat, she apparently pulled the hair of the other. That was all it took. The fight broke out. We have been back to this church many times, and we still remember that event as if it were yesterday. We just always have this understanding: No hair pulling allowed in this church.

And from Charlie Sexton:

Back in the 1980s, I played piano for the Saxon Family, a very popular Pentecostal singing family from Gainesville, Georgia. We were privileged to sing in many camp meetings all over the eastern United States. One year, we were also in charge of the combined choir music for a camp meeting in North Carolina. We had chosen some high-energy tunes that were sure to get everyone on shoutin' ground.

The first night, after about the third song, someone hollered out, "Let Brother Parton sing one!"

They called for him to come to the podium, and this gentle, little man, about eighty-five years old, slowly made his way up to the microphone. I knew we were in for a heaven-sent revival.

I was at the piano, and he turned to me and said, "Page seventy-one, sonny boy." Anyone even remotely familiar with the old red-back Church of God church hymnal knows that page seventy-one is "Sweet Hour of Prayer." Slightly bewildered, I kicked it off, and here we went. I've never seen a slow song move an audience like that before. They were shoutin' and runnin' and fallin' out, and, brother, did the Glory forevermore come down!

At the end of the second verse, Brother Parton stopped me and sweetly and tearfully said, "You know, children, sometimes I just wanna humble myself down, and just wave my hankie before the Lord." He reached in the back pocket of his Duckhead bib overalls and pulled out a perfectly pressed silk hankie and flew it high above his head. I tell you, there was not a dry eye in the place. It was precious.

The next night, about the third song, the same thing took place. The next night, it happened again. By Friday night, there were about two thousand people in attendance, the biggest crowd of the entire series of meetings. A few moments into the service, somebody called out, "Let Brother Parton sing one!" Just as every night before, this precious old man went through the same repartee.

But this night was slightly different. He stopped me at the beginning of the second verse and started into his now-familiar speech. "You know, children, sometimes I just wanna humble myself and wave my hankie before the Lord, just wave my hankie for the Lord."

This time, however, when he reached into his back pocket, instead of his silk hankie, he produced a pair of white Fruit of the Loom underwear and began waving them high over his head, saying, "Come on, children, don't be shy. Wave 'em high before the Lord!"

Everyone totally cracked up, and we never made it through the next verse of "Sweet Hour of Prayer."

And Judy Clapsaddle remembers a special day at a church in Indiana:

We were singing near Kokomo. Shortly after we arrived, we lost the electricity in the sanctuary and half of the church. It was ninety-five degrees outside, and as the day progressed, the temperature kept rising. We ended up running a heavy-duty extension cord from one side of the church to our sound equipment. It worked.

People were arriving, and we tried to make the most of it. Out came the handheld fans for everyone; out came the beautiful Christmas candles that were placed at the stained-glass windows and various other places; off came our jackets; off came the shoes. It looked like a Christmas Candlelight Concert with the McKameys. We asked everyone in attendance to hold their fans up, point them at us, and wave them fast. Boy, that felt good!

L. David Young, who was part of a number of groups, including the Prophets Quartet, tells this story himself:

I was pianist for the Prophets Quartet in early summer of 1961, until being inducted into the US Army in December. The members then were Lou Garrison, tenor; Charles Yates, lead; Ed Hill, baritone; and Jim Boatman, bass.

On a trip up north, I was put in a motel room with Lou. He weighed 350 pounds (a low estimate). We had two double beds and his was nearest the bathroom. He had already taken his turn and was laying in his bed. When I got up to go, he jumped in front of me and blocked my way in. This happened three or four times, and I gave up and laid down. About two a.m., I jumped up, beat him inside the bathroom, and then locked the door. I figured, well, I'll fix him. Looking out the bathroom window, I could see the ground outside. I got on the commode seat, let myself out the window, and dropped. All the way down to the concrete at the next level.

There was an invisible ramp I landed on, but all I could see from the bathroom window was the ground. Stunned and not able to walk, I had to crawl, in nothing but my jockey shorts, and in the dark, all the way around the motel and back down to our room.

I went to doctors, but had no broken bones, and everybody was giving me these electric foot-bath machines.

Lou kept saying, "He's all right—he's just stove up." However, in doing concerts in Ohio; West Virginia; Washington, DC; and Toronto, Canada, to the Peoples Church where Oswald Smith was pastor, I had to be carried and placed on the piano stool.

It was definitely embarrassing and not funny at the time. But in later years, as Charles, Ed, and I talked about it . . . well, it was funny.

STORIES AND
THEIR TELLERS

Inventing a Time Machine
and Other Adventures

Emory Jones, the great storyteller

ARNOLD DYER'S young daughter Krista couldn't believe what she'd just read in the local newspaper. "Daddy," she said, tears in her eyes, "they're going to move Yonah Mountain to Atlanta and put in a lake where the mountain is."

"Let me see that newspaper," Dyer said. "Honey, look who wrote that story." The byline over the column, printed about fifteen years ago in the *White County News* of Cleveland, Georgia, was that of Emory Jones. Krista had nothing to fear, her father assured her. It was just another one of Jones's tall tales.

That's Emory Jones's story of what happened that evening, but that's not exactly the way Dyer remembers the incident. "But," Dyer said, "let's go with Emory's version. He's got a better memory than me, and he's a better storyteller." In fact, Emory Jones is a better storyteller than most people. If you don't believe it, talk to his friends or to his wife, Judy, or to the publisher of his local newspaper. Better yet, sit down with him in his rustic home, nestled nicely in the woods two-thirds of the way up White County's Yonah Mountain, and just listen. The mountain, by the way, hasn't moved an inch.

"The Joneses like to talk," Emory said. Jones's daddy was Dennis Jones of Banks County, Georgia; his mother was Wirtha Meaders of the famous family of potters who lived in the Mossy Creek section of White County. "The Meaderses are quiet people. The typical Meaders can go in the woods

PLATE 93   A perfect face for a jug, but that's not his face.

for six months and never speak to anyone and be happy," he remarked. Emory is definitely more Jones than Meaders. But he does love pottery. As we talked in his home, sixty-one sets of funny-looking eyes looked down on us from a shelf that holds Jones's collection of face jugs.

"I tell people who are interested in starting a pottery collection that pottery is like heroin," Jones said. "You may start with a little pot now and then, and pretty soon you're addicted to the hard stuff." Mostly, it seems, Jones is addicted to having fun. A few examples of his sense of humor:

- Jones wrote a newspaper column saying he didn't think it was right for Sarah Palin to run for vice president of the United States. "If we let people from Alaska run for office," he said, "before you know it, there'll be people from Hawaii and New Mexico wanting to run." One reader took Jones seriously and complained to the newspaper.
- He advocated changing Georgia's state bird from the brown thrasher to the chicken. "What's a brown thrasher ever done for the state?" he wanted to know. The chicken is big business.
- A lot of people have conversation pieces in their homes, but very few build covered bridges in their yards. Jones did. Its only pur-

pose, other than sparking conversation and providing a place for graffiti, is to house a 1986 Ford F-150 pickup, with forty-two thousand actual miles on the clock, that belonged to his uncle Howard.

"Jones obviously loves storytelling," said Billy Chism, a longtime friend and the former editor and publisher of the *White County News*, which published many of Jones's tongue-in-cheek columns: "You can call Emory up and ask him to go to lunch, and he'll tell you three stories before you hang up. That's just in his nature. He has to tell a story just to say hello."

Emory Mitchell Jones was born on May 7, 1950, in the old Downey Hospital in Gainesville, Georgia, and was taken home to Banks County, Georgia, where his father grew up. The Joneses were planning to settle for good in that rural county; in fact, Emory's father was building a house there for his young family when tragedy changed everything.

Dennis Jones and some of his friends and relatives had been blasting out a well on the new homeplace when Bill Griffin, a friend from nearby Lula, went down into the well to remove loose rocks. A short time later, others at the top saw that Griffin had passed out at the bottom of the well, which at the time was about thirty feet deep. They knew he had been sick at work that day, and they thought his passing out was due to sickness. Jones went down after him.

"He took a rope," Emory said, "and put it behind Mr. Griffin's shoulders and looked up at Leonard Jones and my mother and asked, 'How do you think I should tie this knot?' And he just fell over." Both men died. Emory was eleven months old.

The men were using a gas-powered blower to force dust and fumes out of the well, but the blower's exhaust pipe was defective. It had rusted off, causing carbon monoxide to flow back into the well.

After his father's death, Emory and his mother moved to live with his granddaddy, Wiley Meaders, oldest of the Meaders potters of White County, on a farm connected to the old Meaders home place and pottery shop in the Mossy Creek section of White County. But it was a good walk from where the school bus picked up children. Granddaddy didn't want his grandson walking that far, so he built another house close to the road.

"Granddaddy had made a little money in the chicken business," Jones said, "so he built this brick ranch house and spent five thousand dollars on it. People came from all over to see that five-thousand-dollar house."

Jones also spent a lot of time at the home of his aunt and uncle, Lenore and Howard Chambers, in nearby Clermont, Georgia. "I just loved being out in the pasture with Uncle Howard, feeding the cows and chickens, going to cow sales, and stuff like that."

In fact, Emory Jones the little boy thought he was going to be a farmer until he "realized there was a lot of work in it." So Emory Jones the teenager found other opportunities in agriculture. At White County High School, he did about everything that could be done in the Future Farmers of America (FFA) chapter. He showed cattle and pigs. He gave speeches. He served as chapter president and state secretary. He even received the American Farmer Degree, the highest degree given by FFA.

He told stories, too, of course. "I think I've always told stories," he said. "Even in high school, I enjoyed public speaking. I'm not saying I was good at it. I would just get up and tell stories. You can only talk to one person at a time when giving a speech. That set me at ease."

FFA also afforded him a trip to England through its Work Exchange Abroad program. He worked for four months on a farm in the county of Herefordshire, where Hereford cattle originated in the mid-1700s. His first day on the job, the farmer, whose name coincidentally was Hereford, assigned him a chore he didn't quite understand. "I don't know if he was messing with me or not, but the first day I put on work clothes and went out to work, he said this: 'Go get a spanner [a wrench], go out to the lorry [the truck], look under the bonnet [the hood], and check the petrol transport [the fuel line] for stoppage [a leak].'

"I didn't have a clue," Jones said. "I went to England because I thought we wouldn't have a language barrier. The other FFA folks who went to Germany and France dealt with people who spoke perfect English."

After high school, Jones spent a year goofing off, he admitted to it, at Abraham Baldwin Agricultural College (ABAC) in Tifton, Georgia. "I had a grade point average of 1.4 and a [draft] lottery number of thirty-four," he said. He loved airplanes better than school, and flying better than marching, so he spent his next four years in the US Air Force.

Even in the service, Jones used his storytelling talents to win and entertain friends. "I remember sitting up on the top bunk and people coming in and me telling stories from back home," he said. "I read correspondents' columns to the boys from New York and Chicago: 'So and So is visiting So and So.' I made up a character named Wayne, and a lot of Wayne was Emory. People always wanted me to tell a story or a joke."

Jones emerged from the military a changed, more mature man. He entered the University of Georgia, where he majored in agriculture journalism and graduated with a 3.9 grade point average, considerably better than his 1.4 at ABAC.

After college, in 1976, Jones landed the perfect job for someone who likes to write, shoot the bull with people, and travel. He went to work in the public relations department at Gold Kist, Inc. "It was a great job, a great company, like family, and I had a company car, making ten thousand a year. I just went around interviewing farmers, taking pictures, doing stories." At Gold Kist in Atlanta, he met his love and soul mate, Judy Gee, whom he married in 1978.

The Joneses lived in Atlanta for twenty-seven years before they eventually bought their getaway cabin, as Emory calls it, on Yonah Mountain in White County. "I told a Realtor that I want a place where I can run around the house naked if I want to." And when they were shown the house on Yonah, they knew this eventually would be home. "We hadn't even been in the house," Jones said, "and Judy said, 'We'll take it.'"

For several years, the couple spent their weekdays in Atlanta and their weekends on the mountain. Then, in 2000, they moved to White County permanently, and Emory commuted to Atlanta for the next three years. "I didn't hate Atlanta," he said, "but it was a tremendous relief getting out of Atlanta."

Emory Jones retired from the Atlanta job in 2003 and started his own ad agency, working out of his White County home. Today, he is anything but retired and rocking on the back porch. He's always working on a project, a documentary film, a book, a column, a speech, anything that involves telling stories. Whatever he's doing at home, his fifteen-year-old cat, Sylvester, the only cat in the county that can chase a German shepherd up a tree, will be at his side. "I never liked cats until Sylvester showed up one day and stayed," Jones said.

And Judy was there, too, unless she was at work at Yonah Mountain Treasures, a store north of Cleveland that sold everything from pottery to puzzles. "It's been an adventure being married to Emory," she said, standing

PLATE 94   Emory in his time machine

behind the counter of the store, which since has closed. No, she said, she doesn't have her husband's creativeness. "We don't have time for both of us to have that talent. It takes all our time to keep up with his ideas. Sometimes we don't see eye to eye on how to sell things. He's the relationship person. He gets out there and talks and talks. I'm not. I'm going to be over here doing the bookkeeping part of it."

But Judy Jones sells herself short on creativeness. For Emory's fiftieth birthday, she had twenty-two women and two men dress up as Dolly Parton for a party she threw in his honor. Said Emory, "I missed most of it because I passed out when twenty-four Dolly Parton look-alikes yelled *SURPRISE!*"

One strange piece birthed by the man with the snowy-white hair and beard and the sleepy blue eyes used to sit uncomfortably in the middle of the Yonah Mountain store. It was Emory Jones's time machine. "I was kind of concerned about the time machine," Judy said, smiling. "I didn't know if that was going to work out. But he did it." Yep, he did it, all right. He did it with the help of the late Ludlow Porch, a radio personality known throughout Southern Appalachia for his slow, down-home voice and humorous stories.

"I asked him if he would help me write a history book that involved a time machine," Jones said. "What do I have to do?" Porch asked. "First, you have to tell me what a time machine looks like." Porch said, "Give me a week."

PLATE 95   *Zipping Through Georgia . . .* one of Jones's books

This time machine, Porch decided, should consist of two johnboats, one turned upside down on top of the other and held together by four cedar posts. It requires photos of John Wayne and Dolly Parton and is powered by a goat running on a treadmill and facing a basket filled with overripe rutabagas with an "ovulating" fan on the back to blow away the pixie dust. It's operated by the Fleebish system. "We started with Fleebish One, worked up to Fleebish Eight, and decided to settle on the Fleebish Seven," Jones said. "The only difference was the Eight had a horn, and Seven didn't have a horn."

Jones built the full-size, workable model, named the USS *Fred MacMurray*, and equipped it with two rocking chairs from a Cracker Barrel restaurant. "This is the only time machine in Georgia that's publicly operated," Jones quipped. "We could afford permits for only intrastate travel. We charge just a hundred thousand dollars a year, but you don't have to pay until you get back." Customers need only to show proof of insurance and furnish their own goat, which must get the treadmill up to White Max–warp speed, which is three miles per hour.

The result of it all was a book written by Jones and a recording of the story narrated by Jones and Porch. It's titled: *Zipping Through Georgia . . . On a Goat-Powered Time Machine with Ludlow Porch and a Parrot Named Pete*, or *ZTGOAGPTMWLPAAPNP*, for short. Jones read the entire book to Porch, who was in declining health, and the radio man responded, "This ranks right up there with *The Grapes of Wrath* and some other book I read one time."

At first glance, some people think it's a children's book, but it's really for adults with a sense of humor and a love for Georgia history. "The history is very real," Jones said. "We tried to go back to 1733 and see Oglethorpe land on the coast of Georgia, but we didn't set the hob knob right and the first time we go out, we land on top of Stone Mountain in 1920, when they're doing the carving."

The machine also visits Kennesaw, Georgia, where the time travelers saw Yankees steal the Confederates' train *The General* during the American Civil War. They witnessed, among other events, Jefferson Davis, president of the Confederacy, being captured in Irwinville, Georgia; and even the Goat Man clopping through Royston, Georgia.

"We had a lot of fun with the book," Jones said. "Some people get it; some people don't."

Billy Chism said he liked the audio version better than the book. "The audio really gets into the characters, whether it was Emory talking or Ludlow Porch talking," he said. "Emory had all these different voices that he would project, but the whole thing was so full of tomfoolery that he tickled himself doing it, and it came through in the audio."

Said Arnold Dyer, Jones's closest friend for fifty-eight years, "He's as full of crap as a Christmas turkey. But he's sincere. I'm pretty much in awe of Emory."

Awesome may well describe everything Jones accomplished before and after retirement. He was one of a hundred people chosen to photograph rural America for a book titled *Country USA*; he and a White County historian, the late Shirley McDonald, published a book called *White County 101*, about things to do, know, and love about the county; he also wrote a book, and, with videographer David Greear, produced a video titled *Distance Voices: The Story of the Nacoochee Valley Indian Mound*, which brings to life the story of a prehistoric Indian burial mound in the county, its builders, and the valley that spawned it; he turned out *Heart of a Co-op*, a book on the history of Habersham Electric Membership Corporation (HEMC), with sponsorship from HEMC; and he wrote the script for *Experience North-*

east Georgia, a recorded guide, narrated by the late artist John Kollock, to seventy-five places to visit in the region.

More recently, Jones wrote a novel, *The Valley Where They Danced*, a story based on a legend about a medical doctor who moved to White County from middle Georgia after World War I and married a local woman. The book, which has been well received, captures the dialects, words, and sayings of the era, generational knowledge that eventually will be lost. Thanks to Jones's versatility, the book became a play, first performed in June 2017 at Piedmont College in Demorest, Georgia.

Jones's latest project is a film documentary of the old Tallulah Falls Railroad, which operated in the Northeast Georgia Mountains from 1854 until 1961. With David Greear as videographer, the documentary features local people as narrators, most of them from nearby Rabun County.

Emory Jones isn't done yet. His plans include writing a book called *The Well*, about the accident in which his father died; a sequel to *The Valley Where They Danced*; and another screenplay and maybe starting another business, now that Yonah Treasures has closed. What kind of business? The Joneses aren't sure yet.

One of her husband's favorite sayings, Judy Jones said, is "It's something all the time." If Jones is not collecting pottery (he has reduced his collection from about five hundred pieces to half that) or working on a book or a documentary or a speech or a satirical column for the newspaper, you might find him taking one of his kinfolks to the doctor or running an errand for a friend. It's not unusual to hear a good word about Emory Jones. "He's always thinking about somebody else and doing for somebody else," his wife said.

Deep down, said Chism, his former editor, Jones is just a good guy. "And because of that, he can't help but do good things and write good things. That's where it all comes from: There's an inner goodness about him once you get past all that humor."

But don't think that anyone will get past all that wit. It's in Jones's nature to conjure up humor when it's appropriate. Sometimes, of course, conjuring isn't needed. Circumstances themselves are often enough for a laugh. Take, for example, the time Dyer was accompanying Jones on a flight from North Georgia to Tifton, Georgia. Jones was the pilot and Dyer was the sole passenger. But after a while in the air, Jones said he felt sick and might throw up any minute. He asked Dyer to take over.

"Just keep that little airplane on the control board level, and we'll be all right," he told his friend. "Well, we got close to the airport in Tifton," Dyer said, "and I said, 'Emory, you either got to puke, jump out, or we're going to crash, because I ain't landing this thing.'" "Ah, I feel better now," Jones said, and took over after faking his friend into believing he was ill.

When you're with Emory Jones, his wife said, "you're always laughing. He gets in so many situations. Sometimes you can't believe that one person could get in that situation and then get out." And nearly every one of those situations has been turned into a story of some kind.

It might be the story going around that the state planned to dig up Yonah Mountain, move it to Atlanta, and put a lake in its place. Have you heard that one? Let Emory Jones tell it to you some time. He will certainly oblige.

Passing Down Memories

The story of author Dori Sanders

DORI SANDERS had been a reader, "a deep reader," she says, all her life, but she'd never been a serious writer. In the late 1980s, however, she knew it was time to write her own books. She wanted to leave something for her nieces and nephews, she says, "because I know when my generation passes, this farm will pass out of our family."

Her father purchased a farm—at least part of one—in rural Filbert, South Carolina, about 1915, before he married. He had passed by the land of sandy soil many times in his horse and buggy, on his way to the two-room elementary school where he was principal, and thought it would be ideal for farming. Dori and her nine siblings grew up on this land, one of the oldest African American farms in the region. And her father was right: It was great for farming, for growing peaches and okra and corn and tomatoes to feed a family and to provide produce to sell to customers from a stand alongside Highway 321.

Dori Sanders sits in a straight-back chair in her sister's house, about four miles from the Filbert farm, and talks about her family, her childhood, and how she envisioned the story line of her first book. The first idea drove by right in front of her one day while she was sitting at that farm stand, waiting for customers. A funeral procession eased by, and a little black girl waved to her. "She waved a little sweeping wave from an open window, and I thought about that little hand. It was as though the little girl was trying to catch sadness itself out of the very air because she brought her hand in like this," Sanders says, cupping her hand and drawing it in toward her heart. "See, I was a reader, a reader, a reader. My daddy said that if you read, it teases your intellectual curiosity."

Later that same day, down the highway comes another funeral procession, and Sanders watches a white woman dab daintily at her tears with a white laced handkerchief. She was riding in a Bentley. The little girl was in an old car. "And I wondered what would happen if that little girl wound up with that woman," Sanders says. So, in her imagination, she pulled the black girl out of the car and made her ten years old. She pulled the white woman out of her Bentley, "and didn't give her no age, because in South Carolina on the farm, women don't tell age. They say you tell your age, you tell everything."

That first novel, *Clover*, is the story of a ten-year-old black girl in South Carolina named Clover whose father, the principal of the local elementary school, marries a white woman, Sara Kate. Just hours later, the father is killed in an automobile accident, leaving Clover with a stepmother she hardly knows in a community that's foreign to her.

For her book's characters, Sanders watched real people, including those who rode by the farm stand. Some of them were the customers. She wrote down what they said and how they said it, sometimes while they stood at the stand, because she was afraid she'd forget their words. One woman, bless her heart, lectured Sanders for killing a black widow spider. "Didn't you read *Charlotte's Web*?" she scolded. The woman became a character in the book. Sanders also threw in some relatives, friends, and a few drunks and crazy people.

The novel, published in 1990, was a huge success. *Clover* won the Lillian Smith Award for Southern literature that enhances racial awareness and was recommended reading for classrooms across the country. *The New York Times Book Review* called the story "very much the genuine item"—no surprise to Sanders, since she used real people for her characters. *The Washington Post Book World* said the book "sews these family scenes together like a fine quilt maker." In 1997, *Clover* became a made-for-TV movie, "and that," Sanders says, "was a great honor."

Sanders has been a popular speaker and panelist at writers' conferences and other gatherings ever since *Clover* hit the bookstores. She even spoke at universities in Denmark, and she was one of four judges one year for the Robert F. Kennedy Book Award.

She is independent and self-confident, just as her father wanted her to be, but she is also engaging and charming. It's her vitality, her enthusiasm, her wit that attract people to her. And you never know what she will say.

Sanders loves farming, food, and life itself. And, unlike most contemporary writers, she writes of farm life from experience. She knows how to milk cows, how to grow peaches, how to harvest row crops. She knows about hog killings. She knows rural life itself because she has lived it.

Sanders, it is obvious, revered her father. He was stern, strict, disciplined. "It was work, work, work," she says. "Sunrise, sunset, work, work, work. I would say my father was a man for all seasons because he always had something to do." But he was a good man, she adds quickly, someone who believed every child, black or white, should have books to read and an opportunity to be successful in life.

Her father also believed in giving back to the community. He sent his children when a neighbor needed help and wouldn't allow them to accept money for their work. "If the farmer over there happens to be white, or black, you go help them," Sanders says. "Didn't matter. You didn't have to go get anyone. That's the way it was."

Dori Sanders wasn't much for sitting in a classroom learning arithmetic; her vivid imagination was always taking her to foreign places, places she had read about in books. "I was a deep reader," she says again. She read the classics. Hawthorne. Shakespeare. Homer. She talks about books with passion and expression, her voice rising and falling, almost singing at times. Occasionally she takes a breath. Words fascinate her, and her words fascinate whoever is listening.

"Imagine growing up in the country," she says, her eyes widened. "No electricity, but all those books, the classics, all those great writers. Someone asked me, 'So you grew up with the classics?' Of course, I did. What kind of books did you grow up with?' All these wonderful books, and my father had all those books."

As a young woman, reading, working, and cooking mostly consumed Sanders's life. There wasn't much else to do. "The little town of Filbert,"

Sanders writes in a note at the end of *Clover*, "consisted of a general store, a peach packing shed, a cotton gin, two churches, two schools, and a train depot. I can close my eyes and picture that store, with the well-worn wooden floorboards that creaked, particularly the candy section where generations of children had shifted from one foot to the other while trying to decide between B-B Bats, Johnny cakes, and candy sticks of all colors. The smells of cinnamon buns, coffee, and onions mingled with those of cotton seed, Octagon Soap, and fertilizers. Wintertime was best of all, when the aroma of kerosene and burning oak from the big black stove made a pungent potpourri."

After *Clover*, Sanders wrote another novel, *Her Own Place*, published in 1994. It traces the life of Mae Lee Barnes, an African American from rural South Carolina who buys a farm, works it, raises a family, and moves to town. Protagonist Mae Lee, Sanders says, "represents all women who struggled after World War II."

These days, Sanders is a caregiver. She looks after members of the family who call and say, "Oh, Dori, please, can you come and stay an hour over here?"

PLATE 96   Dori on her tractor

or "Can you take this person to the doctor?" She's helping out relatives and old people she knows in the neighborhood. But she's still called on to speak, and on the day of this interview, she was trying to find time to read and critique *Their Eyes Were Watching God*, a 1937 novel by African American writer Zora Neal Hurston. Sanders is on the program at The Big Read in Low Country South Carolina in a couple of weeks, where she "will explore how Hurston infused the characters and their world in the novel with reality and how her descriptions, meanings, and observations mirror truth."

Sanders probably wouldn't have said it that way—it's a bit fancy—but she knows about infusing characters with reality. Decades before *Clover*, she and her siblings gathered at a place they called "the storytelling rock," where they shared stories of all sorts. And when she became a serious writer, she knew, from experience, that storytelling is all about being real, even in fiction.

And that is Dori Sanders: a storyteller, yes, but first a simple farmer from Filbert, South Carolina, someone who still tills the land with her brother Orestus; who still sits at the farm stand during season selling peaches and okra and other produce; who still puts her family's needs before her need to write. She's well-known now. Outside of her family and friends, only her regular customers knew her on the day those two funeral processions passed by her farm stand, triggering a brilliant idea for a novel.

Sometimes, she says, she has "felt like a buzz above the farming," now that she's an author and popular speaker. But then she hears a sharp command from brother Orestus: "Dori, get your tractor over here." And, suddenly, she's a farmer again.

Dr. C. B. Skelton
of Winder, Georgia

Practicing medicine and sharing humorous stories

IT WAS MIDMORNING on the day before his eighty-ninth birthday, and Doc Skelton was sitting in his living room with a hot towel across his face to soothe his weak blue eyes. He'd been up for several hours, watering his tomato plants, tending his okra, piddling.

"Are you not going to get dressed?" his wife, Fran, asked, noticing that he had not changed his dirty shirt after working outside or combed his hair, even though he was expecting company. "No," he said, "I'm going to be dressed just like this." "Well, are you going to zip up your pants?" asked Fran.

The scene sort of describes Charles Bryant "Doc" Skelton of Winder, Georgia, a man comfortable in his own skin, even if it's dirty. No use pretending, no use putting on airs, no use dressing up for an interview. "I'm just me," he said later, during the interview. "I always have been just me." But just being Doc Skelton is quite a story.

Myles Godfrey, a longtime mutual friend and owner of *The Barrow Eagle* newspaper until he sold it, is well familiar with Doc Skelton, his story, and his storytelling. "People who know Dr. Skelton's background are aware that he is an exceptional person," he said. "He finished high school, earned a college degree, and completed a tour in the Army, all before he turned twenty-one. Then he was accepted at Emory Medical School, graduated, and became a doctor when he was twenty-five. All that proves to everyone he is special, except to him. He does not think of himself that way at all."

Doc Skelton is a man of many interests and talents. He is a Bible teacher, local missionary, speaker for Gideon's International, singer, autoharp player, humorist, community leader, family man, philosopher, and optimist, but most people know him as an engaging storyteller. In this role, he's written songs, poems, and five books, in addition to the many stories he's famous for sharing with friends and family. Godfrey remembers the day his daughter, Isabel, came home talking about Doc's speaking to her school's sixth-grade class. "He told stories, recited poetry, played the autoharp, and sang," he said. "The kids were enthralled." Isabel still remembered Doc's stories and one particular poem five years later.

So what does it take to become a good storyteller? Doc struggled a little with his answer, not because he doesn't know, but because storytelling comes so naturally to him, it's hard to put into words. "Well," he said, finally, "a fellow has to know what he's talking about, and yet you need to be able to embellish without it looking like embellishment." Many of his stories come from decades of doctoring in Barrow County, Georgia, and don't need a lot of embellishment. Other stories go back to his childhood, back when he was plowing a mule named Blackie. Anybody who ever plowed a mule knows that you talk to the animal as though he were human. And sometimes you use bad words to get his attention. But one morning, Doc harnessed Blackie and then told him, "Blackie, I'm a Christian now, and I'm not going to talk bad to you anymore." Blackie was not impressed.

"That mule was so cantankerous and my plow caught on so many roots, I could not hold my temper or my tongue," Doc said. "Before I had plowed two rounds, every evil word I knew had come out. I couldn't believe my ears. 'Christians don't talk that way,' I thought. Frustration, anger, disappointment, and doubt were my emotions of the moment. Every day, I vowed to do better, and every day, I failed. Fearing the 'rod of correction,' I dared not tell Mother or Daddy. Months passed, but the problem remained. Finally, taught by a mule, the truth dawned on me. One can only live the Christian life in God's strength—never in our own strength. It didn't hurt that we finally sold Blackie."

In his earliest years, Charles Bryant Skelton thought his first name was Red, and this was long before comedian Red Skelton became famous. "My hair was red, and I was [called] Red from birth," he said, chatting over coffee

PLATE 97   Doc as a happy child

at the Skelton home near Winder. "My first report card in 1931 came out as Red Skelton. They tell me that my teacher asked me, 'What is your name?' And I answered, 'Well, my name is Red, but sometimes they call me Charles.'"

This healthy, red-haired boy was born at nearly fourteen pounds, the tenth of a dozen children sired by Newton Anderson Skelton. Five of the children had been born to the former Ethel White, and after her death, Doc's father married the former Rosa L. Turner, who produced seven more. Doc was her fifth, born in 1926.

Three years later, the Great Depression descended on the Skeltons' family home and on the nation. Being a man of compassion, Newton Skelton had signed bank notes for a couple of men who later went bankrupt, leaving his family broke. The Skeltons eventually lost their home and became tenant farmers, moving from rented farm to rented farm and breaking new ground with a mule-drawn plow. Doc Skelton became a plowhand at eight years old and once plowed land that would become part of the Hartsfield-Jackson Atlanta International Airport. His father worked as a streetcar conductor, and money was tight. "I didn't ask my dad for a penny to buy a pencil with," Doc said. "I'd go through the school yard and I'd find a pencil somewhere."

Neither would he request a penny to buy candy, but he learned to use poetry and boyish guile to sometimes get it for free at a little store close to his home. "I had not learned to write," he said, "but I made up my first rhyme and put a tune to it and sang it to them: 'Charlie, he's a good little boy / Charlie, he's a dandy / Charlie, he's a good little boy / And he likes striped candy.'" He got his candy sometimes, "but most of the time," he said, "they were as poor as we were." So Doc Skelton got his start in poetry out of necessity.

Doc idolized his brother Jimmy, the sixth of the dozen little Skeltons. Jimmy was a great athlete and a man of faith. And when he told his parents he wanted to be a missionary to Africa, Doc declared he wanted to be a medical missionary in Bolivia. "I had no idea where Bolivia was," he said. "In a way, I was copying my brother, but I also knew in my heart I had to become a doctor."

Doc graduated from high school at age fifteen and then worked his way through Mercer University in Macon, Georgia. He had set his sights on medicine, but with World War II raging, the US Army had a different vision for him. At that time, the Navy was educating men for different types of professional work, including medicine, through a program called the V-12. Doc had tried to join the program, but a minor deformity, one he couldn't explain graphically to members of the Women's Missionary Union, disqualified him, and the Navy said no.

The Army, however, said yes, even though Doc had already been accepted to medical school. "I was supposed to be ineligible for the draft, but the Army guy said, 'You're in the Army now.'" It was ironic, he said, that he was not qualified to attend school in the Navy, but he was qualified to lead an Army platoon into combat.

At the encouragement of his captain in basic training, Doc ended up in Officers Candidate School. He had gotten a college degree at eighteen, and it was his duty to become an officer and a leader, the captain said. So Doc completed OCS and became an infantry officer. He was training a platoon of men to invade the islands of Japan, but then US planes dropped atom bombs on Hiroshima and Nagasaki, and Doc Skelton became expendable. He was sent to Europe to lead a crew that traveled from little burg to little burg, locating the graves of American servicemen in France, Germany, Austria, and part of Italy. A few days shy of two years of service, he was discharged and returned home.

Turned out, the Navy had done Doc a favor by not accepting him. The program that would have trained him for a career in medicine had folded; he would have been left with no outside financial support after two years in med school. But the GI Bill had passed Congress, and Doc hitched a full ride as an Army veteran. His education at the Emory University School of Medicine was paid for. "I am probably the most blessed man who ever existed," he said more than once.

While in med school, he married Nora Louisa Hart, who in rapid order would present him with five daughters. He had the perfect squelch for people who kidded him about living in a house with six women: "If the Lord thinks a home needs a man in it, he sends one."

Asked how many babies he delivered as a family-practice doctor, he said, "I didn't keep up with the number, but when I was an intern and assigned to OB in Louisiana, on one occasion I signed twenty-five birth certificates in twenty-four hours. We didn't have room for all of them. We put them butt to butt on the beds and sent them out the next day, which was unheard of at that time."

In 1953, the Skeltons moved to Winder, where Doc began his family practice on July 5. For the next forty-two and a half years (he retired the last day of 1995), Skelton was Doc to everybody in the county. At one time, he did it all: orthopedics, surgery, obstetrics, and even anesthesia. He made house calls and developed relationships that have lasted for decades.

"I pledged to my patients that whatever time you need is what time I'll give you," Doc said. "My office girls didn't like that philosophy that much. If I had a patient in the hospital that I was worried about at night, I'd get up out of bed and go to the hospital and do everything I knew to do. And once I'd done everything I knew to do, I'd go home and go to bed and not worry anymore."

One year, during a severe flu epidemic that nearly paralyzed the town, he arrived home for dinner about ten at night. He was tired and irritable and feeling sorry for himself. "Nora met me at the door, not with dinner, but with a list of three more house calls to make that night," he said. "Disgustedly, I complained, 'By the time these are finished, it will be eleven o'clock and the train should be coming through town. Maybe I should run in front of that train and let you get a husband who will stay home with you sometimes.' Nora replied in her sweetest voice, 'Honey, if you're going to do that, please take the old car.' "

Nora Skelton died in 1987, and Doc later married "Penny" Emory Morris, a widow. Penny died in 2011, and in 2013, he married Fran Peeples Lynch, whose husband had died several years earlier. "I've had three absolutely fabulous ladies in my life," Doc said. "I didn't strike out once." He describes Fran as "Fran-tabulous." But he didn't stop there: "Fran is very pretty; she's one of the most capable people I'd ever seen; she's energetic and she helps *everybody*." Theirs is one of the city's love stories.

Doc enjoys a good love story, obviously, and in one of the five books he

PLATE 98   Doc and Fran Skelton at home

has written, *A Simple Seller of Noodles*, he tells what he calls "the greatest love story I've ever heard of." It's the true story of SamSan, a refugee from Cambodia who, along with nine members of his family, was sponsored by the local First Baptist Church, Doc's church at the time. Doc chaired the sponsoring committee. After several years of menial labor, SamSan opened a restaurant in Winder.

Today, Doc Skelton spends considerable time in front of his computer. He might be writing one of the poems that he emails to several hundred recipients every week. For years, Myles Godfrey published Doc's poems in *The Barrow Eagle*.

"When I was first approached about printing Doc's rhymes," he said, "I was very hesitant. I was aware that every community is awash with amateur poets, and I feared a deluge of submissions from folks who would expect publication. Then I read the samples I had been given. Some were inspirational, with messages that would resonate. Some were sad, but many were funny—no, *hilarious*. I decided to print them."

Here are some of Doc Skelton's favorite humorous stories. And they're all true. Some of them were adapted, with permission, from his book titled Dirty Laundry Don't Take No Doctor's Orders.

Almost everyone called him "Snake," not Lonel, his real name. It must have been because of his thin face and somewhat beady brown eyes. He worked on the construction crew building the Winder-Barrow Hospital and then in the hospital for many years as an orderly. One day, Snake entered a patient's room to give a "four H" enema, which meant one that should be "high, hot, a heck of a lot, and the patient should hold it."

The Director of Nurses knew both Snake's whereabouts and his assigned mission, but she needed to speak to him. She felt her message for Snake could not wait until his task was complete, so she went to the patient's room to have the conversation. We had an intercom system, but for some reason, she chose not to use it.

The doors to our patients' rooms were heavy enough to be virtually soundproof, so our intrepid Director backed up against the door just enough to open a tiny port for sound to pass through, but not enough for her or anyone else to see inside the room. This accomplished, she called out, "SNAKE!"

Meanwhile, at that precise moment, Snake had inserted the enema tube into the patient's backside and begun the flow to get his business done. But with the sound of the woman's voice calling "Snake," seemingly in the room, our patient gave a startled jump and pulled out the enema tube. The contents of the enema bucket, as well as those emitted from the patient, were strewn all over the patient, the bed, and assorted parts of the room.

Doc is not bashful in telling about his "minor deformity," the one that kept him out of the Navy, but received no sympathy from the Army, which drafted him. He told this story during an interview:

The wind had blown the top off of our outhouse, and during that time, I had to go real bad. And I had this deformity. I could stand and pee over tall buildings. My brother Jim wouldn't let me in, and I was about to bust, and I warned him and warned him. I don't think but maybe one or two drops of that yellow liquid had come over the top when Jim busted out of that outhouse, and I forgot having to go. I had to run for my life.

Jim caught me—he was a great athlete and I was slow and clumsy—and he had me down ready to hit me. And then he said, "Well, I should have unlocked the door." That was the kind of guy he was.

Another story is about Lawrence, a grinning, mischievous, happy-go-lucky, rotund kid of about seventy years who appeared to be the kind of fellow who could, and would, have fun at a funeral. Even when he became very ill, he never lost his sense of humor. He came into the office one day with an obviously bad cold.

"Lawrence," I asked, "how did you ever manage to catch such a terrible cold?"

Lawrence grinned. "Well, Doc, I really don't know for certain how I got it, but I think it might be because of these cool nights we've been a-havin' here lately. You know how cold it's been a-gettin' every night these past few weeks, especially early in the mornin'. Well, at that time, I ain't been sleepin' under nothin' but one thin woman."

Then there was Mrs. Sosebee who had been diagnosed as suffering from obsessive-compulsive personality disorder with a fixation on extreme cleanliness. This obsession caused her to sometimes wash her hands more than two hundred times a day, and she often required treatment for a skin disorder brought on by the excessive handwashing.

On this particular visit to my office, Mrs. Sosebee's massively swollen, red, and feverish right leg loomed as a problem. She had blood clots in that leg. But she refused hospitalization and told me, "No! I am not going to any hospital. You will have to find some way to treat me at home."

"I will try to treat you at home," I said, "but you must stay in bed; and I mean *in the bed* to the extent you have all your meals brought to the bed and use a pot at your bedside. Use the remote control for the TV or get someone else to change the channels for you." She was to receive complete bed rest and to keep her leg elevated.

The following Tuesday when Mrs. Sosebee dutifully showed up in my office at the appointed time, it seemed perfectly obvious she had not been in bed. Her leg appeared more swollen than before and the redness and heat had increased. My unhappiness with the entire situation obviously showed. I began to tell her of my displeasure until Mrs. Sosebee gently patted my arm to interrupt me. She explained in the gentlest, softest, sweetest voice, "But, Doctor Skelton, surely you are smart enough to know that dirty laundry don't take no doctor's orders." Her logic overwhelmed me. This lady considered cleanliness the most important thing in the world, even worth the risk of death. Her treatment continued at home, because she still gave me no other option. Mrs. Sosebee got well with no further problems and no permanent damage that we could recognize. What do we doctors know?

Then there was Miss Ocie, a teacher for more than fifty years, who fell at a PTA meeting one night and later complained of severe hip pain. X-rays showed a displaced fracture of the femoral neck in her left hip. An orthopedic surgeon from Athens, Georgia, was called in to perform surgery in the local hospital, where Miss Ocie could be closer to relatives and friends.

Following the surgery, Miss Ocie was not doing her prescribed exercises to build up her muscles. Weeks of no progress turned into a month. As we were about to begin the second month in which she had not taken one single step, it appeared obvious that some type of action must be taken now, and it was my duty to take it.

One Sunday morning, I walked into her room and made my stern statement: "Miss Ocie, the doctors and nurses have done what we can do for you. Your hip is nailed in exceptionally good position, and X-rays show healing is taking place. Two months have passed, and you have not taken one step. You do not seem to be working hard at the exercises we devised for you and are not gaining the strength we had expected." My spiel continued: "I cannot walk for you. The nurses cannot walk for you. In fact, whether or not you ever take another step is strictly between you and The Man Upstairs." Having said my piece, I whirled and left the room, not waiting for a reply. Miss Ocie turned to her sister, Miss Marie, and blustered, "I thought we were on the top floor."

Doc Skelton has an amazing ability to make most anything rhyme. "Rhyming comes easily for me," he said. So, when someone sent him a joke about Grandpa, Doc turned it into a poem:

When Grandpa Croaks

The door to the bedroom was slightly ajar
as Grandpa settled down for his nap.
Lately, it seemed he couldn't go far
before he ran plumb out of zap.

Suddenly, wide open, the bedroom door bolted.
From his nap, poor Grandpa was jolted.
"Grandpa! Grandpa! Make a noise like a frog,"
came a voice, an excited grandson.
"Go away, Son," Grandpa said in a fog,
"we'll talk when my nap is done."
The door hardly closed behind this one,
when it opened real fast like before.
This time, another eager grandson
said as he raced through the door,
"Grandpa! Grandpa! Make a noise like a frog!"
But Grandpa lay there like a log.
"Go away, Son! Can't you see I'm trying to sleep?"
came the voice of an irate grandfather.
As the boy from the bedroom started to creep,
"That's my boy! Now don't be a bother."
A third time, the door was flung open wide,
and in comes his favorite granddaughter.
Even Grandpa admitted he had too much pride
and loved her more than he ought to.
"Grandpa! Grandpa! Make a noise like a frog!"
Her sweet voice made Grandpa's mind slip a cog.
"Make a noise like a frog? Why in this world?"
asked Grandpa, his mind in a whirl.
"Papa said," came the answer from his favorite girl,
"when you croaked, we'd go to Disney World."

IN PURSUIT OF "HOBBINESS"

Eighteen Thousand
Long-Play Albums

Jerry Kendall and his record collection

JERRY KENDALL SEEMED TO BE STALLING. I had asked to see the collection of LP albums in the basement of his home, a modest, mid-1970s house situated high on a hill overlooking Lake Chatuge near Young Harris, Georgia.

For any young people not familiar with the terms, LP stands for "long playing" or "long play"; an album is a phonograph record that contains a number of songs; a phonograph record is a vinyl, microgroove disc that is played on a machine that turns at thirty-three and a third revolutions per minute. And if it hadn't been for technological advances in music presentation, your parents and/or grandparents might still be members of the Columbia Record of the Month Club, from which there seemed to be no escape short of the extinction of the product.

"Can we go down to the basement now?" I asked, again, eager to hear the story of a man obsessed with Southern gospel music, not to mention movie cowboys of yesteryear.

"Well, let me tell you about this right here," Kendall said. He'd already gone through album after album ensconced in pasteboard boxes in his living room, naming singer after singer and musician after musician, many of whom he knew personally, had met at some point, or was related to. His mother had more than 125 first cousins.

"Here's Billy Nicholson on steel guitar," he said, holding an album. "He's

PLATE 99   You can't get eighteen thousand albums in one photo; here are a few of them.

from here. Here's Jimmy Hooper. He's from here. Ken Fuller was a Methodist minister. He was here when he did this record. Now he's retired here.
Cranford Nix was from Blairsville, Georgia, and he played the banjo on a
song by the Supremes in an album called *The Supremes Sing Country, Western and Pop*. Jerry Scoggins sang the *Beverly Hillbillies* theme song, and they
made a movie in the nineties, and he sang it again. Tim Spencer was an original with the Sons of the Pioneers and wrote a bunch of songs. He published
'How Great Thou Art.' "

Kendall pointed to a photo of singing cowboy Roy Rogers hanging on
the wall, right beside a shot of Lake Chatuge before development and huge
boat slips moved in. Roy Rogers was his favorite cowboy, a humble man who
made a lot of money in movies and records, but who wasn't obsessed with
being wealthy, as cowboy Gene Autry was, Kendall said.

Finally, he consented. We could walk down to the basement.

"Just be ready for a shock," he said, reaching the door. A shock because it's
not every day that one can see a collection of *eighteen thousand* LP albums
in a three-compartment basement—yes, eighteen thousand albums: Southern gospel, cowboy, country, and other genres. Albums that fill every room,
some in boxes, some in stacks, some on shelves.

And that number does not include seven thousand 45 rpm records and several hundred 78 rpm records. Kendall also has a collection of VHS and DVD movies, mostly Westerns.

How did his wife feel about his hobby? "Well, I'd already started when we got married," Kendall said of his collection, failing to note that the collection has grown considerably since then.

Fortunately, Glynda Hayes Kendall, his wife of thirty-five-plus years, has a sense of humor. "I warned our neighbors a long time ago that if you see little black discs flying out over the lake, it's not UFOs," she said, laughing. "You can pretty much say, 'Glynda's had it.' And he's handed me one or two every now and then to flip out like a Frisbee."

Is Glynda a fan of Southern gospel music? "Not to his extent," she said, "but I enjoy it."

The obvious question arises: Does this man of thousands of records sing? Alan, the older of the Kendalls' two sons, answered that question a long time ago. "Alan was just a little thing," Glynda Kendall said, "and we would be in the car, and Jerry would start singing with the tape or something. And it would be from Alan, 'Daddy, please don't sing.' Finally, I asked him, 'Why don't you want Daddy to sing?' 'Because Daddy can't sing.'"

Fortunately, the sons, Alan, thirty-five, and Kevin, thirty, *can* sing, very well. Alan has sung with three groups: the Melody Boys Quartet of Little Rock, Arkansas; Freedom of Sevierville, Tennessee; and the Rebels Quartet, a revamp of a quartet in Florida. He has also filled in for the Chuck Wagon Gang on several occasions.

Now that he's the father of two, Alan has gone into a solo ministry, singing in churches, at fairs and festivals, concert settings, and "anybody that'll have me," he said.

Kevin sings at churches and with friends, but not professionally. But he did get to fill in a weekend for his brother as lead singer for the Rebels. Alan and Savannah were in Arizona adopting their daughter Evalee at the same time the Rebels were to sing in Florida, where Kevin lives. "I understand he did a really good job," Alan said. So it's clear that while Jerry Kendall has his albums, his sons have the voices.

Unable to find a place to sit down in the basement, we moved to the kitchen table upstairs to continue the conversation.

Jerry Bruce Kendall grew up in Towns County, Georgia, just down the road from where he lives now. All his relatives from his great-grandparents forward have lived in Towns County, "so I'm probably related to more than half the natives," he said. He never knew his father, Homer Kendall, who was killed in World War II when his Navy ship was hit by a kamikaze plane. Jerry was only two months old.

Kendall's love of Southern gospel music may be partly inherited. His mother, Velma Ree Nichols Kendall, was a fan, and after buying a record player, an RCA Victor machine, in 1950, she started her own small collection of records, mostly of Georgia-based groups: the Statesmen, the Harmoneers Quartet, Homeland Harmony, the LeFevre Trio, and the Sunshine Boys.

Kendall bought his first record when he was six years old. His grandfather had sold a calf and given him a dollar from the profit. "We were going to Gainesville, Georgia, to get shoes at Saul's downtown," he said, "and I bought my first record with that dollar." It was a record by the Statesmen Quartet. On one side was "Listen to the Bells"; on the other, "I Want to Be Ready." As you might expect, he still has that record.

He also kept his first record player, bought in 1958, when he was thirteen. It was that year that records began to pile up in the Kendall home.

Years later, when he had more money, Kendall occasionally would buy a whole box full of albums at a yard or garage sale, not knowing everything that was inside. "Sometimes you get some good ones," he said.

But he's not buying many records these days. He's even sold a few, mainly at the Grand Ole Gospel Reunion in Greenville, South Carolina. But when you've packed more than twenty-five thousand records into your home, it's hard to tell when a few are missing. Kendall pretty much stopped visiting record stores years ago, back when there were such things as record stores, because he had more music than they did.

He's been retired for several years after thirty-three years at Towns County Family and Children Services, twenty-seven as its director. He now has time to scavenge for more records, but where would he put them?

"I'm a little embarrassed about it now," he said. "What in the world was I thinking about, getting all those records? A lot of them are worth a lot of money. It's hard to know what to do. I want to sell some. My sons are into music, but they won't want all those records."

PLATE 100   A shot of Kendall's first record

As it is with other collectors, it's not about the money or the bragging rights. It's about sentimentality and memories.

Kendall can pull out a 1952 album by the Blackwood Brothers, one of his more collectible pieces, and remember just how much he enjoyed that group a few decades ago.

But he seldom plays any of his records, not because he can't find the one he wants—his basement collection is categorized and filed mostly alphabetically—it's just that he'd rather sit back and hear one of his sons sing, maybe at his church, Woods Grove Baptist Church. Music, after all, and certainly Southern gospel music, is best when it's enjoyed as a family. And that's when Jerry Kendall seems most proud: when he talks about his family.

He knows that a collection of records can be worth some money, but a collection of family memories is priceless.

Tractors and Trucks

Carl "Feel Bad" Davis

THROUGH THE KENTUCKY COMMUNITIES of Slat and Murl and Cabell and Stop, Carl Davis is known as "Feel Bad" Davis. That's because when he worked as a guard at the Lake Cumberland Boys Camp near Monticello in Wayne County, Kentucky, he'd sometimes go to work with a bad cold or the flu, and he'd let everybody know he felt bad.

"I'd set down, if I had a chance, and I'd blow, you know. Wheeew! 'I feel bad today. Boy, I feel bad,'" he says. "I done that several times, you know, and somebody just picked up on that 'feel bad' and started calling me that. I was Feel Bad Davis." His fellow workers even gave him a Feel Bad Davis cap. He doesn't have it anymore, but he's kept the name. "It's all over the county now," he says.

The one thing that makes Feel Bad Davis feel good is collecting old tractors. At last count, he owned twenty of them. His daughter, Jerrie Davis Shoemaker, explains why.

"When he first retired from working at the camp," she says, "he didn't know what to do with hisself. He talked to me and my sister and said, 'What am I going to get into to fill this void, not having to work every day?' We told him he needed to get a hobby."

Davis owned four tractors at one time, back when he was farming a lot. But then, his daughters gave him a good reason to buy more.

And buy he did. Davis not only filled the void left by not working, he

PLATE 101   Carl's tractors

and his hobby filled an entire huge barn, part of another barn, and a big shed. He also owns five trucks, three hay balers, three four-wheel wagons, and a 1925 Chrysler automobile with a honeycomb radiator. He even has a blond saddle-mare that he bred with a jack donkey, creating a blond mule. The animals are mainly to remind him of how plowing used to be done. The mare's sire, he was told, is the grandson of cowboy Roy Rogers's horse Trigger.

So why does he enjoy collecting tractors so much?

"Well," he says, almost showing the gold on his front teeth, "it just feels like I was a boy."

Carl Francis Davis was born on January 30, 1940. He grew up in Murl, a community close to Slat, where he now lives in a house he and his brother Calvin built behind their father's home. Slat is so named, Davis says, because a century or two ago people came from near and far to cut down nice, big oak trees to sawmill into boards for houses and slats for paling fences. Most of the people who remember the name Slat are gone now. But "Feel Bad" remembers.

Carl Davis farmed on his own for several years, and then he and his father farmed together on part of the forty-six acres at Slat. The Davises, like

PLATE 102   Carl with an old truck

most farmers, used mules for plowing back in the old days, but a tractor is a lot easier, Davis says.

But collecting tractors can be expensive. Davis bought a 1947 John Deere, Size D, in Canyon, Texas. Gave five hundred dollars for it. Cost him nine hundred dollars to get it hauled to Slat.

He got a better deal on a Size U, 1950 MM—that stands for Minneapolis-Moline. It had sat in a junkyard for thirty years, and Davis claimed it for forty dollars. "I got it to running," he says. In fact, last time he counted, seventeen of his twenty tractors would run.

He eventually got into raising grass-fed Texas Longhorn cattle. His herd grew from six cows and one bull to forty cows in just a few years. Why Longhorns? "Looks, mostly," he says.

But after undergoing heart surgery in 2012, Davis sold all his cattle. Today, he can plow and take care of a garden and tinker with his farm equipment, but he leaves the heavy work of cutting and baling hay to someone else. "We do it on the halves," he says. "He gets half of the hay, and I sell my half."

Our first visit with Feel Bad Davis came in the spring of 2016. We telephoned him in the summer of 2017 to get an update. Here's a portion of that conversation:

Have you bought any more tractors? "Yeah, I bought me another tractor, a 130 International" (built by International Harvester from 1956 to 1958; that makes twenty-one tractors for Davis).

Which one is your favorite tractor? "My favorite is a 1961-model Size 65 Massey Ferguson. We've had it for fifty years, and it's been all over the road. We've really done lots of work with that tractor. I just love it. It'll start and go anytime you touch it."

What about your favorite truck? "It's a '60 model Chevrolet two-ton truck that me and my daddy bought. Daddy used it till he got sick and had to quit."

Did you ever have an accident driving a tractor? "No, not bad. One time, I was trying to blow my nose, and I run out of the road and hit a culvert. But I never turned over or wrecked or nothing bad."

What have you been doing since we saw you last? "Well, lately, we've got a 127 yard sale going on. Flea market stuff. It's a big outfit in everybody's yard, nearly, all up and down that 127 highway. It goes plumb all the way to Ohio. I'm looking mostly for old tools and stuff. I hadn't found anything that I don't have."

Are you still tinkering with your trucks and tractors? "Yeah, I got six of 'em out the other day, drove them around a little and put 'em back in the barn. I'm still tinkering with them."

Are you still visiting the Kennett store and the Dairy Queen? "Yeah, I was probably at the Dairy Queen last night when you called. I loaf up there about every night. A bunch of farmers gather up there, and we talk."

What do you talk about? "We talk about farming. The other night we talked about weed killers and bush killers, how to spray weeds, Johnson grass, stuff we don't like."

Is there a tractor that you're just dying to own? "I'd like to have me a Ford tractor. I don't have one on the farm here. I need a Ford."

Jerrie Shoemaker and her sister, Janie Hicks, are still pondering what to do with the monster they helped create by suggesting their daddy get a hobby.

"Them tractors are mine and my sister's legacy," Shoemaker says. "We get to inherit all of them."

"What are you going to do with them?"

"We don't know," she says. "We've not yet decided. Sometimes we get a little aggravated and tell him we're just going to sell them all. You know, he's got quite a bit of money tied up in them tractors." But wait a minute, ladies. It might not be over.

"Have you still got the itch?" Feel Bad Davis is asked. "If you saw an old tractor in somebody's yard, one you didn't own, would you go see if you could buy it?"

"Yeah," he says without flinching. "I probably would."

Snaking Logs Through
the Kentucky Woods

Hollis Thrasher and his mules

WHEN HOLLIS THRASHER was five years old, his father would harness two mules and hand the lead reins for one to Hollis and the reins for the other to Hollis's brother, Curtis, who was six. The boys' job was to lead those stubborn animals about a mile through the woods to their grandfather's place, while their daddy drove a truck on the road to meet them.

A few years later, Hollis and Curtis were riding, not leading, the mules to Granddad's, and sometimes even farther away. And then, a few years after that, they were plowing with a mule, just like the grown-ups. "We worked those old mules every year, summer and winter," Hollis remembers.

That's because their daddy, trying to eke out a living for his growing family, would rent every old tobacco patch he heard about, even if it was just a half-acre ten miles away. That meant Hollis and Curtis, as soon as they were big enough, were riding mules bareback for ten miles, plowing and working most of the day, and then riding ten miles back home. At night, the insides of their legs were so galled, they could barely walk.

One day, Curtis, in a fit of mule-induced exasperation, said, "Hollis, when I'm grown and I get gone, I'm never going to look one of these in the butt again."

But it didn't happen that way with Hollis. "When I got out of the service and out of college," he says, "the first thing I wanted to buy myself was a pair of mules. Now, that was before a home or a car or anything. I wanted a good

PLATE 103   Hollis and his mules

pair of mules." He stresses a *good pair* because the mules his daddy owned are what Hollis calls junk. "He'd have a red one with a black one or a white one with a black one. He'd have a little one and a big one."

But Hollis Thrasher doesn't buy junk, at least not intentionally. Most of his mules stand head and shoulders above the others. He owns two blond ones, Sam and Bert, whose mamas were Belgian mares. The Belgian Heavy Draft horse can reach seventeen hands or sixty-eight inches tall, but Sam is already slightly more than eighteen hands tall. And he's not fully grown.

When his mule-buying fever first began raging, Thrasher found himself the proud owner of ten mules, but his wife, Carolyn, suggested he pare down his herd. "He sold two and bought three," she says, "and I told him he needed to work on his math." At the time of this writing, Thrasher was down to only six mules.

Elvin Hollis Thrasher was born at home on August 29, 1948, the second of seven children of Kendle and Arvella Thrasher. After living a year and a half in a chicken-coop-type house behind his parents' home, Kendle bought a 130-acre farm in Clinton County, Kentucky. A creek with the unlikely name of Ill Will ran behind the house and flowed into Dale Hollow Lake about a quarter mile away. Hollis remembers chasing minnows up and down Ill Will Creek when he was just big enough to walk.

He also remembers his daddy's unpredictable, unmatched mules. For whatever reason, when it was time to lead them, brother Curtis always got the one that was difficult. The boys and their mules had to conquer a steep hill on the way to their grandfather's farm, and the mules would get tired.

"I remember that old mule of my brother's would just stop," Thrasher says, smiling. "He couldn't get him to go. You could figure on about five minutes when he was just going to stand there, and then he'd go on. Curtis would get so mad. My brother looked that mule in the eye one day and said, 'When I get big, I'm gonna whip you.' And him six years old at the time."

"Dad would remind us, 'Boys, never trust a mule a hundred percent. He'll work for you for forty years to get a chance to kill you.'" Hollis learned the truth of that warning when he was five or six years old.

Egged on by Curtis, one day he stuck his head through a hole in the barn and continuously poked a mule with one of his mother's bean sticks. The agitated animal ran by, kicked, and plastered the boy right in the head. Hollis was out cold. "Mama said it was a good thing the mule didn't have his shoe on," Hollis says, "because it probably would have killed me."

Thrasher recalls his parents as good, hardworking people. "Mom is a good example of hard work won't hurt you," he says, "because I never knew anybody that worked harder than my mom did. She was the last one to go to bed after working out in the fields with us."

Kendle Thrasher occasionally would travel to Louisville, Kentucky, to find seasonal work while his wife stayed behind to put out the crops, cook meals, and look after the children.

Arvella was a good mother, Thrasher says, but her way of tending to the baby—and with seven children, there was always a baby—would not get the seal of approval today from children's services. She would leave it in a baby pen on the back porch and go to work chopping tobacco. But she always stayed within earshot. Today, "they would have you down in the courthouse for negligence," Thrasher says.

A good mule, a well-trained mule, Thrasher says, is one "that'll listen to you, one that's not always wanting to run off from you. He's the kind that you can take him to the woods and lay your lines down, pick up your saw, cut a tree

PLATE 104   Sign says it all.

down, and he's still standing there. You need one that you can 'whoa' at him to stop and he'll stop."

Still, even with a good mule, it pays to use caution when approaching the animal from his blind side. Thrasher didn't do that one day—he forgot to "whoa" the critter or let him know he was coming. "And just as I laid my hand on his side, he kicked me in the fat part of my leg and kicked me about ten feet backwards on the ground." Fortunately, the leg was not broken, only bruised and sore for a few days. "You know," he says, "I never did forgive that mule for that. I kept him on for two years, but I never did forgive him. I ended up selling him."

But Hollis Thrasher was not deterred. He still relies on each of his mules to be, well, maybe not his best friend, but at least a companion he can depend on when he's needed. In fact, he thinks a mule may be smarter than a horse. He says he's seen a mule in danger, such as getting a leg hung in a fence, but not stupid enough to keep pulling and squirming if he's being hurt. "A horse will tear a leg off before they quit," he says.

And a mule can learn commands if he hears them repeatedly. "Gee" and "haw" are examples, the words used to get a mule to turn right or left. "Pulling a log is the best way to teach that," Thrasher says.

It's hard to say what a mule driver is supposed to look like, but if being physically fit is part of the description, then Hollis Thrasher, now in his late sixties, looks like a mule driver. He also has the commanding voice of a drill sergeant—he was trained as one in the Army—so no mule can claim he didn't hear his instructions.

Tough as he is, though, Thrasher obviously is a real softie when it comes to children. He likes to tell about the hayride he ran in his community about fifteen years ago. Thrasher and his mules had been hauling kids for some time when a little girl, maybe five years old, brought him a hamburger and Coke.

Just for that, he told the girl, you can ride as many rides as you want, free of charge. "Now that girl is grown and going to vet school," he says. "But she still remembers that."

Thrasher has competed in a lot of contests and won. In 2002, he entered the wagon class in Columbia, Tennessee's Mule Day, an annual celebration that began in 1840 as "Breeder's Day," a meeting for mule breeders, and now draws more than two hundred thousand people for a four-day event. He was driving a covered wagon.

"The others could see better," he recalls, "because they sat up high and didn't have a cover to look around." He was the last of eleven competitors to run an obstacle course. Seven of the eleven had been disqualified because their wagons touched one of the obstacles. Three drivers and their mules had performed perfectly.

"I *ran* those mules," Thrasher says. "I had to look out the side windows on the covered wagon." He won. And when it was over, the contest judge said, "We've never seen one that fast in this contest."

He also won the individual-mule class that year, pulling a sled through an obstacle course. Unlike most competitors, he used no lines, guiding the mule solely by voice commands.

But with all his skills, Thrasher doesn't claim to be the greatest mule handler in his circle of friends. For that honor, he names Billy Coomer of Edmonton, Kentucky, who estimates he's won a hundred or more mule contests. So what's the secret to being a good mule man? "I don't know, buddy,"

PLATE 105   Hollis and grandson John Paul Dubarry III

Coomer says. "Probably have to be smarter than the mule. You just got to know your animal."

Animals are a lot like children, Coomer says. When a kid gets up about fifteen years old, and he doesn't want to work, it's hard to get him to do anything. "And that's just about the way a mule or a horse is. If you don't break him when he's young, a lot of time he won't have a lot of sense. You got to study your animal when you're working it. And if it wants to goof up, you can tell it if you watch him before he goofs up."

A mule has his own personality, Coomer says, and there are some good ones and some that are of no-account. "I've had a lot of sorry mules," he says.

Working with mules, however, "is sort of leaving out of here," according to Coomer. "Used to go to a mule sale and there'd be a thousand head of mules down there. That was twenty years ago. Now you go down there and they'll be two or three hundred."

Thrasher calls Coomer the best driver he's ever seen. "When I say he's good, I mean he's got good hands. When you drive a team, you've got to have good hands. You've got to know how much pressure you need to put in a mule's mouth to get him to respond to you." So when Coomer wants to help Thrasher snake a few logs, he's certainly welcome.

Thrasher's wife is often there on the job, too, not to do any snaking, but to make sure her husband doesn't get hurt out there in woods all alone. It's dangerous work, Carolyn Thrasher says, but "it's a good, slow-down kind of life."

But Hollis Thrasher doesn't say anything about slowing down. He doesn't want to work every day, of course, but it's not unusual in the wintertime to see him out in the woods three days a week geeing and hawing a mule or two, or maybe even four, if he's using a two-wheel log cart.

"You know," he says, "it's kind of nice to do what you enjoy doing and make money at the same time."

To Hollis Thrasher, there's nothing like training a mule to do what he's supposed to do, and then watching him do it. His wife supports him, but may not get the same enjoyment.

"I think the day I die," he says, "she'll call somebody to bring their horse trailer and come get these mules."

Family History

Jerry Taylor on tracing other people's genealogies

WHEN JERRY TAYLOR was in the sixth grade, his teacher told his class, "You all had ancestors at Valley Forge, and you can find out about them. They're not in the history books, but you can find out about them."

That teacher at Hiawassee Elementary School, Kieffer Garrett, was speaking metaphorically, Taylor said. But he was hoping his students would be intrigued enough to at least *think* about George Washington at Valley Forge during the American Revolution. Maybe, just maybe, they were actually related to someone there.

Jerry Taylor, who became a teacher himself, took Mr. Garrett at his word. He went home and told his parents, "We're going to Grandma Taylor's this afternoon to find out about my ancestors that were at Valley Forge with George Washington."

John and Helen Taylor humored their inquisitive son. They took him to town and stopped by the dime store to buy a notepad to record all the great stories his grandmother would tell him. Turns out, Grandmother Rosa Nicholson Taylor didn't know of any ancestors who were at Valley Forge, but she told him as much as she could about the family.

Young Taylor wasn't satisfied. Thanks to a friend, Alexander Burns, a genealogist who hired him to copy census records, he learned as a student how to find applications for Revolutionary War pensions. "If I could find someone in census records who was born before the Revolution, and if they were soldiers, they probably had a pension," said Taylor, now in his sixties. "And Alexander Burns showed me where to look for who got pensions," information available in archives in Washington, DC.

By the time he was fourteen, Taylor had tracked down eight ancestors who fought in the Revolutionary War. "And believe it or not," he said, "one of them was John Peter Corn, who was actually at Valley Forge. So, my teacher was speaking metaphorically, and it came out that it really was. I made it turn out to be the truth."

It was a warm Tuesday in early June in the mountains of Northeast Georgia, and Jerry Anthony Taylor was sitting at a reading table inside the Towns County Public Library in Hiawassee, a convenient place for an interview because it is next door to the courthouse, where Taylor spent countless hours researching the history of his county and its people. Following the interview, sure enough, he headed for the courthouse. After all, he is the official county historian.

Let's get one thing clear about this man, a retired teacher after thirty-two years at Towns County High School. A lot of people are interested in gene-alogy and in the history of their region, but few of them are obsessed with studying heritage as Jerry Taylor is. Thirty years ago, years before Google and the Internet facilitated family research, Taylor, with help from Thomas Flanagan, a fellow teacher, spearheaded the production of a heritage book for Towns County, Georgia. Researching the original settlers back then was tremendously time-consuming. The county was established in 1856, so, naturally, he concentrated on the 1860 census.

Then someone challenged him. Taylor does not take challenges lightly. "What about those people who settled here before the county became Towns?" he was asked. "Don't they count?" So Taylor is working on volume two of *Hearthstones of Home*, tracking down people who lived in the area from 1832 until 1856. "My goal," he said, "is to have a tidbit on every settler from 1832 to the 1860 census."

Taylor grew up on a chicken farm, first in Hog Creek Community and then in the Fodder Creek Community. "They say I was studious," he said, "but I grew up country like everybody else." But Taylor didn't spend his time like everybody else. His mother worked in Hiawassee at an egg hatchery, and he usually rode home with her after school. Between the time classes ended and his mama's quitting time at five o'clock, he could be found at the local library, when it was open, which wasn't every day.

When school was out for the summer, his parents would take him to Atlanta to spend several weeks with an aunt and uncle. The uncle worked at the big Sears Building on Ponce de Leon Avenue, which served for decades as a warehouse facility as well as a retail store for Sears, Roebuck. At six o'clock in the morning, Taylor was at the Sears store. "I would find my way to the state archives and be waiting at the door, chomping at the bit, when they opened at nine o'clock." He would walk from Sears to the capitol, where his uncle would pick him up after five o'clock. "When that uncle got tired of me," he said, "I had another uncle at Forest Park," near Atlanta.

After high school, it was no surprise that Taylor, an exemplary student, received a scholarship to attend nearby Young Harris College. After Young Harris, he attended the University of Georgia in Athens, where he majored in, not surprisingly, history. He attended UGA on a scholarship that was half grant, half loan. But if the recipient taught in certain areas in "poverty-stricken Appalachia," as the program put it, the loan part was forgiven after seven years. Taylor's was forgiven.

So, what kind of teacher was Jerry Taylor? Quilla Thomas-Bradley of Towns County, now a teacher herself, remembers well. In Taylor's social studies class, he delighted in posting on a bulletin board the genealogies of several families of the county. He would put up four or five of these genealogies, all drawn, lined off, and written by hand, and invite students to see if they could find their names. Thomas-Bradley was interested in her own family tree, mainly because her mother, Jean Sosebee Thomas, was heavily into genealogy. But Taylor expanded her interest to include the whole county. "It was thrilling to students to see how we were all connected," she said.

Taylor was also adviser to the Coed Y Club, a Christian group that Thomas-Bradley led as president for three years. Taylor was also a tour guide. "He would take us all over Northeast Georgia on field trips," Thomas-Bradley said. He would escort students to Rock Eagle at Eatonton, Georgia, to different conferences, to singing or talent shows, you name it. And he took it upon himself to pick up students who lived in the Young Harris area so they could come, too. "I think maybe he had a Ford Granada," Thomas-Bradley said, "and he'd cram eight or nine people into his car. You couldn't do that today, of course."

What was the purpose of the trips? "Well," she said, "he wanted quality. He wanted upstanding citizens, and he wanted people to have more knowledge, period. He wanted us to see not just Towns County, but to be with other people and learn new things."

After becoming a teacher, Thomas-Bradley was working in her classroom one day while her older daughter, Jeannie, then a fourth grader, was looking over a printout of several genealogies that Taylor had digitized as a favor to his former student. Examining the family trees, Jeannie learned just how tightly connected her family is to other families in the county.

Not only does Taylor know genealogies, he knows beaucoup stories from the county's past. One of them from 1887 involves a man named James B. Goddard. Taylor doesn't know much about him, but he knows this much: Goddard ran a tippling house on the square in Hiawassee, where he sold liquor by the drink. Thirsty folks would walk up to the window in the door and order. Goddard was often fined, Taylor said, for keeping his business open on the Sabbath.

One day, Goddard was walking down the road when he met Tilman Justice and a friend. The story goes that Justice was a moonshiner and that Goddard had turned him in. "The story in the court minutes," Taylor said, "is that Tilman went up to Goddard, who immediately got down on his knees, held up his hands to pray, and said, 'Lord, have mercy; don't hurt me, Tilman.'" Justice shot the man in the face and beat him unmercifully with the stock of the gun.

"Tilman is the only person in Towns County who received a death sentence by hanging, and my grandmother was there," Taylor said. "She was about eight. Everybody went to the hanging. Back then, capital punishment was to be a deterrent to crime. People got to see what happened to you if you were bad. So hangings were public spectacles. The amazing thing is that my great-grandparents took their eight-year-old daughter and put her up on the back of a wagon so she could see." Fortunately, he said, someone fired a gun off in the distance and onlookers turned away just as Goddard was hanged. When they turned back around, it was all over.

This is just one of Taylor's many stories about the county. "Jerry's got so much of this stuff in his head, he doesn't need to do tons of research," said Debbie Phillips, manager of the library where the interview was held. "He's such a unique person in how he can remember and know a person's genealogy, and for several generations."

Taylor has also formed some strong opinions about the importance of historical events, like how the Civil War affected education, for example. Before the war, he said, the penmanship of people in the county was excellent. But if you look at Southern court records a generation afterward, you can see how unimportant education had become. "They were scraping to get by," said Taylor, "and going to school was not part of the scraping. So the education went down."

But about the 1880s, he said, a concentrated effort was made to educate citizens once again. National church organizations started academies in the Northeast Georgia Mountains, and some of those academies are now colleges. People began going back to school to become qualified to do something: to be a teacher, a preacher, a doctor, a lawyer. But where would these people teach, preach, doctor, and do their lawyering? They would leave the mountains for better opportunities elsewhere.

"By the 1920s," he said, "a brain drain had been created in the area. Even if you weren't educated, you still wanted to get out because there was nothing to make a living at." People went to Gainesville, Georgia, to work at textile mills, or to Asheville, North Carolina, or to Detroit, Michigan, or to Canton, Ohio. Taylor's great-grandfather, Esco Burch, was one of them. After putting his crops by in the summer, he would go to Murphy, North Carolina, get a train ticket for twenty-nine dollars, and go to Canton, Ohio, to work in a factory.

Taylor's aunt, Pauline Taylor Funderburk, went to Hiawassee Academy and got a teacher's certificate. After teaching at a three-month school, she used her pay to buy a train ticket to Charlotte, North Carolina. "She got her a job and never came back," he said. "That Hiawassee Academy was her ticket out of here to a better life."

Fortunately, by 1940, Taylor said, the level of education in Hiawassee was astoundingly good. "We looked like a little academic town." Public high school education found a home in the mountains. In Towns County, the county bought a school building started by a church home mission board and turned it into a public high school.

Jerry Taylor is a product of that improved education system, and he stayed in Towns County to continue the trend. Unfortunately, he said, penmanship again is being kicked to the side, this time in favor of computer training. "This generation is growing up and they won't be able to read cursive. It'll be akin to something like hieroglyphics in Egypt. If it's not spit out of a computer, they can't read it."

Taylor occupies a bully pulpit for his opinions on education. He's a member of the county's board of education. And even school boards could stand some improvements, he said. Board members should have to meet certain qualifications before they can seek election. If we're demanding that students pass statewide tests every year, shouldn't we demand that school policy makers meet some requirements, too?

PLATE 106 Taylor often is asked to play at concerts and churches.

His days as a teacher may be over, but Taylor stays busy with his research, his reed organs, his concerts, and his speaking engagements. "He gets around," said Towns County Commissioner Bill Kendall, who has known Taylor since he was a high school student. "I see him at the courthouse, at historical society meetings, and I attended a meeting at a church in Hayesville, North Carolina, and he was a piano soloist."

Music is a big part of Taylor's life. "Being a Taylor," he said, "music is supposed to be in your blood. Growing up, all I heard was, 'Oh, you're Jeremiah Taylor's grandson. He was a great singer.'" And Jerry Taylor has lived up to everyone's expectations. He was fascinated by the pump organ, an old Sears, Roebuck model, he saw in his grandmother's house, and took music lessons through high school and college. Taylor is called on occasionally to give concerts, and he's given tours of the thirty-one reed organs that occupy their own room at the Taylor home.

PLATE 107   Jerry Taylor's loft at his home contains thirty-one reed organs.

You may be wondering what happened to John Peter Corn, the Taylor ancestor who was traced to Valley Forge Camp during the Revolutionary War.

Corn, according to family lore, was detailed one day to get apples for the Army. And when he came to a certain farm, he spotted a pretty young girl and fell madly in love with her right there in the orchard. After the war, he went back and married the apple of his eye and moved to Hendersonville, North Carolina. By the next generation, Native Americans had been moved out of Northeast Georgia, and some of Corn's sons moved to what became Towns County. The names of Corn's relatives have been found in a family Bible. John Peter Corn died in the 1840s and received a military funeral. He was eighty-something years old. It's stories like this one that keep Jerry Taylor digging into records at the courthouse, records in state and federal archives, and notations in family Bibles. They're what keep him, along with an assistant, Jason Edwards, working on volume two of *Hearthstones of Home*.

"Who knows?" he said. "After I get through volume two, I may get on a roll and pump out a bunch more."

No one in Towns County would be surprised at all.

ABOUT THE AUTHORS

Phil Hudgins has worked as a reporter, editor, and publisher at several newspapers for more than fifty years. He retired as senior editor for Community Newspapers Inc. of Athens, Georgia, where he coached writers at CNI newspapers in three Southern states. He was a 1974 Nieman Fellow at Harvard University, where one of his studies was folklore. He and his wife, Shirley, have two daughters and four grandchildren. Former residents of Rabun County, Georgia, where Phil served on Foxfire's community board, they now live in Gainesville, Georgia, in the foothills of the Blue Ridge Mountains.

A student at Piedmont College in Demorest, Georgia, where she is pursuing a degree in dermatology, Jessica Phillips is the recipient of the 2017 Julia W. Fleet Foundation's Foxfire scholarship. Foxfire has been a part of her life since she was a little girl, when her parents would tell her stories from the books and magazine.

Grateful acknowledgment is made to the following for permission to reprint previously published material:

Bill Landry: Excerpt of "Forming the Great Smoky Mountains National Park" from *When the West Was Tennessee* by Bill Landry. Reprinted by permission of Bill Landry.

Geneva Dabney Llewellyn: Recipes from *Smokehouse Ham, Spoon Bread, & Scuppernong Wine* by Joe Dabney. Reprinted by permission of Geneva Dabney Llewellyn.

Kate Long: Excerpt of interview with Phil Hudgins and excerpt of "Who'll Watch the Home Place?" written by Kate Long. Reprinted by permission of Kate Long.

Dori Sanders: Recipes from *Country Cooking: Recipes and Stories from the Family Farm Stand* by Dori Sanders. Reprinted by permission of Dori Sanders.

C. B. Skelton: Excerpt of "When Grandpa Croaks" from *Fil-osophy/Phool-osophy* by C. B. Skelton. Reprinted by permission of C. B. Skelton.

Illustration Credits

Photographs provided by the authors, with exception to the following: Plates 18 (Greg Hamby), 24 (Joy Phillips), 25 (micajahclarkdyer.org), 36 (Amanda McClure), 48 (Charles Phillips), 52 (Steve Stoyer), 57 (Ann M. Woodford), 77 (Ethan Phillips), and 96 (Katherine Stoyer) were provided by the people credited and are used with permission. Plates 1, 2, 5, 7, 8, 12, 13, 19, 21, 22, 23, 34, 41, 46, 47, 49, 50, 54, 55, 56, 58, 61, 62, 63, 64, 65, 66, 68, 70, 71, 72, 73, 76, 79, 84, 86, 87, 88, 90, 91, 92, 97, 104, 106, and 107 were provided by the interviewees and are used with permission.